The Greek Philosophical Vocabulary

The Greek Philosophical Vocabulary

J.O. Urmson

Duckworth

First published in 1990 by
Gerald Duckworth & Co. Ltd.
The Old Piano Factory
43 Gloucester Crescent, London NW1 7DY

© 1990 by J.O. Urmson

ISBN 0 7156 2335 4

British Library Cataloguing in Publication Data

Urmson, J.O. (James Opie).
    The Greek philosophical vocabulary.
    1. Greek philosophy, ancient period. Language
    I. Title
    180

    ISBN 0–7156–2335–4

Photoset in North Wales by
Derek Doyle & Associates, Mold, Clywd.
Printed in Great Britain by
Biddles Ltd, Guildford and King's Lynn

Introduction

This book is designed to be an aid to students of ancient Greek philosophy who have some, but not necessarily a profound, knowledge of the Greek language. It contains five or six hundred paragraphs, each aiming at providing useful information about some word used by Greek philosophers. Each paragraph starts with a Greek word, transliterated, in English alphabetical order. Information about each word is given, so far as possible, in quotations from the philosophers, all with a translation added. The translations are all the author's own; they are intended to be helpful rather than literal, and sometimes contain extra, explanatory, matter. These quotations are not merely illustrative; they frequently contain the philosophers' own statements about the meaning and use of the word in question. The statements of Plato or Aristotle, or, indeed, of any philosopher, about the meaning of the words he uses are more valuable than those of others, even though they do not always adhere to their own definitions. The paragraphs are not designed to replace the lexicon, nor to discuss adequately any philosophical theory, but merely to give such basic philological and philosophical information as seems likely to be most useful to most readers.

Quotations range from the fifth century BC to the sixth century AD. When one considers how much the English language has changed in a period of similar length, one cannot but be impressed by the homogeneity of philosophical Greek over that period. More and more terms acquired technical uses, more and more abstract nouns were coined, minor grammatical changes came about; but such late writers as Syrianus and Simplicius knew the works of Plato and Aristotle intimately, and Plato and Aristotle would have read their works with some surprise, but no difficulty. It is often said that the great changes in English and English spelling are to be explained through conquest, the absence of printed books and the like; but such factors seem to have had little effect on the Greek of scholars.

One must, of course, be cautious about using a quotation from a writer of one period as evidence for its meaning in the writings of a philosopher of another period. But one should be similarly wary about such inferences from one philosopher to a contemporary, or even from one passage to another by the same philosopher. The usage of philosophers of all periods has often departed from their own definitions and explanations. But the veneration of the neoplatonic writers for Plato and their respect for Aristotle led them to adhere more closely to the usage of the fourth century BC than did many philosophers at intervening times. So, for example, a statement by Simplicius about the meaning of a word in Aristotle is, while not definitive, very likely to be correct. So, while quotations will sometimes illustrate variation in use, mere difference in date is not of overriding importance.

Conventions of transliteration

Most of the transliteration requires no explanation. But the following points should be noted:

omega and eta have a circumflex accent, thus: *ô, ê*
an *i* following *ô* or *ê* represents iota subscript
terminal alpha with iota subscript is written *aï*
gamma is always transliterated as *g*; thus *aggelos*, not *angelos*
chi is transliterated as *kh*; words beginning with chi are under '*k*'

All words occur in the English alphabetical order. Thus words beginning with a zeta come at the end of the book, and words beginning with theta appear under 't'. This, like all transliteration, is annoying, but seems the best policy. Without transliteration most readers would not have been able to afford this book.

Abbreviations

The use of abbreviations has been kept to a minimum. Names of all authors except Plato and Aristotle are written in full, as are names of works rarely quoted in this book. Aristotle is written Ar., Plato Pl.

Introduction

Aristotle's works

An. Po.	Analytica posteriora	Posterior Analytics
An. Pr.	Analytica priora	Prior Analytics
Cat.	Categoriae	Categories
Col.	De Coloribus	On Colours
De An.	De Anima	On the Soul
De Gen. et Cor.	De Generatione et Corruptione	On coming to be and passing away
De Int.	De Interpretatione	On Interpretation
De Juv.	De Juventute	On Youth
De Mem.	De Memoria	On Memory
E.E.	Ethica Eudemia	Eudemian Ethics
E.N.	Ethica Nicomachea	Nicomachean Ethics
Gen. An.	De Generatione Animalium	On Generation of Animals
H.A.	Historia Animalium	Enquiry about Animals
Met.	Metaphysica	Metaphysics
Part. An.	De Partibus Animalium	On the Parts of Animals
Phys.	Physica	Physics
Pol.	Politica	Politics
Rhet.	Rhetorica	Rhetoric
S.E.	De Sophisticis Elenchis	On Sophistical Refutations
Top.	Topica	Topics

Other titles are given in full.

Plato's works

Alcib.	Alcibiades	Alcibiades
Apol.	Apologia	Apology
Charm.	Charmides	Charmides
Clit.	Clitophon	Clitophon
Crat.	Cratylus	Cratylus
Def.	Definitiones	Definitions
Ep.	Epistolae	Letters
Euthyd.	Euthydemus	Euthydemus
Gorg.	Gorgias	Gorgias
Hip. Min.	Hippias Minor	Hippias Minor

Parm.	*Parmenides*	*Parmenides*
Phil.	*Philebus*	*Philebus*
Pol.	*Politicus*	*The Statesman*
Rep.	*Respublica* (*Politeia*)	*Republic*
Soph.	*Sophistes*	*The Sophist*
Theaet.	*Theaetetus*	*Theaetetus*
Tim.	*Timaeus*	*Timaeus*

Other titles are given in full.

In general, the titles of works by other authors are either given in full or are otherwise self-explanatory. Where an inexperienced reader finds that this is not so, he could look up the author in the list of authors and works at the beginning of the Greek lexicon of Liddell and Scott as revised by H. Stuart Jones, which is referred to in this book by the initials *LSJ*, as is usual. There he will find, for example, that the work here called the *Physics* of Simplicius is officially *In Aristotelis Physica Commentaria* ed. Diels, in volumes 9 and 10 of the Berlin edition of the *Commentaria in Aristotelem Graeca*. Quotations from Proclus *In Platonis Rem Publicam* are from Kroll's Teubner edition. Quotations from his *Elements of Theology* give the theorem number in Dodds's edition, not page and line as in Dodds's index. Quotations from Plotinus are, inevitably, from the *Enneads*. The initials *OCT* abbreviate *Oxford Classical* texts; *SVF* abbreviate *Stoicorum Veterum Fragmenta*, a collection of Stoic texts edited by H. von Arnim.

When a further discussion of another word occurring in a quotation may be helpful for the understanding of the principal word, that word has been printed in bold. But the fact that a word is not printed in bold does not mean that it has not its own individual paragraph, but only that its meaning is not closely germane to the matter under discussion.

A

adiaphoros has two distinct applications. (1) To things that are indistinguishable from each other, particularly members of the same species: *t'auton gar pantôn tôn adiaphorôn eidei genos* – all things indistinguishable in species are of the same genus (Ar. *Top*. 121b 17); *adiaphoron d'hôn adiaireton to eidos kata tên aisthêsin* – things are indistinguishable whose species cannot be differentiated by perception (Ar. *Met*. 1016a 18); see also Ar. *Top*. 121b 15. (2) Esp. in neuter plural, to things that are indifferent as neither good nor bad. This latter use is mainly Stoic: *adiaphora d'einai legousi ta metaxu tôn agathôn kai kakôn* – they [the Stoics] say that things between good and bad are indifferent (Stobaeus 2.79.1 W); see also Epictetus, *Encheiridion* 32. The Stoics also made a distinction within these *adiaphora*: *dikhôs de legesthai adiaphora· hapax men ta mête pros eudaimonian mête pros kakodaimonian sunergounta, hôs ekhei ploutos, doxa, hugieia, iskhus kai ta homoia. allôs de legesthai adiaphora ta mête hormês mête aphormês kinêtika, hôs ekhei to artias ekhein epi tês kephalês trikhas ê perittas* – things are called indifferent in two ways; first those things that do not contribute either to the good life or to wretchedness, as is the case with wealth, reputation, health, strength and the like. In another way things are called indifferent if they do not move to choice or rejection, as is the case with having an even or odd number of hairs on one's head (Diogenes Laertius of the Stoics, *Lives* 7.104). But also a distinction made by Epicureans, *hugieian tisi men agathon, tisi de adiaphoron* – to some health is good, to some indifferent (*Vita Epicuri* 120b). Not used by Plato in either sense.

adiastatos, adiastatôs has two distinct applications. (1) Continuous, without distinction or interval: *hola di'holôn phoitônta adiastatôs* – wholes interpenetrating without spatial interval (Proclus, *Elements of Theology* 176); cf. Plotinus, *Enneads* 3.7.2 and Damascius, *De principiis* 105, 370. More commonly (2) not extended: *enulôs te to* **aülon** *apotupoutai kai* **diastatôs** *to* *adiastaton* – [nature] copies the immaterial materially and extend-edly the unextended (Proclus, *Republic* 177.18); *eidê adiastata te kai amerista* - forms that are unextended and indivisible (Simplicius, *Physics* 231.30). The contrary is *diastatos*. Not in Plato.

adikein, adikia, adikos: in a narrower sense, unjust, unfair: *ho t'adikos anisos kai to adikon anison* – the unjust man is unfair and injustice is unfairness (Ar. *E.N.* 1131a 10); in a wider sense, unrighteous, contrary to accepted practice (*nomos*): *ho paranomos adikos* – the lawbreaker is unrighteous (Ar. *E.N.* 1129b 11). The contrary of *adikos* is *dikaios*, of *adikein, dikaiopragein*. Plato appears notably to confuse these two senses in *Republic* 1. According to Aristotle, one may *adikein* – behave in a way that is objectively unfair to someone – without having the specific badness of character that is *adikia*: *estin adikounta mêpô adikon einai* – one may act unjustly without being an unjust person (Ar. *E.N.* 1134a 16). For fuller discussion see *dikaios*.

aei: constantly used to mean 'everlasting', 'for ever', in distinction from the timelessly eternal (*aiônion*): *pros ton aei khronon* – throughout all time (Pl. *Critias* 112d). But it also means constantly, over and over, on each occasion: *ho to pleon ekhôn aei* – he who has too much on each occasion (Ar. *E.N.* 1136b 26); *hai hêmas aei ek tôn kindunôn sôzousin* – that over and over save us from dangers (Pl. *Gorg.* 511b). *aiei* is a common alternative spelling.

aêr: conventionally, air, but applied to any vapour, especially mist. Anaximenes is said to have called it the basic material of the world; in Empedocles, Aristotelian physics and most later Greek and scholastic philosophy it is one of the four elements (*stoikheia*) or simple bodies (*hapla sômata*) in the sublunar region, lighter than and above earth and water, heavier than and below fire. Of the four basic characteristics of body, the moist (*hugron*), the dry (*xêron*), the hot (*thermon*) and the cold (*psukhron*), it is the essentially hot and damp, *ho aêr thermon kai hugron* (Ar. *De Gen. et Cor.* 330b 4). It was recognised that air, like other simple bodies, was rarely in a pure state but, as mist contains air and water, mixed with another element and thus composite (*suntheton*), not simple (*haplon*).

agathos: good. The highest term of commendation whether of what is to be praised (*epainetos*) or what is to be prized (*timios*). In general use it can refer to good birth, bravery or other qualities according to context when applied to persons. What is *agathos* has excellence (*aretê*). Sometimes moral: *dikaion onta kai andreion kai hosion, agathon andra einai teleôs* – being just and brave and pious to be a completely good man (Pl. *Gorg.* 507c). Often with regard to high capacity or achievement in other areas: *ton de agathon eu te kai kalôs prattein ha an prattêi* – the good man does what he does well and finely (*Gorg.* 507c); *agathos* in argument (Pl. *Hip. Min.* 367c); *agathos* runner (Pl. *Hip. Min.* 373d); to make a man an *agathos* citizen is to make him 'most capable of acting and speaking on the affairs of the city' (Pl. *Prot.* 319a). This use can conflict with use to indicate moral excellence. Thus at *Gorg.* 470e the *agathos* is opposed to the unrighteous (*adikos*), but at *Rep.* 348d Thrasymachus says that the *adikos* is *agathos*, cynically rather than as an abuse of language. In neuter singular *to agathon* is the ultimate goal of man, as in *E.N.*, Book 1, Ch. 2. In *Rep.* Books 6 and 7 *auto to agathon* – the good itself – is the highest principle and the source of being and understanding: *touto toinun to tên alêteian parekhon tois gignôskomenois kai tôi gignôskonti tên dunamin apodon tên tou agathou idean phathi einai* – count that which provides its truth to what is known and gives the faculty of knowing to the knower as the form of the good (Pl. *Rep.* 508e). Aristotle famously denied the Platonic form of the good and claimed in *E.N.*, Book 1, Ch. 6 that *agathos* was ambiguous; but his clearest account of the alleged ambiguity is *skopein de kai ta genê tôn kata t'ounoma katêgoriôn, ei t'auta estin epi pantôn· ei gar mê t'auta, dêlon hoti homônumon to legomenon, hoion to agathon en edesmati men to poiêtikon hêdonês, en iatrikêi de to poiêtikon hugieias, epi de têi psukhêi to poian einai, hoion sôphrona ê andreion ê dikaion· homoiôs de kai epi anthrôpou. eniakhou de to pote, hoion to en kairôi agathon· agathon gar legetai to en tôi kairôi. pollakis de to poson, hoion epi tou metriou· legetai gar kai to metrion agathon. hôste **homônumon** to agathon* – but one must inspect the types of category in which the word occurs, to see if they are the same throughout. If they are not the same it is clear that there is ambiguity. For example, the good is in eating that which produces pleasure and in medicine that which produces health; of the soul it is a quality, such as being temperate or brave or just, and similarly of a person. Sometimes it is a time, as that which is opportune is good, and often a quantity, as of the moderate; for the moderate is also said to be good. So that 'good' is ambiguous (Ar. *Top.* 107a 2). In neoplatonic theology the *agathon* is

11

equated with *to hen*, the supreme deity: *to agathon tôi heni t'auton* – the good is identical with the One (Proclus, *Elements of Theology* 13). For the distinction of *agatha* into things praised (*epaineta*) and things prized (*timia*) see e.g. Ar. *E.N.*, Book 1, Ch. 12. The usual abstract noun for goodness is *aretê*; the etymologically related *agathotês* is late: *hê tou pro pantôn henos agathotês* – the goodness of the One before all things (Syrianus, *Metaphysics* 59.13).

agnoein: to be ignorant; *agnoia*, ignorance. As in English, *agnoia* can be simple unawareness, as the common man is unaware of the world of forms in Plato, or as Aeschylus was ignorant that it was forbidden to speak of the mysteries (Ar. *E.N.* 1111a 10); or it can be mistaken opinion, as when the bad man is ignorant of how to behave (Ar. *E.N.* 1110b 31). It is unclear in which, if either, of these senses Plato says *mê onti mên agnoian ex anagkês apodidomen* – we necessarily assign ignorance to that which is not (Pl. *Rep.* 478c).

agroikos: literally, one who lives in the country. Usually treated as one who is boorish and uncouth as in the 4th of Theophrastus' *Characters*; but in *E.N.* at 1104a 23 Aristotle takes the *agroikos* to be typical of those who are insensible (*anaisthêtos*) with regard to bodily pleasures and thus lack temperance (*sôphrosunê*).

aïdios: in common use and generally in philosophy, everlasting, temporally without beginning and end, as opposed both to what has a beginning and end and to the atemporally eternal, which is called *aiônios*. Thus *tôn mentoi arkhôn ouk estin heteron aition aïdiôn ousôn* – there is no further cause of first principles, which are everlasting (Ar. *Phys.* 252b 4); the heavens (*ouranos*) are *heis kai aïdios* – one and everlasting (Ar. *De Caelo* 283b 28); *ouk ara endekhetai sunekhê kinêsin einai epi tês eutheias aïdion* – there cannot be an everlasting continuous motion in a straight line (Ar. *Phys.* 263a 3). But Plato *Tim.* 37d-e appears to use *aïdion* as a synonym of *aiônion*, contrasting the eternal reality (*aïdion ousian*) with the temporal. Proclus, *Elements of Theology* 55, says that the *aiônion* and the temporal (*kata khronon*) are two kinds of the *aïdion*. The noun is *aïdiotês* (Ar. *De Caelo* 284a 1).

aidôs: shame, bashfulness. Aristotle says it is not a disposition (*hexis*) but an emotion (*pathos*) with physical manifestations (Ar. *E.N.* 1128b 10). He says that it is not an excellence (*aretê*) and befits only the young. Plato also says that it is not always a good thing: *estin ara, hôs eoiken, aidôs ouk agathon kai agathon* – so, as it seems, shame is both not good and good (Pl. *Charm*. 160e ff.).

aiôn: generally, a life-span, or a long time: *empeiria men gar poiei ton aiôna hêmôn poreuesthai kata tekhnên* – experience makes our life proceed in accordance with skill (Pl. *Gorg*. 448c); the heavens have no end *tou pantos aiônos* – through all time (Ar. *De Caelo* 283b 28). But in Plato's metaphysics and in neoplatonism the *aiôn* is timeless eternity: *khronou tauta aiôna mimoumenou* – time imitating eternity in these respects (Pl. *Tim*. 38a); *pantôn tôn aiôniôn proüparkhai ho aiôn, kai pantôn tôn kata khronon ho khronos proüphestêken* – eternity precedes everything eternal and time preceded everything temporal (Proclus, *Elements of Theology* 53).

aiônios: colloquially applied to anything lasting a long time. Thus Plato writes *methên aiônion* – an everlasting drinking-party (Pl. *Rep*. 363d). But it is strictly applied to the timelessly eternal. Thus body and soul are indestructible (*anôlethra*) but not *aiônia* (Pl. *Laws* 904a). *pan to aiônion holon hama esti* – everything eternal is a simultaneous whole (Proclus, *Elements of Theology* 50). See *aidios, aiôn*.

aiskhros: applied without any apparent thought of ambiguity both to physical ugliness and to the morally base and shameful. Thus we pity the ugly (*aiskhrous*), the small and the weak (Pl. *Prot*. 323d). But, also, the life of the male prostitute (Pl. *Gorg*. 494e), flattery (Pl. *Gorg*. 503a) and theft (Pl. *Gorg*. 515e) are *aiskhra*, and it would have been *aiskhron* for Achilles not to have avenged Patroclus' death (Pl. *Apol*. 28c). All deeds that are *aiskhra* are *kaka*, but it is not clear whether all moral faults are *aiskhra*, or only, perhaps pre-eminently, those that are sordid, base and shameful and thus aesthetically repugnant. Thus the *adikon* (the unjust) and the *anosion* (the impious) are listed alongside the *aiskhron* at *Prot*. 325d, not as cases of it, and uncontrolled temper is less *aiskhron* than lack of control of bodily appetites (Ar. *E.N*. 1149a 24-5). *aiskhros* is the contrary of *kalos*.

aisthanesthai. See *aisthêsis*.

aisthêsis: sensation, perception; *aisthanesthai*: to sense, to per-

13

ceive; *to aisthêton*: the object of perception; *to aisthêtêrion*: the sense-organ. *to aisthanesthai legomen dikhôs· to te gar dunamei akouon kai horôn akouein kai horan legomen, k'an tukhêi katheudon, kai to êdê energoun* – we use 'perceive' in two ways; for we say that what is capable of hearing and seeing hears and sees, even if it happens to be asleep, as well as the actual perceiver (Ar. *De An.* 417a 10); *katholou de peri pasês aisthêseôs dei labein hoti men hê aisthêsis esti to dektikon tôn aisthêtôn eidôn aneu tês hulês* – generally concerning all perception it must be understood that perception is the reception of forms without matter (Ar. *De An.* 424a 17). Also more loosely of any awareness: *aisthômetha geloioi ontes* – we perceive we are being laughable (Pl. *Theages* 122c). Not only perception in a narrow sense, but also emotions: *hai men oun aisthêseis ta toiade hêmin ekhousin onomata, opseis te kai akoai kai osphrêseis kai psukheis te kai kauseis kai hêdonai ge dê kai lupai kai epithumiai kai phoboi keklêmenai, aperantoi men hai anônumoi, pamplêtheis de hai ônomasmenai* – such *aisthêseis* as the following have names, being called sights and sounds and smells and cold and heat and distress and pleasures and fears; the nameless are countless, but very many have names (Pl. *Theaet.* 156b). Aristotle distinguishes *koina aisthêta* (common sensibles) that are perceptible by more than one sense, such as shape and motion from *idia aisthêta* (proper sensibles) that are perceptible to only one sense, such as colour and smell: *to men [aisthêton] idion estin hekastês aisthêseôs, to de koinon pasôn* – one kind of percept is private to each sense, the other is common to all (Ar. *De An.* 418a 11). *aisthêsis* may also be a form of perception, a sense: *hekastê men oun aisthêsis tou hupokeimenou aisthêtou estin* – each sense is of the sense-object falling under it (Ar. *De An.* 426b 6).

aitêma: an assumption or postulate in logic or mathematics. In Aristotle it is something provable that is assumed and used without proof: *ho an tis apodeikton on lambanêi kai khrêtai mê deixas* (Ar. *An. Post.* 76b 33). In Euclid it is a postulate that certain constructions can be made, or an axiom (the axiom of parallels is called an *aitêma*). Non-technically, a demand: *to dê turannikon aitêma to poluthrulêton* – the often mentioned demand of tyrants [for a bodyguard] (Pl. *Rep.* 566b).

aithêr: non-technically, the heavens or the sky. Identified by Empedocles and Anaxagoras with the outermost fire: *Anaxagoras de*

14

katakhrêtai tôi onomati toutôi ou kalôs· onomazei gar aithera anti puros – Anaxagoras misuses this word, not well: for he says 'ether' instead of 'fire' (Ar. *De Caelo* 270b 24). In Plato's *Epinomis* 981c it is the fifth element, in addition to earth, water, air and fire. In Aristotelian and neoplatonic cosmology the other four elements are to be found in the sublunar region and the aether in the spheres of the planets and in the outermost sphere of the fixed stars. Etherial bodies are ungenerated (*agennêta*), indestructible (*aphtharta*) and in everlasting circular motion. There is a full discussion in Ar. *De Caelo*, Book 1, Ch. 3. See also Simplicius, *Physics* 594.27 ff.

aitia (not to be confused with plural of **aition**). (1) Responsibility in the moral sphere: *aitia helomenou, theos anaitios* – the responsibility is his who chooses, god is not responsible (Pl. *Rep.* 617e). (2) Cause or explanation: *hosoi men oun mian tina legousin aitian kai stoikheion hen* – those who hold that there is some single cause [of everything] and a single element (Ar. *De An.* 405b 17); *tou megistou agathou aitia tê polei hê koinônia* – community is the cause of the greatest good to the city (Pl. *Rep.* 464b).

aition: appears to be synonymous with **aitia** in its second sense. It is traditionally translated 'cause', but 'explanation' is often more idiomatic. Thus Aristotle's 'four causes' are best understand as four types of explanation: there is the material cause – *ex hou gignetai* – the *hulê*, the material of which the thing is made; the formal cause – *to eidos* – that explains what sort of thing it is; the efficient cause – *he arkhê tês metabolês* – that tells what or who brought the thing about; and the final cause, the *telos*, the end for which the thing exists. These four causes are systematically listed and explained in *Physics*, Book 2, Ch. 3. In later literature *hulikon aition*, *eidikon aition*, *poiêtikon aition* and *telikon aition* are commonly used to refer to the material, formal, efficient and final causes respectively: *poiêtikon esti aition kai eidikon kai telikon* – there is an efficient and a formal and a final cause (Syrianus, *Met.* 2.6). The different kinds of *aition* are discussed in Ar. *Met.*, Book 4, Ch. 2. Used thus as a substantive, *aition* is derived from the adjective *aitios*, responsible.

akhôristos: unseparated, inseparable. Used only once by Plato: *ou gar akhôrista ge duo enoei, all'hen* – for if they were undivided he would have thought of them not as two, but one (Pl. *Rep.* 524c). In

Aristotle, inseparable: *akhôrista pephukota kathaper en têi periphereiaï to kurton kai to koilon* – naturally inseparable like the convex and concave of a circumference (Ar. *E.N.* 1102a 30). But in neoplatonic thought used mainly of *eidê* – forms – and other intelligible entities taken as not separated or inseparable from that in which they are present: *ei oun ti kat'ousian estin akhôriston, kai kat'energeian homôs ê kai eti mallon akhôriston* – so anything inseparable [from body] in existence is equally or even more inseparable in its activity (Proclus, *Elements of Theology* 16); *kai gar tên mathêmatikên ousian mesên legousi tôi men katholou to khôriston ekhon tês hulês, tôi de diastatôi kai diakekrimenôi to akhôriston* – for they also say that mathematical existence is intermediate, being separable from matter as universal but, as extended and distinct, inseparable (Simplicius, *Physics* 1).

akinêtos: unchanging, usually with reference to change of place and thus immovable or motionless: *akinêton megalôn en peirasi desmôn* – motionless in the limits of mighty bonds (Parmenides, fr. 8). But 'motionless' is often, at best, unidiomatic. Thus *to prôton kinoun akinêton auto* (Ar. *Met.* 1012b 31), usually translated 'the prime mover is itself unmoved' is better translated as 'the prime source of change is itself unchanging'; *tôn ta akinêta kinountôn* – those who try to change the unchanging (Pl. *Theaet.* 181a); *pan ara ê akinêton estin ê autokinêton ê heterokinêton* – everything is either unchanging, self-changing or changed by something else (Proclus, *Elements of Theology* 14). See *kinêsis*.

akolastos: in Aristotelian ethics the person who exhibits the fault of excess in relation to the excellence of *sôphrosunê*, which is excellence in respect of the pleasures of the body that involve the sense of touch (*haphê*) and taste (*geusis*), notably food, drink and sex; excessive indulgence in pleasures of sound and sight is not included. It is frequently translated 'self-indulgent'; *akolasia* is self-indulgence: *peri tas toiautas d'hêdonas ... hê akolasia estin hôn kai ta loipa zôa koinônei ... hautai d'eisin haphê kai geusis* – self-indulgence is concerned with such pleasures as other animals share in, and these are touch and taste (Ar. *E.N.* 1118a 23-5). In Aristotle the *akratês* has to be distinguished from the willingly self-indulgent, since he acts unwillingly *dia pathos*: *dio ho akolastos kheirôn tou akratous* – therefore the self-indulgent man is worse than the weak-willed (Ar. *E.N.* 1150a 30). Plato and other

16

philosophers also treat *akolasia* as opposed to *sôphrosunê*: *sôphrosunê men eggignêtai, akolasia de apallattêtai* – temperance will enter [the soul] and self-indulgence be ended (Pl. *Gorg.* 504e 6-7); but Plato does not define it so narrowly or distinguish it from *akrasia*, see *Rep.* 431a-b. Etymologically *akolastos* is derived from the verb *kolazein,* to punish, with a privative prefix, and can thus mean less technically simply 'badly brought up'. See Ar. *E.N.*, Book 3, Chs 10-11 for general discussion.

akolouthein: in general, to follow in all senses. In logic it is the general term for logical consequence: *duoin men gar ontôn akolouthei euthus to hen einai* – if there are two it follows immediately that there is one (Ar. *Cat.* 14a 31). But the noun *akolouthêsis* means 'sequence': *proteron de dokei to toiouton einai aph'hou mê antistrephei hê tou einai akolouthêsis* – that thing seems to be prior which precedes in irreversible sequence (Ar. *Cat.* 14a 34-5).

akousios: translated variously as involuntary, unwilling, unintended, contrary to intention. None of these is wholly satisfactory in every context, but in Aristotle's ethics 'contrary to intention' is usually best. It is the contrary of *hekousios*, which presents the same problem: *to de di'agnoian oukh hekousion men hapan estin, akousion de to epilupon kai en metameleiaï* – acts done through ignorance are all unintentional, the contrary to intention is distressing and regretted (Ar. *E.N.* 1110b 18-19). The person who performs acts that are *akousia* does so *akôn* (not intending) and *akousiôs* (unintentionally). See *E.N.*, Book 3, Ch. 1 for general discussion. For the sense of 'unwilling' in adverbial form: *hômologêsen kai mal'akontôs* – he agreed very unwillingly (reluctantly) (Pl. *Prot.* 333b).

akrasia: in Aristotle and later writers, lack of self-control, the condition of being *akratês*. The verb is *akrateuesthai* – to lack, or exhibit the lack of, self-control. Sometimes translated 'incontinence'. In Plato, except in spurious *Definitions*, used more loosely and always written *akrateia*, as in *Rep.* 461b: *meta deinês akrateias gegonôs* – born in terrible licentiousness. In Aristotle *akrasia* is the condition of the man who has right principles but whose appetite leads him to act contrarily to them, whereas the *egkratês* controls his appetite. Both the *egkratês* and the *akratês*

17

are to be distinguished from the **agathos** and the **kakos** who act well or ill without internal conflict, though Plato does not make this sharp distinction. *ho akratês epithumôn men prattei, proairoumenos d'ou –* the uncontrolled man acts in accordance with his appetite, not with his choice (Ar. *E.N.* 1111b 13-14). *akrasia* proper is lack of self-control with regard to the bodily pleasures of touch and taste; if self-control is lacking in other spheres the term must be qualified: *hêtton **aiskhra** akrasia hê tou thumou* – an uncontrolled temper is less disgraceful (Ar. *E.N.* 1149a 24).

akros: in general, an extreme: *epi ta akra tês thalattês aphigmenos* – having arrived at the edge of the sea (Pl. *Phaedo* 109d). In formal logic the *akra* are the extreme terms of the syllogism that appear also in the conclusion, each of which is predicated of, or has predicated of it, a middle term in the premises. The *meizon akron* – the major term – is that *en hôi to meson estin*, the *elatton* that which is *hupo to meson* – contained in the middle term (Ar. *An. Pr.* 26a 21-3). The names for the terms apparently derive from the fact that in the syllogism in the first figure – if *A* is predicated of all *B*, and *B* is predicated of all *C*, necessarily *A* is predicated of all *C* – the middle term appears between the others in the two premises and the extension of the major term *A* is greater than that of the minor term *C*. In geometry and mathematics the extremes of lines and the extreme terms in proportions are also termed *akra*.

alêthês: true; **alêtheia**: truth; **alêthôs**: truly; **alêtheuein**: to tell the truth. In line with its derivation from *lanthanein* with privative prefix, *alêthês* has a wider use than the conventional translation 'true' would allow. It can have a sense rather like 'non-deceptive' and thus be applied to persons and things: *alêthês tis* – a candid, truthful person (Ar. *E.N.* 1108a 20); the *gnôston* (knowable) exceeds the *doxaston* (object of opinion) in *alêtheia*, is less deceptive (Pl. *Rep.* 510a). In Plato the non-deceptive can be simply the real, genuine: *diêirêsthai alêtheiaï te kai mê, hôs to doxaston pros to gnôston, houtô to homoiôthen pros to hôi hômoiôthê* – that the copy is distinguished from the original in reality or not as the opinable to the known (Pl. *Rep.* 510a). But *ouden allo pephuke alêtheuein ê pseudesthai plên phaseôs kai apophaseôs* – nothing can properly be true or false save assertion and denial (Syrianus, *Metaphysics* 78.27).

alloiôsis: etymologically, 'becoming *allos* – different'. In Aristotle and most later writers it has the technical sense of change in the category of quality only, as opposed to changes in other categories and to coming and ceasing to be: *hê alloiôsis kinêsis kata to poion* – it is qualitative change (Ar. *De Caelo* 270a 27). Plato also calls *alloiôsis* a *kinêsis: hotan … sklêron ek malakou gignêtai, ê tina allên alloiôsin alloiôtai, ara ouk axion heteron eidos phanai kinêseôs?* – when something becomes hard instead of soft, or undergoes some other alteration, is it not right to call this another type of change [in addition to motion]? (Pl. *Theaet.* 181d). The verb is *alloiousthai* – to change qualitatively; the thing thus changed is *alloiôtos*.

alogos: applies etymologically to that which is without *logos*. It can mean both irrational – contrary or opposed to reason, or merely non-rational. Thus in general use animals other than man can be called *aloga* as being (reputedly) incapable of reasoning: *ou gar koinon hê proairesis kai tôn alogôn, epithumia de kai thumos* – animals do not share in rational choice, but do in appetite and anger (Ar. *E.N.* 1111b 12). In the sense of 'non-rational', applied also to parts of the soul (Ar. *E.N.* 1117b 24) and to the *aloga pathê* of men (Ar. *E.N.* 1111b 1). Frequently as 'irrational' with regard to arguments and opinions: *deinon kai alogon* – a strange and irrational [statement] (Pl. *Theaet.* 203d). Adverb *alogôs* – irrationally, *ou dê alogôs* – not without reason (Pl. *Rep.* 439d). The modern mathematical term 'irrational' derives from the application of *alogon* to incommensurables: *hê de geômetria ti to alogon* – geometry [assumes] what the incommensurable is (Ar. *An. Po.* 76b 9).

amerês: without parts, simple, indivisible. Derived from *meros* with privative prefix: *ouden tôn sunekhôn ameres* – nothing continuous is indivisible (Ar. *Phys.* 233b 32); the *kinoun prôton* (prime source of change) is *ameres* (Ar. *Phys.* 266a 10). *ameristos* seems to be a synonym: *mia tis idea ameristos sullabê* – the syllable [would be] an indivisible form (Pl. *Theaet.* 205c).

amethektos: unparticipated. An important neoplatonic word, not found in Plato but derived from his doctrine of the *methexis*, participation, of sensible things in the intelligible *eidê*, forms. Neoplatonic authors distinguished between intelligible entities in the world of being in which nothing in the world of becoming

19

participated, which are the *amethekta*, the unparticipated, and the *metekhomena*, participated: *pan to amethekton huphistêsin aph' heautou ta metekhomena, kai pasai hai metekhomenai hupostaseis eis amethektous huparxeis anateinontai* – all that is unparticipated produces out of itself the participated, and all participated substances reach up to existences not participated (Proclus, *Elements of Theology* 23); *pantakhou pro tôn metekhontôn esti ta metekhomena kai pro tôn metekhomenôn ta amethekta* – everywhere prior to the participants there are the participated, and prior to the participated there are the unparticipated (Proclus, *Elements of Theology* 53); *hôs ekhei pros tên zôên ho aiôn ho amethektos, houtôs ekhei pros psukhên ho prôtos houtos khronos* – as the unparticipated eternity is related to life, so this primary time stands towards the soul (Simplicius, *Physics* 784.34).

anagein: in general use, to bring (lead) up. It also has various technical uses of a non-philosophical character. In logic it has the technical sense of reduction of an argument in one figure of the syllogism to another, or to put an argument into syllogistic form. Thus one can *anagein* the second figure syllogism 'if no *P* is *M* and all *S* is *M*, then no S is *P*' to the first figure by simple conversion of the major premiss to 'no *M* is *P*': *esti de kai anagein pantas tous sullogismous eis tous en tôi prôtôi skhêmati katholou sullogismous* – it is possible to reduce all syllogisms to the universal syllogisms in the first figure (Ar. *An. Pr.* 29b 1); *tous ex hupotheseôs sullogismous ou peirateon anagein* – one should not try to reduce hypothetical arguments [to the figures of syllogism] (Ar. *An. Pr.* 50a 17).

anagkê: is necessity of many different sorts; *anagkaios*: necessary; *anagkazein*: necessitate. (1) Logical necessity and validity: *aneu te eikotôn kai anagkaiôn apodeixeôn* – without likely and necessary proofs (Pl. *Tim.* 40d); *sullogismos de esti logos en hôi tethentôn tinôn heteron ti tôn keimenôn ex anagkês sumbainei* – a syllogism is an argument in which, some things being premised, something different follows of necessity (Ar. *An. Pr.* 24b 18); *ei gar to A tini tôi B, kai to B tini tôi A anagkê huparkhein* – if *A* belongs to some *B* it is necessary that some *B* should belong to some *A*. (Ar. *An. Pr.* 25a 21). (2) Metaphysical necessity: *esti en tois ousi ta men aei hôsautôs ekhonta kai ex anagkês, ou tês kata to biaion legomenês all'hên legomen tôi mê endekhesthai allôs* – among things that are, some are always the same and from necessity, not the sort of necessity

20

arising from force but that predicated of what cannot be otherwise (Ar. *Met*. 1026b 27). (3) The necessity arising from force, compulsion: *ei de tis ta hêdea kai ta kala phaiê biaia einai* (*anagkazein gar exô onta*) – if somebody should say that pleasant and fine things were forcible, since they compel from the outside (Ar. *E.N.* 1110b 9). (4) Necessary as indispensible or minimum requirement: *hê anagkaio-tatê polis* – the minimal city (Pl. *Rep.* 369d); *hosa anagkaia ê phusika sumbainei tois anthrôpois* – things necessary or natural for men (Ar. *E.N.* 1135b 21). Ar. *Met.*, Book 4, Ch. 5 is on senses of *anagkê*.

anaisthêsia, anaisthêtos: (1) Lacking the power of perception or sensation (from *aisthêsis* with privative prefix): *dia stereotêta anaisthêsian empoiousai* – causing lack of sensation through their density (Pl. *Tim*. 74e). (2) The defect of character of not enjoying food and drink as required by and compatible with health: *elleipontes de peri tas hêdonas ou panu gignontai ... estôsan de anaisthêtoi* – people deficient with regard to these pleasures scarcely occur ... let them be called insensitive (Ar. *E.N.* 1107b 7).

analogia, analogos, analogôs: (1) Proportion, proportionate, proportionately. *a*:*b*::*c*:*d* is an *analogia*: *kalousi de tên toiautên analogian geômetrikên hoi mathêmatikoi* – mathematicians call such a proportion geometrical (Ar. *E.N.* 1131b 14). (2) Analogy, analogous, analogously. Used especially with regard to the meaning of terms: a term *B* is applied analogously to *C* if it is so applied because *B* stands to *C* in the same relation as it does to *A*. Thus the term 'foot' is applied analogously to the lowest extremity of a mountain since it is so applied because the foot stands to the mountain in the same relation as it does to a human being: *ê mallon kat'analogian? hôs gar en sômati opsis en psukhêi nous* – or is [the use of the word 'good'] rather analogical? For intelligence is to the soul as sight to the body (Ar. *E.N.* 1096b 28); *en tais metaphorais legomenon tais analogon* – used in those metaphors made analogically (Ar. *Rhet*. 1408a 8). *analogon* is the usual adverbial form as in the preceding quotation from the *Rhetoric*; the form *analogôs* occurs only in later writers. This notion of analogy underlies that which became so important in later Christian theology.

analuein: non-technically, to undo. In logic, to reduce [an argument] to one of the *skhêmata*, to put into logical form: *tous gegenêmenous analuoimen eis ta proeirêmena skhêmata* – we may reduce [the arguments] constructed into the forementioned figures (Ar. *An. Pr.* 47a 4). Not in Plato. Also a form of mathematical analysis: *analuein ton eirêmenon tropon hôsper diagramma* – to analyse in the way stated as one does a diagram (Ar. *E.N.* 1112b 20). See *analusis*.

analusis: (1) Any sort of reductive analysis: *tôn stoikheiôn ontôn stereôn mekhri epipedôn poieitai tên analusin* – [Plato] makes the reduction from the solid elements to planes (Ar. *De Gen. et Cor.* 329a 22. (2) Reduction to logical form: *ean d'en merei lêphthêi to sterikon, ouk estai analusis* – if a particular negative premiss be taken, reduction to logical form is impossible (Ar. *An. Pr.* 51a 18). Not in Plato.

analutika: as a noun, 'logic'. It is the title of the two works that we call the *Prior* and *Posterior Analytics* but Aristotle treats as one; it is the analysis of the characteristics of valid arguments and part of the *organon* or tool which Aristotle considered indispensable for accurate thought: *di'apaideusian tôn analutikôn touto drôsin* – they do this [sc. confuse metaphysics and epistemology] through not being taught logic (Ar. *Met.* 1005b 4). *analutikôs*: Ar. *An. Post.* 84a 8, Simplicius, *Physics* 328.14. Not in Plato.

anamnêsis: recollection, recall; *anamimnêskesthai*: to recall the forgotten: *legêtai tis ek lêthês eis anamnêsin metaballein* – someone is said to change from forgetfulness to recollection (Simplicius, *Physics* 839.23). Distinguished from *mnêmê* (memory) which is not to have forgotten. A work of Aristotle is entitled *Peri Mnêmês kai Anamnêseôs* – 'Concerning memory and recollection': *hotan analambanêi hên proteron eikhen epistêmên ê aisthêsin ê hou pote tên hexin elegomen mnêmên, tout'esti kai tote to anamnêskesthai tôn eirêmenôn ti* – when one regains knowledge or perception or that the possession of which we called memory, that is then the recollection of one of the things mentioned (Ar. *De Mem.* 451b 3). Especially in Plato, recollection of things known before birth and forgotten, a theory offered as an explanation of discovery of truth by pure thought and thought of the inexperienced like the absolutely just and absolutely equal: *to de analambanein auton en hautôi epistêmên ouk anamimnêskesthai estin?* – is retrieving oneself knowledge in oneself not to recollect? (Pl. *Meno* 85d); *hêmin hê mathêsis ouk allo ti ê anamnêsis* – for us learning is nothing other than remembering (Pl. *Phaedo* 72e); cf. *Phaedo* 92d 6.

anarkhos. (1) In Plato and Aristotle, without government, anarchic: *hêdeia politeia kai anarkhos* – [democracy is] a pleasant and anarchic form of state (Pl. *Rep.* 558c). ***anarkhia***, anarchy: *hubrin kai anarkhian* – insolence and anarchy (Pl. *Rep.* 560 e); *anarkhian poiein* – to bring about anarchy (Ar. *Pol.* 1272b 12). (2) Not in Plato and Aristotle, without beginning: *estin anarkhon apauston* – [reality] is without beginning and without end (Parmenides, fr. 8.27); *agenêton kai anarkhon* – uncreated and without beginning (Simplicius, *Physics* 1192.24).

andreia: etymologically, an abstract noun from *anêr* – adult male – meaning manliness and, especially, bravery; ***andreios***: brave. Cf. the Latin *virtus* from *vir* with similar original meaning. This sense always remained central: *kuriôs dê legoit'an andreios ho peri ton kalon thanaton adeês … toiauta de malista ta kata polemon* – the central sense of 'brave' is 'fearless concerning a glorious death' … which happen particularly in war (Ar. *E.N.* 1115a 32). The dialogue in Plato's *Laches* about *andreia* is mainly concerned with bravery in war. But other types of bravery may be called *andreia*: *oukh hê autê sôphrosunê gunaikos kai andros, oud'andreia* – the temperance of a woman and a man is not the same, nor their bravery (Ar. *Pol.* 1260a 22). The translations 'courage' and 'courageous' are common but less good; perhaps 'brave' has a greater suggestion of fearlessness, 'courageous' of endurance.

anisos: the contradictory of *isos*, with two meanings. (1) Unequal: *anisa tmêmata* – unequal segments (Pl. *Rep.* 509d). (2) Unfair: *dokei dê ho te paranomos adikos einai kai ho pleonektês kai anisos … to d'adikon to paranomon kai to anison* – both the lawbreaker and he who is grasping and unfair seem to be unjust … and injustice is both the unlawful and the unfair (Ar. *E.N.* 1129a 32).

anô: upwards, above: *topou de eidê kai diaphorai to anô kai katô kai emprosthen kai opisthen kai dexion kai aristeron* – the forms and varieties of place are the above and below, in front and behind, and right and left (Ar. *Phys.* 205b 31). In Aristotelian physics upwards is a straight line from the centre of the earth, which is the middle of the universe, to the sphere of the fixed stars: *to de pros to eskhaton anô* – [the limit of the universe] towards the extremity is the above (Ar. *Phys.* 212a 27); *eutheia d'hê anô kai katô· legô d'anô tên apo tou mesou* – upwards and downwards are in a straight line; I call upwards that from the middle (Ar. *De Caelo* 268b 21). The six directions listed above are called *diastaseis*.

antikeisthai: to be opposed or opposite to, particularly in logic. In particular (a) one proposition may be opposed to another in two ways: they may be *enantia*, contrary, as in 'All *A* is *B*' and 'No *A* is *B*', or they may constitute an *antiphasis*, a contradiction, as in 'All *A* is *B*' and 'Some *A* is not *B*'; and (b) a predicate may be opposed to another as *enantion*, contrary, as are good and bad, right and wrong. But *legetai de heteron heterôi antikeisthai tetrakhôs, ê hôs to pros ti, ê hôs ta enantia, ê hôs sterêsis kai hexis, ê hôs kataphasis kai apophasis* – things are said to be opposite to each other in four ways – as relatives [double and half], as contraries [good and bad], as privation and possession [blindness and sight], or as affirmation and negation (Ar. *Cat.* 11b 17). For contradictory and contrary propositions see also Ar. *De Int.* 17b 16 ff. Aristotle discusses the various senses of *antikeisthai* in *Met.*, Book 4, Ch. 10.

antiparektasis: reciprocal coextension, interpenetration. See *antiperistasis*.

antiperistasis: in physics, the exchange of position by one body with another or others. It is used to explain the possibility of movement in a plenum and also, conjecturally, to explain movement *biaï* – by force – as opposed to movement *phusei*: *antiperistasis de estin, hotan exôthoumenou tinos sômatos hupo sômatos antallagê genêtai tôn topôn* – *antiperistasis* comes about when one body is pushed out by another body and an exchange of places takes place (Simplicius, *Physics* 1350.32); *hê d'antiperistasis hama panta kineisthai poiei kai kinein* – *antiperistasis* makes everything move and be moved at once (Ar. *Phys.* 267a 18). The Stoic Chrysippus held that bodies could occupy the same place, and introduced the notion of *antiparektasis* or mutual penetration as an alternative to *antiperistasis*: *mixin d'einai duo ê kai pleionôn sômatôn antiparektasin di'holôn* – mixture is the mutual penetration of two or more bodies throughout each other (Stobaeus 1.153.24).

antiphasis: contradiction; *antiphatikôs*: contradictorily; *kai estô antiphasis touto, kataphasis kai apophasis hai antikeimenai* – so let a contradiction be this, an affirmation and negation opposed to each other (Ar. *De Int.* 17a 33). See *antikeisthai*.

24

antistrephein: in logic, to be convertible; **antistrophê**: conversion. Ross, in his note to Ar. *An. Pr.* 25a 6, distinguishes six uses of the verb *antistrephein* in the *Analytics*. In particular, *antistrophê* is the conversion, or the possibility of conversion, of a proposition by exchange of position of its subject and predicate. The negative propositions 'No *A* is *B*' and 'Some *A* is not *B*' and the particular affirmative proposition 'Some *A* is *B*' may all be converted validly without change of quantity, but 'All *A* is *B*' may be validly converted only into the particular 'Some *B* is *A*': *tên de katêgorikên [protasin] antistrephein men anagkaion ou mên katholou all'en merei* – the affirmative proposition is validly convertible, but not as a universal, but in part (Ar. *An. Pr.* 25a 7). In traditional logic the valid conversion from all to some is called conversion *per accidens* as distinct from simple conversion.

aoristos: indeterminate, indefinite, undefined: *mê toinun mêd'ho legomen einai paideian aoriston genêtai* – what we call education must also not remain undefined (Pl. *Laws* 643d); *hê men oun dunamis hôs hulê katholou ousa kai aoristos tou katholou kai aoristou estin* – potentiality [of knowledge] as matter is universal and indeterminate and of the universal and indeterminate (Ar. *Met.* 1087a 17); *Anaximenês ... hetairos gegonôs Anaximandrou mian men kai autos tên hupokeimenên phêsin hôsper ekeinos, ouk aoriston de hôsper ekeinos all'hôrismenên, aera legôn autên* – Anaximenes, a companion of Anaximander, also says that the substance is single like him, but not indeterminate like him but determinate, saying that it is air (Simplicius, *Physics* 24.28); *panta men gar ta plêthê têi heautôn phusei aorista onta* – all manifolds being of their own nature indeterminate (Proclus, *Elements of Theology* 117).

apagôgê has two senses in logic. (1) *apagôgê eis to adunaton* – *reductio ad impossibile* in traditional logic – which is a way of proving a syllogism not in the first figure when ordinary reduction to the first figure (*anagein*) is impossible. Thus to prove that if no *P* is *M* and some *S* is *M* then some *S* is not *P*, one argues that if all *S* is *P* we have the first figure syllogism that if no *P* is *M* and all *S* is *P* then no *S* is *M*, which contradicts the original minor premiss: see *An. Pr.* 29a 30 ff. (2) Substitution of a more probable premiss for another less acceptable. The complicated methods and aims of this process are described in *An. Pr.*, Book 2, Ch. 25. Plato uses the verb *apagein*, but only in the non-technical sense of leading away.

apatheia: used of people in the sense of being insensible to something or other. We connect time with, among other things, *tois pathesi kai tais apatheiais* – emotions and absences of emotions (Epicurus, *Letter to Herodotus* 73). It is common in the Stoics to mean freedom from emotion. More widely, *apatheia* is not being affected in any way and is applicable to anything animate or inanimate, and also, by neoplatonics, to transcendent entities. In this use it is commonly translated 'impassivity': *tên khôristên ekeinôn apatheian* – the separate [from becoming] impassivity of the transcendent (Proclus, *Republic* 2.118.22); *poiêtika kata de to sklêron kai malakon pathous kai apatheias* – producing passivity if soft and impassivity if hard (Ar. *Phys*. 217b 25). See ***apathês***.

apathês: generally, with genitive, not subject to or inexperienced in something: *apatheis kakôn* – not subject to evils (Pl. *Phaedrus* 250c). In metaphysics, impassive, or impassible, in the technical sense of being unaffected by other things: *apatheis kai akinêtoi dokousin einai hai ideai tois legousin ideas einai* – forms seem to be impassive and unchanging to those who believe in them (Ar. *Top*. 148a 20); *ho nous isôs theioteron ti kai apathes estin* – perhaps the intelligence is something more divine and impassive (Ar. *De An*. 408b 29); *to men homoion apathes phêsin hupo tou homoiou* – [Xenophanes] says that the like is impassive to the like (Simplicius, *Physics* 23.1); *to de asômaton haplon on apathes estin* – the incorporeal, being simple, is impassible (Proclus, *Elements of Theology* 80). In Aristotle's *Poetics* it means that there is no catastrophe: *kai ou tragikon· apathes gar* – it is not tragic, for there is no catastrophe (Ar. *Poetics* 1453b 39).

apeiros: lacking an end, boundary or limit, from ***peras***, a bound, with privative. Often translated as infinite. In particular used in neuter singular *to apeiron*, the infinite, unlimited, boundless, or indefinite, and, in the construction *eis apeiron*, without limit, *ad infinitum*. Anaximander is said to hold that the basic stuff was *to apeiron*, in the sense of being indefinite, and of no specific nature: *arkhên te kai stoikheion eirêke tôn ontôn to apeiron … legei d'autên mête hudôr mête allo ti tôn kaloumenôn einai stoikheiôn, all'heteran tina phusin apeiron* – [Anaximander] said that the indefinite was the principle and element of things … he says that it is not water nor any other of the things called elements but some other indefinite nature (Simplicius, *Physics* 24.14); *ei gar pan to on en* *topôi, dêlon hoti kai tou topou topos estai, kai touto eis apeiron* – for if all that is is in a place it is clear that there will also be a place of place and so without limit (Ar. *Phys*. 209a 25). This sense of *apeiros* must not be confused with that in which it means 'without experience' as the opposite of *empeiros*, experienced, which is common in Plato: *anagkê pantôn apeiron gegonenai* – he will inevitably have become totally inexperienced (Pl. *Gorg*. 484c).

aphairesis: in general, taking away, removal: *tôn orthôs dothentôn aphairesis ouk estin* – taking away legitimate gifts is not allowed (Pl. *Phil*. 19e). Philosophically, abstraction, especially in the phrase *ex aphaireseôs*: (a) of mathematics, *ho mathêmatikos peri ta ex aphaireseôs tên theôrian poieitai· perielôn gar ta aisthêta theôrei ... monon de leipei to poson kai to sunekhes* – the mathematician makes his study of things in abstraction; for he studies them stripped of perceptible qualities ... leaving only quantity and continuity (Ar. *Met*. 1061a 18), and (b) conceptually, *to katholou hoi men polloi kata to koinon noousi to en tois kata meros ex aphaireseôs autou psilên tên idiotêta lambanontes* – people in general intuit the universal by what is common in the particulars, taking the special feature on its own by abstraction (Simplicius, *Physics* 18.5).

aph'henos: literally, from one thing. To be *aph'henos* is, in Aristotle, one way in which two or more meanings of a term may be different but related and not chance *homônuma*. The meanings of a term are *aph'henos* if the others derive from one central meaning. A standard example is that a place, a diet, a complexion etc. may all be called healthy derivatively from the central case of a healthy person. In *E.N.*, having claimed that *agathos* has many senses, he says that the senses may be related *tôi aph'henos einai ê pros hen hapanta suntelein* – by being from a single case or from all contributing to a single case (Ar. *E.N.* 1096b 27). Contributing to and being from one case seem to be the same thing looked at from different angles. See also the discussion in Ar. *Met*., Book 11, Chs 3-4.

aphthartos: indestructible, from *phtheirein*, to destroy, with privative. Not in Plato. Used usually in conjunction with *agenêtos*, without beginning: *agenêton kai aphtharton* – [the universe] is without beginning and indestructible (Ar. *De Caelo* 270a 13); *ên gar an aphtharta kai agenêta* – they would be indestructible and

27

without beginning (Proclus, *Elements of Theology* 178). For Proclus *pasa psukhê anôlethros kai aphthartos* – every soul is imperishable and indestructible (op. cit. 187), since it is eternal and without beginning. Christian writers used *aphthartos* less strictly of the created human soul (e.g. St Paul, Epistle to the Romans 2:7).

aplanês: not wandering, fixed, has a special application in astronomy to both the fixed stars themselves and to the sphere of the fixed stars: *hos'aplanê tôn astrôn* – such of the stars as are fixed (Pl. *Tim.* 40b 4), *pôs hê aplanês peri ekeino [to kentron] strephetai?* – how does the fixed sphere move round the centre? (Proclus, *Republic* 2.228). The feminine *hê aplanês*, with or without the noun *sphaira*, refers normally to the sphere itself: *ou gar dê kai hê aplanês* – for the fixed sphere also is not [in place] (Simplicius, *Physics* 482.20). Used of an embryo by Plato: *eupages aplanes hêsukhaion te en mêtraï* – compact, motionless and quiet in the womb (Pl. *Laws* 775c). Metaphorically: *toutôn ... aplanês theôria* – the undeviating awareness of these things (Epicurus, *To Menoeceus* 128).

apodeiknunai, apodeixis, apodeiktikos: to prove, proof, demonstrative. In technical contexts the terms are usually confined to strict demonstrations, though they are sometimes used more loosely: *ti an tis ekhoi tekmêrion apodeixai ... poteron katheudomen ... ê egrêgoramen?* – what indicator would one have to prove whether we are asleep or awake? (Pl. *Theaet.* 158c). But by later writers arguments from *tekmêria* were not regarded as being strictly *apodeixeis*: *dêlon hoti tekmêriôdês estin hê gnôsis hê peri tôn arkhôn all'ouk apodeiktikê* – it is clear that knowledge of first principles is based on indicators and not demonstrative (Simplicius, *Physics* 18.23); *hê men gar apodeixis sullogismos tis, ho* **sullogismos** *de ou pas apodeixis* – proof is a kind of argument, but not every argument is a proof (Ar. *An. Pr.* 25b 30); *oute pasan epistêmên apodeiktikên einai, alla tên tôn amesôn anapodeikton* – nor is all knowledge demonstrative, since that of the immediate is undemonstrated (Ar. *An. Po.* 72b 19); *ek proterôn dei tên apodeixin einai kai* **gnôrimôterôn** – demonstration should be from the prior and better known (Ar. *An. Po.* 72b 26). The noun and verb are both common in Plato, but he does not use *apodeiktikos*.

aponia: in earlier writers, laziness: *hai rhathumiai kai hai aponiai kai hāi ameleiai* – slackness, laziness and carelessness (Ar. *Rhet.*

1370a 14). But it acquired a technical sense of freedom from distress and pain (*ponos* being the most common medical term for the distress of the sick): *hê men gar ataraxia kai aponia katastêmatikai eisin hêdonai* – freedom from mental and physical distress are constitutive pleasures [and not such as involve change] (Epicurus, fr. 1).

apophansis: a categorical proposition: *kataphasis de estin apophansis tinos kata tinos*. *apophasis de estin apophansis tinos apo tinos* – an affirmation is a proposition affirming something of something. Negation is a proposition denying something of something (Ar. *De Int*. 17a 25). Confusingly, there is an attested spelling of *apophansis* as *apophasis*; *LSJ* gives Ar. *Rhet*. 1365b 27 as an example of this, but the *OCT* has *apophansis* with many MSS.

apophantikos: categorical: *esti de heis logos apophantikos ê ho hen dêlôn ê ho sundesmôi heis* – a single categorical statement either declares something single or what is single by conjunction (Ar. *De Int*. 17a 16). *apophantikos logos* is a synonym of *apophansis*: *anagkê de panta logon apophantikon ek rhêmatos einai ê ptôseôs rhêmatos* – every propositional utterance must contain a verb or a tense of a verb (Ar. *De Int*. 17a 11).

apophasis: negative proposition: *phasin kai apophasin* – affirmation and negation (Pl. *Soph*. 263e); *hê apophasis logos apophatikos* – a negation is a negative statement (Ar. *Cat*. 12b 8). See *apophansis*.

apophatikos: negative. See *apophasis*.

apoproêgmenon: the contrary of *proêgmenon*, that which while not properly counted as *kakon*, bad, one would none the less prefer to avoid. A Stoic notion, applied to things exhibiting *apaxia*, disvalue: *ta men oun pollên ekhonta axian proêgmena legesthai, ta de pollên apaxian apoproêgoumena* – those things having much value were said [by Zeno] to be preferable, those having much disvalue to be preferably absent (*SVF*).

aporia: literally, absence of a way through; a difficult terrain may be *aporos*. In general use the noun and the verb *aporein* refer to not knowing what to do: *aporounti autôi erkhetai Promêtheus* – when

[Epimetheus] did not know what to do Prometheus came (Pl. *Prot.* 321c). This sense is explained by Aristotle in the *Topics* at 145b 16 ff. But usually in Aristotle and most later philosophy an *aporia* is a puzzle arising from the difficulty of reconciling two or more accepted or plausible beliefs. Aristotle believed the solution, or dissolution, of such puzzles to be a main task of philosophy: *dei d'hôsper epi tôn allôn, tithentas ta phainomena kai prôton diaporêsantas houtô deiknunai malista men panta ta endoxa peri tauta ta pathê, ei de mê, ta pleista kai kuriôtata· ean gar luêtai te ta duskherê kai kataleipêtai ta endoxa, dedeigmenon an eiê hikanôs –* we must, as elsewhere, state the apparent facts and, having first raised the *aporiai*, establish preferably all the received opinions about these states, or, if not all, the majority and most important; for if the difficulties are resolved and the received opinions remain, that would be a sufficient proof (Ar. *E.N.* 1145b 2); *aporêseie d'an tis pôs hupolambanôn orthôs akrateuetai tis –* one may raise the puzzle about what sort of correct understanding is possessed by the weak-willed (*E.N.* 1145b 21); *ekhei de pollas aporias ti pote estin ho topos –* there are many puzzles about what place is (Ar. *Phys.* 208a 32). The quotation by *LSJ* of the definition in the *Topics* (145b 1) of an *aporia* as *isotês enantiôn logismôn* is misleading, since Aristotle rejects it on the ground that one argument may have false premisses.

apsukhos: inanimate: *ean de apsukhon ti psukhês anthrôpon sterêsêi …* – if an inanimate object deprives a person of life … (Pl. *Laws* 873e); *legomen … diôristhai to empsukhon tou apsukhou tôi zên –* we say that the animate is distinguished from the inanimate by life (Ar. *De An.* 413a 20). In some non-philosophical literature plants are treated as *apsukha* in distinguishing a vegetable from a meat diet, but in philosophy only non-living matter is called *apsukhos*.

aretê: excellence or goodness of any kind. It is an abstract noun connected with **aristos**, excellent; the equivalent abstract noun **agathotês** from **agathos** is late and rare; *aretê* is commonly translated virtue, a transliteration of the Latin *virtus*, but neither *aretê* nor *virtus* means virtue, except in such archaising expressions as 'the virtues of the internal combustion engine', where 'excellences' would be equivalent: *oukoun kai aretê dokei soi einai hekastôi hôiper kai ergon ti prostetaktai?* – do you not think that everything to which a function is assigned has an excellence? (Pl. *Rep.* 353b); *dendra pantodapa kallos hupsos te daimonion hup'aretês tês gês ekhonta* – having all kinds of trees fantastic in beauty and height through the excellence of the soil (Pl. *Critias* 117b); *agathoi ontes pasan aretên* – being good in respect of every excellence (Pl. *Laws* 900d); *adikia* is an *aretê* because it pays (Pl. *Rep.* 348c); *dittês dê tês aretês ousês, tês men dianoêtikês, tês de êthikês* – excellence [of human soul] being of two kinds, of intelligence and of character (Ar. *E.N.* 1103a 14). The opposite of *aretê* is *kakia*. The translation of Aristotle's account of *eudaimonia* as *energeia kat'aretên* (*E.N.* 1098a 17) into 'activity in accordance with virtue' is particularly unfortunate. *kat'aretên* is an adverbial expression meaning 'excellently', and *energeia kat'aretên* is activity excellently performed, whatever the as yet undetermined activity may be.

aristeros: left, one of the six *diastaseis*, directions, recognised in Aristotelian physics. See Ar. *Phys.* 205b 32 and *anô* for details.

aristokratia: in general use, rule by what are called aristocrats in ordinary English (Aristotle says that *eugeneia estin arkhaios plutos kai aretê* – good birth is ancient wealth and excellence (Ar. *Pol.* 1294a 21)). In strict philosophical use it is rule by the best, who are the disinterestedly good and wise. Thus Plato says that rule by his guardians would be *aristokratia* (Pl. *Rep.* 445d). It is the *alêthinên kai prôtên* – the true and first type of aristocracy – based on *aretê* (Ar. *Pol.* 1294a 20, 24). This is correct etymologically, since the *aristos* is one who has *aretê*.

aristos: is grammatically treated as the irregular superlative of *agathos*; it means 'excellent' or 'best' and is applied to whosoever and whatsoever has any *aretê*. The supreme goal in life is *to ariston*, the highest good (Ar. *E.N.* 1094a 22).

arithmos: number; *arithmêtikê*: the science of number. Zero was unknown as a number and one also was not counted as a number, the first number being the *duas* – two. From the Pythagoreans, *ton arithmon nomizontes arkhên einai* – who consider number to be the first principle (Ar. *Met.* 986a15) – number played a great part in metaphysics, especially in Plato's unwritten doctrines, involving obscure distinctions of e.g. *sumblêtoi* and *asumblêtoi* – addible and non-addible numbers. For these and other distinctions see Ar. *Met.*, Book 13, Ch. 6. Numbers were written as letters of the alphabet, which made calculation difficult and perhaps explains why Greek geometry progressed so much more rapidly than arithmetic.

arkhê has a great number of meanings, but they can all be seen to derive from the basic meaning of a beginning or starting point: *kai gar hê pêgê kai hê kardia kai monas kai sêmeion kai to hêgoumenon en polei arkhê legetai, tosouton allêlôn têi phusei diapheronta* – a spring, the heart, an individual, a point and the government are all called *arkhê*, though they differ from each other so much in nature (Simplicius, *Physics* 1097.2); *hê autê moi arkhê estin ... hêiper arti* – I start from where I started just now (Pl. *Prot.* 318a); *arkhê de ex hês kai ha nundê elegomen panta êrtêtai* – the basis also of all our recent statements (Pl. *Theaet.* 156a); *arkhê d'estin apodeixeôs protasis amesos· amesos de hês mê estin allê protera* – the starting point of a demonstration is an immediate premiss: it is immediate if there is none prior to it (Ar. *An. Po.* 72a 7); *prôtos autos arkhên onomasas to hupokeimenon* – [Anaximander] having first called substance the first principle (Simplicius, *Physics* 150.23); *hoti men eisin arkhai ... diôristhai houtôs. palin d'allên arkhên arxamenoi legômen* – that there are first principles is thus demonstrated. Now let us speak making a fresh start (Ar. *Phys.* 192b 2); *ei mê hê arkhe dia takheôn kateluthê* – if the leadership (government) had not been speedily dissolved (Pl. *Apol.* 32d).

asômatos: incorporeal: in a lyre *hê men harmonia aoraton kai asômaton, kai pagkalon ... hautê d'hê lura kai hai khordai sômata te ... kai tou thnêtou suggenê* – the tuning is invisible and incorporeal and most beautiful, but the lyre itself and its strings are bodies and akin to the mortal (Pl. *Phaedo* 85e); *ta gar asômata, kallista onta kai megista* – the incorporeal things that are the most beautiful and greatest (Pl. *Pol.* 286a); *hulên tên arkhên legousin, an te mian an te pleious hupothôsi, kai ean te sôma ean te asômaton touto tithôsin* – who say that the first principle is matter, whether they postulate one or many and whether they suppose it to be body or incorporeal (Ar. *Met.* 988a 25); *pasa psukhê asômatos estin ousia kai khôristê sômatos* – every soul is incorporeal and separable from body (Proclus, *Elements of Theology* 186).

atelês: incomplete. Frequent in Plato in non-technical use, e.g. in

Rep. 495c and d. In Aristotle being *atelês* is one of the marks that distinguish a **kinêsis** (change, process) from an **energeia** (activity): *hê te kinêsis energeia men einai tis dokei, atelês de* – change seems to be a sort of activity, but incomplete (Ar. *Phys.* 201b 31). A *kinêsis* has an end outside it, as house-building, for example, has the existence of a house as its end, and is so in itself *atelês*, whereas metaphysical and aesthetic contemplation, for example, have no ulterior **telos**, but are complete, being *energeiai: ouden gar ateles esti tôn tês eudaimonias* – no element in happiness is incomplete (Ar. *E.N.* 1177b 25).

athlios: wretched, miserable, the contrary of **eudaimôn**. Like *eudaimôn, athlios* refers to the value and worthwhileness of a person's life in general and not to a state of feeling in particular. To call a man *athlios* is to say that his life is not worth living: *athlios men oudepote genoit'an ho eudaimôn* – the happy man could never become wretched (Ar. *E.N.* 1101a 7); when asked whether the unjustly killed is *athlios* Socrates replies *hêtton ê ho apokteinus* – less than the killer (Pl. *Gorg* 469b). *athliotês* is wretchedness.

atomos: indivisible, from *temnein*, to cut, with privative. Used of many things, either as being strictly indivisible in any way or as being the smallest unit of its kind: *ou gar khalepon anelein tas atomous grammas* – it is not difficult to dispose of indivisible lines (Ar. *Phys.* 206a 17); *nomôi gluku, nomôi pikron, nomôi thermon, nomôi psukhron, nomôi khroiê, eteêi de atoma kai kenon* – sweet, bitter, hot, cold and colour are conventional, in truth there are atoms and the void (Democritus in Sextus Empiricus, *Adversus Mathematicos* 7.135); in the plural *ta atoma*, with no substantive, as in Democritus, the omitted noun being *sômata* as in *atoma sômata legontas* – saying that there are indivisible bodies (Ar. *De Caelo* 303a 21); *atomon gar to eidos* – for the species is indivisible (Ar. *Met.* 1034a 7).

aülos: having no matter, from *hulê*, matter, with privative. Not to be confused with the noun *aulos* which is the name (not of a flute but) of any pipe or conduit and, most often in the philosophers, of the double-reed ancestor of the oboe. Not in Plato and doubtfully once in Aristotle, but common in later philosophy: *kai to eidos de to enulon saphôs oimai paradidôsin en hois kai to aülon eidos* – [Plato] clearly teaches of the form in matter where he also does of the matterless form (Simplicius, *Physics* 26.19); *pasês merikês psukhês to okhêma aülon esti* – the vehicle of every particular soul is immaterial (Proclus, *Elements of Theology* 208).

autokinêtos: self-changing, self-moving: *duo ontôn arkhikôn tês kinêseôs, tou te akinêtou kai tou autokinêtou* – there are two sources of change, the unchanging and the self-changing (Simplicius, *Physics* 1220.34); *monôs gar houtôs hoion ti autokinêton einai* – only thus can a thing be self-changing (Ar. *Phys.* 258a 2). The verbal form is customarily spelt as two words as in *to auto hauto kinoun* – that which moves itself (Ar. *Phys.* 208a 6-7). The word does not occur in Plato except in one papyrus fragment of the *Phaedrus* where the codices read *aeikinêton*. The *zôion* – animal – including man, the soul being responsible for the bodily motion, was the common recipient of the adjective *autokinêtos*: *ti oun an eiê kata tautên tên kinêsin autokinêton kuriôs ê to zôion?* – what could be self-changing strictly in this way except an animal? (Simplicius, *Physics* 1249.22). For the translation 'self-change' as well as the common 'self-motion', see *kinêsis*.

automatos: generally, of its own accord, spontaneous, automatic: *ean pou automatoi peritukhôsin têi aretêi* – if perhaps they might of their own accord come upon excellence [without education] (Pl. *Prot.* 320a). Aristotle discusses how the notion fits in with his types of explanation in *Physics*, Book 2: *to men gar apo tukhês pan apo t'automatou, touto d'ou pan apo tukhês* – the chance is all spontaneous, but not all the spontaneous is by chance (Ar. *Phys.* 197a 35); *phaneron hoti en tois haplôs heneka tou gignomenois, hotan mê tou sumbantos heneka genêtai hôn exô to aition, tote apo tou automatou legomen* – it is clear that in the field of things that in some way come about for something, if something comes about with an external cause and not for the sake of what results, then we say it happens spontaneously (Ar. *Phys.* 197b 18).

autos: himself, itself, as in the famous *autos epha* – [Pythagoras] himself said it. Philosophically important in the form **auto to** + neuter adjective: *auto to ison* – the equal itself (Pl. *Phaedo* 74c); *auto to hen* – the one itself (Pl. *Parm.* 143a). It is hard to determine whether *auto to ison* as a form is a universal or a perfect non-sensible particular. Thus in *auta ta isa estin hoti anisa soi ephanê, ê hê isotês anisotês?* – have the equals themselves ever

34

appeared unequal or equality inequality? – it has been disputed whether *auta ta anisa* are two or more perfect particulars while *isotês* is equality, or whether the phrase should be taken as a hendiadys, with an explicative *kai* – the equals themselves, that is equality. Sensibly equal things are said to *elleipein kata tên homoiotêta* – fail in likeness – to *auta ta isa*. Aristotle frequently speaks (hostilely?) of *to autoagathon* (Ar. *Met.* 1099c 28), the *autoanthrôpos* (Ar. *E.N.* 1096a 35), and even the *autohekaston* – the so-and-so itself (Ar. *E.N.* 1096a 35) rather than of *auto to agathon* and similarly.

auxêsis: increase in size, the contrary being *phthisis*, decrease in size. The verb is *auxanein*: *auxanomenê selênê* – the waxing moon (Ar. *De Caelo* 291b 19); *to auxanomenon hapan auxanetai hupo suggenous prosiontos* – everything that increases does so by the arrival of something of the same nature (Ar. *De Caelo* 270a 239). *auxêsis* is one of the three kinds of *kinêsis kata topon*, change of place: *phora*, *auxêsis* and *phthisis*: *tautês de to men phora, to de auxêsis kai phthisis* – of [change of place] there are locomotion and increase and decrease (Ar. *Phys.* 211a 15); *meizonos men pragmatos kai elattonos metaxu auxêsis kai phthisis, kai kaloumen houtô to men auxanesthai, to de phthinein* – between a body being greater and smaller there is increase and decrease, and we thus call the one 'to increase', the other 'to decrease' (Pl. *Phaedo* 71c).

axiôma: an assumption or an axiom. Assumption: *houtô gar to te anagkaion estai, kai to axiôma endoxon* – thus necessity will be achieved and the assumption will become accepted belief (Ar. *An. Pr.* 62a 13). Axiom: [*arkhê amesos*] *hên anagkê ekhein ton hotioun mathêsomenon, axiôma* – [an immediate principle] that one must have in order to acquire any knowledge is an axiom (Ar. *An. Po.* 72a 16); *ta d'axiômata autôn· peri pantôn gar adunaton apodeixin einai* – some of them are self-evident principles; for there cannot be proof about everything (Ar. *Met.* 997a 8). Euclid's axioms are called by him *koinai ennoiai* and his postulates are *aitêmata*. Not in Plato.

B

baros: weight; *barus*: heavy. The contraries are *kouphotês*, lightness, and *kouphos*, light. Book 4 of Aristotle's *De Caelo* is *peri de bareos kai kouphou, ti t'estin hekateron kai tis hê phusis autôn –*

concerning the heavy and the light, what each is and what their nature (Ar. *De Caelo* 307b 28). A thing may be said to be heavy relative to another – *pros heteron* – or *baruteron*: *baru de haplôs to katô kai pros to meson* – the absolutely heavy is [what moves of its own nature] downwards and towards the middle [of the universe] (Ar. *De Caelo*, 308a 30). The views of the atomists about weight are uncertain because of apparently conflicting evidence: *kaitoi baruteron ge kata tên huperokhên phêsin einai Dêmokritos hekaston tôn adiairetôn* – Democritus says that each of the indivisible bodies is heavier in proportion to its excess [of bulk] (Ar. *De Gen. et Cor.* 326a 9); *Dêmokritos ta prôta phêsi sômata ... baros men ouk ekhein* – Democritus says that the primary bodies ... have no weight (Aetius 1.3.18). On this problem, see Kirk and Raven, *The Presocratic Philosophers*, 414-15.

bathos: depth; *bathus*, deep: *diastêmata ... tria, mêkos kai platos kai bathos, hois horizetai sôma pan* – three dimensions ... length, breadth and depth, by which all body is defined (Ar. *Phys.* 209a 5); *megethous de to men eph'hen grammê, to de epi duo epipedon, to de epi tria sôma* – of magnitudes the one-dimensional is a line, the two-dimensional a plane, the three-dimensional a body (Ar. *De Caelo* 268a 7). In transferred sense, e.g. *kai moi ephanê bathos ti ekhein pantapasi gennaion* – [Parmenides] seemed to me to have a certain noble depth (Pl. *Theaet.* 184a).

bia: force; *biaios*, forcible; *biazein*, to force. *bia* can be used to mean pressure of a non-physical kind in a non-technical context, as when contrasted with *hekôn*: *mêdamôs pros bian boulêthêis mallon ê hekôn legein* – not wishing to speak under pressure rather than willingly (Pl. *Phaedrus* 236d). But in philosophical use it means physical force: *anagkê gar ê biaion einai tên kinêsin ê kata phusin* – the motion must either be forced or natural (Ar. *De Caelo* 300b 18). In the ethical writings Aristotle gives as examples of *akousia biaï* – unintended because of violence – only physical force: *biaion hou hê arkhê exôthen* – forcible where the source is external (*E.N.* 1110a 1). *bia* is one form of *anagkê*; thus *biaias anagkês* – necessity of a forceful kind (Ar. *De Caelo* 284a 15).

bios: life, usually as a social rather than a merely biological phenomenon, which is usually *zôê*. Thus Plutarch and Diogenes Laertius wrote *Bioi* and not *Zôai*. *ton bion apolaustikon* – the life of pleasure (Ar. *E.N.* 1095b 17). Aristotle also speaks of the *bios politikos* and the *theôrêtikos bios*. But there is no clear-cut distinction between *bios* and *zôê*. *bios* as life has a paroxytone accent; *bios* with an oxytone accent is a bow.

blabê: harm; *blaptein*: to harm. In Book 5, Ch. 9 of the *E.N.* Aristotle makes the distinction, important in all later jurisprudence, between suffering harm (*damnum*) and suffering injustice (*injuria*); hence the Latin tag *damnum, non injuria, fit volenti*. *blaptetai men oun tis hekôn kai t'adika paskhei, adikeitai d'oudeis hekôn* – one is therefore harmed with one's consent and fares unjustly, but nobody who consents suffers injustice (Ar. *E.N.* 1136b 5).

boulesthai: to wish; *boulêsis*: wish, wishing; *boulêtos*: object of wish. The nature of *boulêsis* is discussed by Aristotle in *E.N.*, Book 3, Ch. 2. Aristotle recognises three kinds of *orexis*, appetition: *orexis men gar epithumia kai thumos kai boulêsis* – appetition is either desire [for the pleasant] or anger [seeking revenge] or rational wish [for the good] (Ar. *De An.* 414b 2); *haplôs men kai kat'alêtheian boulêton einai t'agathon* – absolutely and truly, the good is the object of wish (Ar. *E.N.* 1113a 24); unlike *bouleusis*, *boulêsis d'esti kai tôn adunatôn* – wish is also for the impossible (Ar. *E.N.* 1111b 22). Plato uses the terms in a less technical way.

bouleuesthai: to deliberate; *bouleusis*: deliberation. The use of these concepts is carefully discussed in *E.N.*, Book 3, Ch. 3. *bouleuometha de peri tôn eph'hêmin kai praktôn* – we deliberate about things that are in our power and practicable (Ar. *E.N.* 1112a 30). *bouleusis* is a prerequisite of *proairesis* – choice: *hê proairesis an eiê bouleutikê orexis tôn eph'hêmin* – choice is a deliberative appetition of things in our power (Ar. *E.N.* 1113a 10); *bouleuometha d'ou peri tôn telôn alla peri tôn pros to telos* – we do not deliberate about success but about how to achieve it (Ar. *E.N.* 1112b 11).

C

There is no letter C. For words beginning with the Greek letter χ and words anglicised with a C, see under K.

D

dei: it is needful, one needs, it is requisite, and similar expressions; *to deon*: what is needed, requisite. There is no notion of logical necessity or ethical obligation involved, unless contextually. Logical necessity is *anagkê* and ethical need is expressed by *khrê*.

deilos, deilia: coward, cowardly, cowardice. Usually opposed to *andreios*: *hêttôn deilos andreiou* – a coward is inferior to the brave (Pl. *Phaedrus* 239a). In Aristotle, one of the two *kakiai* opposed to the *aretê* of *andreia*: *ho de en tôi men phobeisthai huperballôn tôi de tharrein elleipôn deilos* – he who is excessive in fear and deficient in confidence is a coward (Ar. *E.N.* 1107b 3); *enantion andreia deiliaï* – bravery is the opposite of cowardice (Pl. *Prot.* 360b).

deinos in general use has a variety of meanings corresponding very roughly to those of 'terrific' or 'formidable', ranging through the fearful and terrifying, the strange and the accomplished. In the sense of frightening: *ta deina gignôskein kai ta tharralea* – to recognise the frightening and the heartening (Pl. *Laches* 195e). In philosophy it is sometimes used dyslogistically of the clever: *hê de dê apodeixis deinois men apistos, sophois de pistê* – the proof will be unconvincing to the clever, convincing to the wise (Pl. *Phaedrus* 245c). But frequently, where usually translated 'clever', 'capable' might be better, since it refers to executive ability: *deinoi makhesthai* – capable fighters (Pl. *Laches* 191d); *deinos eis tous logous tous eis ta dikastêria* – an able speaker in the law courts (Pl. *Euthyd.* 304d); *deinotês* is defined as executive ability by Aristotle: *esti dê dunamis hên kalousi deinotêta· hautê d'estin toiautê hôste ta pros ton hupotethenta skopon sunteinonta dunasthai tauta prattein kai tugkhanein autou* – there is a capacity that they call *deinotês*; this capacity is such as to be capable of doing the things necessary to the proposed goal and to attain it (Ar. *E.N.* 1144a 23).

dêmokratia: democracy. Theoretically democracy was the direct rule of the whole free populace (male), but it was thought of usually as the rule of the many poor rather than of the few rich, which was oligarchy: *esti dêmokratia men hotan hoi eleutheroi kai aporoi pleious ontes kurioi tês arkhês ôsin, oligarkhia d'hotan hoi plousioi kai eugenesteroi oligoi ontes* – a democracy is when the free and without substance are in the majority and have the rule in their power, an oligarchy when the rich and better born and few have it (Ar. *Pol*. 1290b 18). Plato was no admirer of democracy: *dêmokratia dê oimai gignetai hotan hoi penêtes nikêsantes tous men apokteinôsi tôn heterôn, tous de ekbalôsi, tois de loipois ex isou metadôsi politeias te kai arkhôn, kai hôs to polu apo klêrôn hai arkhai en autêi gignontai* – I think that there is democracy when the poor conquer and kill some of the others, exile others, and give to the rest an equal share in citizenship and offices, and generally in it offices are gained by lot (Pl. *Rep*. 557a).

den: a word, not in *LSJ*, coined by Democritus forensically as an opposite to *ouden* and as a synonym of *on*; presumably aimed at Parmenides who held that *to mê on* – that which is not – is a meaningless expression: *Dêmokritos ... prosagoreuei ... tôn de ousiôn hekastên tôi te deni kai tôi nastôi kai tôi onti* – Democritus called each thing that exists a *den* or a solid or an entity (Simplicius, *De Caelo* 295.1) The translation 'hing' has been suggested as an opposite to 'nothing'.

diadokhos: successor. Plato's Academy continued without interruption until its closure by Justinian in the sixth century AD. Thus later heads are called *diadokhoi*. In book titles *Proklou diadokhou* and *Damaskiou diadokhou* give the author.

diairein (in past tense, *dielein*), *diairesis*: to divide, division, used in as many contexts in Greek as in English. In philosophy particularly the logical division of a genus into species. In the *Phaedrus* and the *Sophist* Plato speaks of a method of *sunagôgê* – collection – and *diairesis* – division – as the supreme method of philosophy: *toutôn dê egôge autos te erastês, ô Phaidre, tôn diaireseôn kai sunagôgôn hina hoios te ô legein kai phronein* – and, Phaedrus, I myself am a lover of divisions and collections in order to become able to speak and think (Pl. *Phaedrus* 266b); *ean mê tis ... kat'eidê te diaireisthai ta onta kai miaï ideaï dunatos ê kath'hen hekaston perilambanein, ou pot'estai tekhnikos logôn peri kath' hoson dunaton anthrôpôi* – unless one is capable of dividing things and subsuming each thing individually under a single form, one will never become skilled in discussion to the limit of human capacity (Pl. *Phaedrus* 273d); *tês tôn genôn kat'eidê diaireseôs palaia tis ... argia* – a long-standing laziness about dividing genera into species (Pl. *Soph*. 267d). Common in Aristotle's logical works in a similar sense: *esti gar hê diairesis hoion asthenês sullogismos* – a division is a sort of weak argument (Ar. *An. Pr*. 46a 32). Also used of distinguishing the meanings of terms: *dielomenon auton posakhôs legetai to en tôi horismôi apodothen* – when he has distinguished how many senses there are of the term in the definition (Ar. *Top*. 139b 28).

diakrinesthai: separate; *diakrisis*: separation. The contrary of *sugkrinesthai, sugkrisis*. Also distinguished from *ekkrisis*, which is the separation out of something from a mixture: *kai panta houtô ... diakrinesthai kai sugkrinesthai ... gignesthai te auta ex allêlôn, genesis te einai hekastou eis allêla* – everything thus separates and mixes ... and these come from each other and each thing becomes the others (Pl. *Phaedo* 71b); *houtô gar kai Dêmokritos kosmopoiei kai Empedoklês kai Anaxagoras, hoi men sugkrinesthai kai diakrinesthai ta atoma sômata kai ta tettara stoikheia legontes, Anaxagoras de ekkrinesthai tas homoiomereias apo tou migmatos legôn* – that is how Democritus constructs the cosmos, and Empedocles and Anaxagoras, the former saying that the atoms (D.) and the four elements (E.) are conjoined and Anaxagoras that the homoeomeries are separated out from the mixture (Simplicius, *Physics* 1120.20). Also used of conceptual discrimination: *diakrinas tên kath'hautên metabolên apo tês kata sumbebêkos* – having distinguished essential from accidental (contingent) change (Simplicius, *Physics* 804.13).

dialektikê, dialektikos: dialectic, dialectician, from the verb *dialegesthai*, which normally retains its non-technical sense of conversing. For the overriding importance of dialectic: *hôsper thrigkos tois mathêmasin epanô keitai* – [dialectic] rests like a coping stone on other studies (Pl. *Rep*. 534e); *alla mên to ge dialektikon ouk allôi dôseis hôs eg'ôimai, plên tôi katherôs te kai dikaiôs philosophounti* – you will not, I think, give the title of dialectician to anyone save to him who philosophises purely and righteously (Pl. *Soph*. 253e). But it is less clear what dialectic is; in the earlier dialogues it seems to be the attempt to reach definitions by conversational question and answer, as in *Republic* 532 ff.: *ê kai dialektikon kaleis ton logon hekastou lambanonta tês ousias?* – do you take the dialectician to be him who gets an account of the nature of everything? (Pl. *Rep*. 534b). But later the method of *sunagôgê* and *diairesis* is identified as dialectic: *tous dunamenous touto dran* (sc. *sunagein kai diairein*) *ei men orthôs ê mê prosagoreuô, theos oide, kalô oun mekhri toude dialektikous* – those who can collect and divide, god knows whether I speak correctly or not, I have so far called dialecticians (Pl. *Phaedrus* 266b). Aristotle distinguishes dialectical from scientific argument: *dialektikos sullogismos ho ex endoxôn sullogizomenos* – a dialectical argument is one argued from accepted beliefs (Ar. *Top.* 100a 30); *esti de protasis dialektikê erôtêsis endoxos ê pasin ê tois pleistois ê tois sophois* – a dialectical proposition is a proposal accepted either by all or by the majority or by the learned (Ar. *Top.* 104a 9).

dianemein, dianemêtikos, dianomê: distribute, distributive, distribution. Used in all natural contexts by both Plato and Aristotle. Especially in Aristotle, of one of the two kinds of *dikaiosunê en merei* – justice as one particular excellence: *to men gar dainemêtikon dikaion tôn koinôn aei kata tên analogian estin tên eirêmenên* – justice distributive of common goods is always in accordance with the [geometrical] proportion stated (Ar. *E.N.* 1131b 27). The other variety of particular justice is *to diorthôtikon*.

dianoia: intelligence, mind. Plato and Aristotle use the term sometimes in a general sense: [*nosêma*] *kata to sôma ê kata tên dianoian* – a disease of body or mind (Pl. *Laws* 916a); *ouden paskhontos tou sômatos alla mallon tês dianoias* – nothing happening in the body but rather in the mind (Ar. *E.N.* 1117b31). Of thought, including practical thought: *dianoia d'autê outhen kinei* – thought itself initiates no change (Ar. *E.N.* 1139a 35); *ho entos tês psukhês pros hautên dialogos aneu phônês genomenos, tout'auto hêmin epônomasthê dianoia* – the converse of the soul with itself, without speech, is what we called thought (Pl. *Soph.* 263e). Sometimes, as in *hôs metaxu ti doxês kai nou tên dianoian ousan*, which may mean 'discursive knowledge is between immediate apprehension and fallible opinion' (Pl. *Rep.* 511d), it seems to have a narrower meaning. Also some specific thought or intention of an individual: [*skopein*] *pros tên dianoian tou nomothetou* – look to the intention of the lawgiver (Ar. *Rhet.* 1374b 13). The verb is *dianoeisthai*.

diaphora: difference, from the verb *diapherein*, to differ. Used generally in obvious ways. The technical name in logic for the feature which distinguishes one species within a genus. Thus to define any species is to give the genus and difference: if man is generically an animal and the feature distinguishing him from all other animals is his rationality, then the definition 'rational animal' uniquely defines man among all other things. Informally anticipated by Plato: *tên diaphoran hekastou an lambanêis hêi tôn allôn diapherei, logon, hôs phasi tines, lêpsêi* – if you take the difference of each thing by which it differs from other things you will, as some say, get its account [definition] (Pl. *Theaet.* 208d). Formally in Aristotle: *dei gar ton horizomenon eis to genos thenta tas diaphoras prosaptein* – for the definer must put things into their genus and add the differences (Ar. *Top.* 139a 28); *ek gar tou genous kai tôn diaphorôn ta eidê* – species come from the genus and the differences (Ar. *Met.* 1057b7). The traditional Latin tag is that definition is *per genus et differentiam*. The varieties of *diaphora* are discussed by Aristotle in *Met.*, Book 4, Ch. 9.

diaporein: to go through the *aporiai*: *dei ... prôton diaporêsantas houtô deiknunai malista men panta ta endoxa* – one must first run through the difficulties and then establish at best all the accepted beliefs [when making a philosophical investigation] (Ar. *E.N.* 1145b 2).

diastasis: interval, extension, direction, dimension; see *diastatos, diastêma, diistasthai*. (1) As interval, *hêmiholiôn de diastaseôn kai epitritôn kai epogdoôn genomenôn* – intervals of a half and 4:3 and an eighth having come about (Pl. *Tim.* 36a; see also 36b-d); also used of musical intervals. (2) As extension: *sôma men gar estin to pantêi ekhon diastasin* – body is what has extension in every way (Ar. *Phys.* 204b 20). (3) As direction: *anô ê katô ê en allêi tini diastasei tôn hex* – up or down or in any of the six directions (Ar. *Phys.* 206a 6). (4) As dimension, *ei de mê sôma esti to tas treis ekhon diastaseis, logou deêsei· peisthênai gar ou rhaïdion einai ti asômaton treis ekhon diastaseis* – if the thing having the three dimensions is not a body, that will need argument; for one is not easily convinced that there is something incorporeal that has three dimensions (Simplicius, *Physics* 531.9). The slide between senses (2), (3) and (4) can be seen in such phrases as *pasas gar ekhei tas diastaseis* – it is extended in all the directions *or* it has all the dimensions (Ar. *De Caelo* 268b 6).

diastatos: extended: *ou gar diastaton to periekhon* – for what contains them is not extended (Proclus, *Elements of Theology* 176);

tôn de asômaton legontôn, hoi men pantêi **adiastaton***, hoi de diastaton legousi* – of those who say that [place] is incorporeal, some say that it is altogether unextended, others that it is extended (Simplicius, *Physics* 601.16). Not in Plato or Aristotle, but common in later writers.

diastêma: dimension, interval, sometimes translated extension. As dimension: *diastêmata men oun ekhei tria, mêkos kai platos kai bathos, hois horizetai sôma pan* – it [place] has then three dimensions, length, breadth and depth, by which all body is defined (Ar. *Phys.* 209a 4). As interval: *en hekastôi diastêmati* – in each interval (Pl. *Tim.* 36a); *ê gar morphê ê hulê, ê diastêma ti to metaxu tôn eskhatôn, ê ta eskhata ei mê esti mêden diastêma para to tou eggignomenou sômatos megethos* – [place] is either form or matter or some interval between the extremities [of a body] or the extremities if there is no interval beyond the magnitude of the body in it (Ar. *Phys.* 211b 7). Aristotle here and elsewhere entertains the notion of the *diastêma* as something independent. Compare *to de diastêma touto hoi men peri Dêmokriton kai Epikouron kenon einai legousin, hôste pote men plêrousthai sômatos pote de kai kenon apoleipeisthai, hoi de Platonikoi kai hoi Stôikoi einai men allo para ta sômata phasin, aei de sôma ekhein* – this interval the followers of Democritus and Epicurus say is void, so that it is sometimes filled with a body and sometimes left empty, but the Platonists and the Stoics say that it is something other than body but always contains a body (Simplicius, *Physics* 571.27); *en metakosmiôi, ho legomen metaxu kosmôn diastêma* – in the intercosmic, which is what we call the interval between universes (Epicurus, *To Pythocles* 89.4). A *diastêma* may be a one-dimensional distance, or a volume: *diastêma de legô tôn grammôn hou mêden estin exô labein megethos haptomenon tôn grammôn* – I call the interval (length) of a line that such that there is no magnitude joined to the line beyond it (Ar. *De Caelo* 271b 30); *tou megistou topou kai diastêmatos en hôiper estin ho ouranos* – the greatest place and interval in which the heavens are (Simplicius, *Physics* 576.19).

diathesis: condition: *diapherei de hexis diatheseôs tôi polu khroniôteron einai* – a disposition differs from a condition by being much longer-lasting (Ar. *Cat.* 8b 28); *mnême diathesis psukhês* – memory is a condition of the soul (Pl. *Def.* 414a). More especially, the order or manner of arrangement: *diathesis legetai tou ekhontos merê taxis ê kata topon, ê kata dunamin, ê kat'eidos* – the arrangement of what has parts, either spatially or potentially or in form is called *diathesis* (Ar. *Met.* 1022b 1); *ameinôn diathesis tês politeias* – a better arrangement of the constitution (Pl. *Laws* 710b); *tôn men toioutôn ou tên heuresin alla tên diathesin epaineton* – of such it is not the invention but the style that is to be praised (Pl. *Phaedrus* 236a). In *pros tous alêthinous philosophous tên diathesin* (Pl. *Rep.* 489a) attitude is the best translation – the attitude towards true philosophers. The varieties of *diathesis* are discussed by Aristotle in *Met.*, Book 4, Ch. 19.

diathigê: a term meaning order, used by the atomists: *diapherein gar phasin to on rhusmôi kai diathigêi kai tropêi monon. toutôn de ho men rhusmos skhêma estin, hê de diathigê taxis, hê de tropê thesis. diapherei gar ... to de AN tou NA taxei* – they say that what is differs only in rhythm, touching and turning, of which rhythm is shape, touching is arrangement and turning is position; for *AN* differs from *NA* in arrangement (Ar. *Met.* 985b 15).

didaskein, didaskalia, didaktos: teach, teaching, taught. Apart from frequent use in obvious ways, Plato often asks whether *aretê is gained by teaching: ara didakton hê aretê, ê ou didakton all'askêton, ê oute askêton oude mathêton alla phusei paragignetai?* – is excellence taught, or not taught but acquired by training, or neither acquired by training nor learnt, but something that comes naturally? (Pl. *Meno* 70a). Aristotle answers that of two sorts of *aretê*: *hê men dianoêtikê to pleion ek didaskalias ekhei kai tên genesin kai auxêsin ... hê de êthikê ex ethous perigignetai* – excellence of intelligence is mostly acquired and increased by teaching ... excellence of character by custom (Ar. *E.N.* 1103a 15).

dikaiosunê, dikaios, dikaiopragein: conventionally, justice, just, act justly. The opposites are *adikia, adikos, adikein*. In fact *dikaiosunê* and cognates have a wider sense, perhaps 'righteousness', and a narrower sense of 'fair dealing'. These senses are explicitly distinguished by Aristotle: *eoike de pleonakhôs legesthai hê dikaiosunê kai hê adikia* – both ... seem to be used in different senses (Ar. *E.N.* 1129a 26); *dikaios estai ho te nomimos kai ho isos* – the *dikaios* will be both the law-abiding and the fair dealer (Ar. *E.N.* 1129a 34); in the wider use: *hautê men oun hê dikaiosunê aretê men esti teleia, all'oukh haplôs, alla pros heteron* – this sort of *dikaiosunê* is complete excellence [of character] but not simply, but in relation to other people (Ar. *E.N.* 1129b 26). Aristotle says that *dia to suneggus einai tên homônumian autôn lanthanei* – because the two senses are closely connected the ambiguity escapes notice (Ar. *E.N.* 1129a 27); thus when in the *Republic* Polemarchus offers the definition *to ta opheilomena hekastôi apodidonai dikaion esti* – giving to each man his due is just (Pl. *Rep.* 331e) – Socrates objects that returning something to somebody who is insane might be *adikon*; but it is clearly not unjust, but improper in some wider sense. There is a full discussion of all aspects of *dikaiosunê* in *E.N.*, Book 5, where *dianemêtikê* and *diorthôtikê* justice are distinguished within *dikaiosunê en merei* – justice as a part of *holê dikaiosunê* – the whole of righteousness. It is clear that the standard legal accusation against Socrates, *Sôkratês adikei* ... (Pl. *Apol.* 19b) was not an accusation of injustice in the narrow sense, but of something wider, in his case of corrupting the young and introducing strange gods.

dikhotomein, dikhotomia: (1) Cut in two: *sômatos dikhotomêthentos* – the body having been cut in two (Ar. *Problems* 913b 31). (2) Bisect: *dikhotomêsas tas tou trapeziou gônias* – having bisected the angles of the trapezium (Simplicius, *Physics* 62.25); *ep'apeiron einai tên dikhotomian tou apeirou* – the division of the unlimited is without limit (Simplicius, *Physics* 1289.7). (3) Logical dichotomy: *to paranomon kai ennomon hekastên dikhotomei toutôn* – being lawless or law-abiding divides each of these [constitutions] into two (Pl. *Pol.* 302e). Aristotle gives no formal account in his logical works of traditional dichotomous division (e.g. of the class of *A*s into *B* and not-*B*); he regards it with contempt: *eti sterêsei men anagkaion diairein kai diairousin hoi dikhotomountes* – also it is necessary for users of dichotomous division to divide by negation and they do so [but a negative characteristic cannot provide a *diaphora* for a definition] (Ar. *Gen. An.* 642b 22); so *to dikhotemnein têi men adunaton têi de kenon eirêtai* – dichotomous division has been declared in one way impossible and in another empty (Ar. *Gen. An.* 644b 20).

dinê, dinos: vortex, whirl, a concept used by the atomists to explain the joining together of atoms to form bodies: *tês dinês aitias ousês tês geneseôs pantôn* – [Democritus said that] the vortex was the cause of the coming to be of everything (Democritus, fr. 565); also of rotation: *tas de kinêseis autôn ouk adunaton men gignesthai kata tên tou holou ouranou dinên* – it is not impossible that [the rising of the sun and moon] may be due to the revolution of the whole heaven (Epicurus, *To Pythocles* 92.8). Simplicius tells us that Anaxagoras explained the extreme position of fire and the centrality of earth *hoti dia ton dinon meson hê gê krateitai* – since earth occupies the middle because of the vortex (Simplicius, *Physics* 386.24).

diorizein, diorismos: to distinguish, define, distinction, definition: *diorieis oun autois akousia te kai hekousia adikêmata?* – will you distinguish between intentional and unintentional wrongdoings? (Pl. *Laws* 860e); *peri energeias diorisômen ti te estin hê energeia* – concerning actuality, let us define what actuality is (Ar. *Met.* 1048a 26); *hêlios kai selênê ... eis diorismon kai phulakên arithmôn khronou gegonen* – the sun and moon came into existence for the distinction and maintenance of the measures of time (Pl. *Tim.* 38c); *ho men tou plêthous ekei diorismos entautha diaspasmos gegonen* – the distinction of the manifold there [in the intelligible world] here [in the sensible world] has become a dispersal (Simplicius, *Physics* 774.14).

diorthôtikos: corrective. *diorthôtikê dikaiosunê*, corrective justice, is one of the two types distinguished by Aristotle, in which someone who has gained unfairly restores the gain to him who lost: *hen de to en tois sunallagmasi diorthôtikê* – one [type of justice] is that which is corrective in transactions (Ar. *E.N.* 1131a 1). See *dianemêtikos*.

doxa, doxastos, doxazein: opinion, opinable, to opine. Particularly in the *Republic*, Plato made a sharp distinction between the intelligible world of forms of which *gnôsis*, knowledge, was possible and the perceptible world of becoming which is only *doxastos*. This distinction was the basis of neoplatonism: *ep'allôi ara tetaktai doxa kai ep'allôi epistêmê* – opinion has one object and knowledge another (Pl. *Rep.* 477b); *oukoun ei to on gnôston, allo ti an doxaston ê to on eiê?* – surely, if what is is knowable, something other than what is is opinable? (Pl. *Rep.* 478b); *all'hen ge ti doxazei ho doxazôn?* – but he who opines opines some object? (Pl. *Rep.* 478b); *pan gar to on ê aisthêton esti, kai dia touto doxaston, ê ontôs on, kai dia touto noêton* – everything that is is either perceptible and therefore opinable, or true being, and therefore an object of intellect (Proclus, *Elements of Theology* 123); *hoti de allo to doxazein kai allo*

46

ti to epistasthai edeixen en tôi Theaitêtôi Sôkratês ex tou doxan men kai alêthê kai pseudê einai, epistêmên de monôs alêthê – Socrates showed in the *Theaetetus* that opining is one thing and knowing another through opinion being both true and false, knowledge only true (Simplicius, *Physics* 13.10).

duas: dyad. The dyad was thought to be the first of numbers, one not being a number, since not a plurality: *prôtê tôn arithmôn hê duas* – the dyad is the first of numbers (Ar. *Met.* 999a 8); *ei de ge hen monon estin, duas de mê estin, hapsis ouk an eiê* – if there is only one and there is no dyad, there could be no connection (Pl. *Parm.* 148b); *ho gar arithmos estin ek tou henos kai tês duados tês aoristou* – number is from the one and the indefinite dyad (Ar. *Met.* 1081a 14). What the indefinite dyad is is uncertain and much discussed.

dunamis: generally, power, capacity: *phêsomen dunameis einai genos ti tôn ontôn hais dê kai hêmeis dunametha ha dunametha* – we shall say that powers are a kind of thing by which we are able to do what we are able to do (Pl. *Rep.* 477c); *dunameôs d'eis ekeino monon blepô eph'hôi te estin kai ho apergazetai* – in a power I look only to its scope and to its results (Pl. *Rep.* 477d). For Aristotle *dunamis* is one of his *arkhai* – basic principles. It is potentiality as distinct from *entelekheia* – actuality: *hekaston gar tote legetai hotan entelekheiaï êi, mallon ê hotan dunamei* – for each thing is called what it is when it is in actuality, rather than when potentially (Ar. *Phys.* 193b 8). It is also contrasted with *energeia*: *hotan oun eipômen 'to ginomenon ex ontos gignetai', ek tou dunamei ontos phamen to energeiaï ginesthai* – when we say 'what becomes comes from what is', we say that what actually is comes from what is potentially (Simplicius, *Physics* 241.3). The varieties of *dunamis* are discussed by Aristotle in *Met.*, Book 4, Ch. 12.

E

ê: or. No problems, except that the *ê* is occasionally what grammarians call the *ê corrigentis*, the corrective *ê*, where a more accurate expression replaces a less accurate one. Thus Aristotle, referring to a situation where a kidnapped man is forcibly moved from one place to another, says that the situation is such that *mêden sumballetai ho prattôn ê ho paskhôn* (Ar. *E.N.* 1110a 2) which does not mean, as some translations say, that nothing is contributed by either the agent or the patient, but that the agent, or, more accurately, the patient, contributes nothing.

egkratês: self-controlled, strong-willed, or, in old translations, continent; *egkrateia*, self-control. Plato does not distinguish the *egkratês* from the *sôphrôn*: *sôphrona onta kai egkratê auton heautou* – being temperate and self-controlled (Pl. *Gorg*. 491d). In Aristotle being *sôphrôn* is incompatible with being *egkratês*, since the *sôphrôn* has, but the *egkratês* has not, an *epithumia*, non-rational appetite, to act in accordance with his *proairesis* – rational choice: *ouk esti d'oud'hê egkrateia aretê* – nor is self-control an excellence (Ar. *E.N.* 1128b 33); *ho d'egkratês eidôs hoti phaulai hai epithumiai ouk akolouthei dia ton logon* – the self-controlled, knowing that his desires are bad, does not follow them because of reason (Ar. *E.N.* 1145b 13). But *egkrateia*, though imperfect, has merit; the opposed defect is *akrasia*, lack of self-control. *egkrateia* unqualified is in the sphere of bodily appetites, in other areas it is qualified, as in *egkratês thumou* – having anger under control: *akrasia kai egkrateia esti monon peri haper akolasia kai sôphrosunê* – weakness and strength of will [unqualified] are concerned only with the same things as intemperance and temperance (Ar. *E.N.* 1149a 21).

eidos has a variety of connected meanings, from the way a thing looks (the word is etymologically connected with *video*), through its shape or form, a species or kind of thing, to the intelligible form of Platonism. As bodily appearance: *houtôs to eidos pagkalos estin* – he is so very beautiful in appearance (Pl. *Charm*. 154d). As the bodily form itself: *antepideiknunai to eidos apoduomenos* – to strip and display one's body in turn (Pl. *Theaet*. 162b). In Aristotle it is sometimes form in a wider sense in contrast to *hulê* – matter: *eti hê hulê esti dunamei hoti elthoi an eis to eidos* – also matter is that which potentially might come to be form (Ar. *Met*. 1050a 15). As a kind, *tritê [idea] de enudrion eidos* – a third [type] was the aquatic race (Pl. *Tim*. 40a); *ho boulomai legein to eidos* – the sort of thing I mean (Pl. *Rep*. 477e). As species in the technical sense: *ta de genê diaireta eis eidê* – the genera may be divided into species (Ar. *Met*. 999a 4). As the Platonic intelligible form, of which sensible things are imperfect copies: *tois horômenois eidesi proskhrôntai ... ou peri toutôn dianooumenoi all'ekeinôn peri hois tauta eoiken* – they make use of the visible kinds ... not thinking about them but about those to which they are like (Pl. *Rep*. 510d); *touto toinun noêton men to eidos elegon* – it was of that intelligible form that I spoke (Pl. *Rep*. 511a). For connection of the *eidos* with **paradeigmata**: *estai de pleiô paradeigmata tou autou, hôste kai eidê* – there will be several paradigms of the same thing, and therefore forms also (Ar. *Met*. 991a 27); *ta men eidê tauta hôsper paradeigmata hestanai en têi phusei, ta de alla toutois proseikenai kai einai homoiômata* – that these forms stand in nature like paradigms and other things are like them and copies (Pl. *Parm*. 132d). Some treat the Platonic form as being a universal, rather than a perfect exemplar, but many of the texts, such as those given here, do not support this. See also *autos* and *idea*.

eikasia is important mainly for its use by Plato in his simile of the divided line in the *Republic*: *kai tôi teleutaiôi [tmêmati] eikasian [apodos]* – and assign *eikasia* to the final section (Pl. *Rep*. 511e). The objects in the final section are (here physical) *eikones*, images. The precise meaning of *eikasia* is much disputed, but it seems to be the attempt to gauge the nature of objects from awareness of their images alone. *eikôn* is common in neoplatonism with reference to the doctrine that the sensible world is an image of the intelligible: *eikona dei tou aiônos ton khronon [einai]* – time must be an image of eternity (Plotinus 3.7.11).

eikôn. See *eikasia*.

einai: to be, to exist; *to on*: that which is, the real; *ousia*: being, essence. This verb caused great philosophical difficulty to the Greeks and consequential difficulties for us. Much of the trouble arises from the fact that one can say *Platôn esti* – Plato exists – or *Platôn esti philosophos* – Plato is a philosopher – making use of the same verb, whereas in English 'Plato is' is at best an unidiomatic way of saying that he exists. This double use led some earlier Greek philosophers to think that a sentence beginning *Platôn ouk esti ...* must deny the existence of Plato even if the next word is *barbaros*. This leads to translation difficulties for us, as for instance with the sentence *ei ti phaneiê hoion hama on te kai mê on, to toiouton metaxu keisthai tou eilikrinôs ontos kai tou pantôs mê ontos* (Pl. *Rep*. 478d), which might be translated either as 'if something should appear such as both to have and not to have a certain

49

predicate [we said that] such a thing would lie between being clearly of that sort and not being so at all' or as 'if something should appear such that it simultaneously exists and does not exist [we said that] such a thing would lie between clearly existing and not existing at all'. It was presumably these difficulties that led Parmenides to say such things as *khrê to legein te noein t'eon emmenai· esti gar einai, mêden d'ouk estin* – that of which one can speak and think must be: for it is possible for it, but not for nothing, to be (Parmenides in Simplicius, *Physics* 117.4). In an impersonal use *esti* frequently means 'it is possible' as in *estin adikounta mêpô adikon einai* – it is possible to do what is unjust without being an unjust person (Ar. *N.E.* 1134a 17), and in the quotation from Parmenides above. There are also adverbial expressions such as *estin hote*, sometimes, and *estin hôs*, in some ways. See *on, ousia*.

eirôneia: dissimulation or affected ignorance, *not* irony. It was regarded as bad: *kataphronêtikon gar hê eirôneia* – for dissimulation is supercilious (Ar. *Rhet.* 1379b 31). Thrasymachus refers to *hê eiôthuia eirôneia Sôkratous* – the accustomed affected ignorance of Socrates (Pl. *Rep.* 337a) – as an accusation; *ton men haploun mimêtên tina, ton de eirônikon mimêtên thêsomen* – we shall count the one a sincere, the other a dissimulating imitator (Pl. *Soph.* 268a). The verb is *eirôneuesthai*: *eirôneuoiso kai panta mallon poiêsois ê apokrinoio* – you would affect ignorance and do anything rather than answer (Pl. *Rep.* 337a).

ekei: generally, there. In neoplatonic philosophy it is used to refer to the intelligible world as distinct from the sensible world of becoming which is *enthade*, here: *saphôs tou Platônos ousias tas ideas legontos kai mêde ta entautha sumbebêkota hoion dikaiosunên kai sôphrosunên kai epistêmên sugkhôrountos en allôi einai ekei* – Plato clearly says that the ideas are substances and does not agree that things like justice and temperance and knowledge, that here belong to something, are there in something else (Simplicius, *Physics* 476.3). This precise use is not in Plato himself, but he writes of the life of the soul after death: *eukhesthai ge pou tous theous exesti te kai khrê tên metoikêsin tên enthende ekeise eutukhê genesthai* – presumably it is permissible and indeed proper to pray to the gods that our removal from here to there will be fortunate (Pl. *Phaedo* 117c). *ta ekeina* is also used of the transcendent: *pros tên khôristên ekeinôn apatheian epairomena* – aspiring to the separate impassibility of things there

(Proclus, *Republic* 2.118.22).

ekhein. As Aristotle says: *to ekhein pollakhôs legetai* – it has many meanings. None are specifically philosophical, but see the distinctions made by Aristotle in *Met.*, Book 4, Ch. 23 and *LSJ*.

ekkrisis: in Anaxagoras, the separating out of the homoeomeries from the original confusion; this is distinct from the *sugkrisis* and *diakrisis*, conjunction and separation, that occur as individual bodies come into or go out of existence: *Anaxagoras de ekkrinesthai tas homoiomereias apo tou migmatos legôn· kai hê sugkrisis de kai hê diakrisis kai hê ekkrisis kinêseis tines eisin* – Anaxagoras says that the homoeomeries are separated out from the mixture; and conjunction, separation, and separation out are all processes (Simplicius, *Physics* 1120.22).

elegkhos: usually refutation, sometimes proof, but then normally in an adversative situation: *elegkhos esti tou Pittakou rhêmatos* – it is a refutation of the saying of Pittacus (Pl. Prot. 344b); *khalepon de se elegxai, ô Sôkrates* – it is hard to refute you, Socrates (Pl. *Gorg.* 470d). As proof: *hôste toutôi tôi tropôi k'an tauta elegkhois, ei bouloio, hôs hapanta estin homoia allêlois* – so in this way you could prove, if you wanted to, that everything is like everything else (Pl. *Prot.* 331e). *Peri Sophistikôn Elegkhôn* – 'Concerning Sophistical Refutations' – is the title of one of Aristotle's logical works; the phrase therein: *tên tou elegkhou agnoian* (168a 18), was translated into Latin as *ignoratio elenchi*, but Aristotle was referring to the whole variety of ways in which refutations may go wrong, whereas the Latin phrase is now used to mean 'a logical fallacy consisting in disproving some statement different from that advanced by an opponent' (*Shorter OED*); so it would be better to translate the Greek as 'not understanding the nature of refutation'.

eleutheriotês: in a wide sense, behaviour suitable to an *eleutheros* – a free man, but its important use in philosophy is in the sense of liberality with regard to money: *pros tên tôn khrêmatôn eleutheriotêta thaumastos* – remarkable in regard to liberality with money (Pl. *Theaet.* 144d). It is one of the *êthikai aretai*, excellences of character, discussed by Aristotle: *dokei dê einai hê peri khrêmata mesotês* – [liberality] seems to be the mean with regard to money (Ar. *E.N.* 1119b 22); *hê asôtia kai aneleutheria peri khrêmata **huperbolai*** *kai elleipseis* – lavishness and illiberality are excesses and deficiencies about money (Ar. *E.N.* 1119b 27).

elleipsis: in general, any deficiency, the opposite being *huperbolê*, excess: *kai tis allê anaxia hêdonêi pros lupên estin all'hê huperbolê allêlôn kai elleipsis?* – what other demerit has pleasure with regard to distress except their relative excess and deficiency? [i.e. pleasure is bad only if it is relatively small and causes greater distress] (Pl. *Prot.* 356a). In Aristotle's ethics, *êthikê aretê*, excellence of character, is *mesotês duo kakiôn, tês men kath'huperbolên, tês de kat'elleipsin* – a mean between two faults, one of excess, the other of deficiency (Ar. *E.N.* 1107a 2); it is thus opposed in different ways to an excellence and to a fault at the opposite extreme.

empeiros: experienced; *empeiria*: experience. Usually in a good sense: *dei prosekhein tôn empeirôn kai presbuterôn ê phronimôn tais anopodeiktais phasesi kai doxais oukh hêtton tôn apodeixeôn· dia gar to ekhein ek tês empeirias omma horôsin orthôs* – one must attend to the unproved sayings and beliefs of the experienced and older or wise; for through their experience they have an eye and see correctly (Ar. *E.N.* 1143b 11). *empeiria* is also used, often disapprovingly, of a practice denied to be a skill or craft because it lacks a theory, as in Socrates' attack on rhetoric: *ouk estin tekhnê all'empeiria kai tribê* – it is not a skill but a practice based on experience (Pl. *Gorg.* 463b). Used especially of those who in medicine rely on experience rather than scientific theory, sometimes with disapproval: *iatros tôn tais empeiriais aneu logou tên iatrikên metakheirizomenôn* – one of those physicians who on the basis of experience take part in the medical craft without rational basis (Pl. *Laws* 857c). But some physicians accepted the name and called themselves *empeirikoi* – empiricists – in opposition to the dogmatic and methodical schools of medicine, like Sextus Empiricus, who was a sceptic in philosophy and an empiricist in medicine.

empsukhos: having a soul, animate. Usually in neuter *empsukhon, empsukha*, with *sôma*, body, understood: *legomen ... diôristhai to empsukhon tou apsukhou tôi zên ... kai ta phuomena panta dokei zên* – we say that the ensouled is distinguished from the soulless by living ... and all things that grow seem to be alive (Ar. *De An.* 413a 21); *empsukhon ekeino legetai to psukhês metekhon* – that thing is said to be ensouled that has a share in soul (Proclus, *Elements of Theology* 188); *hothen hê kinêsis kai hou heneka kai hôs ousia tôn empsukhôn sômatôn hê psukhê* **aitia** – the soul is the efficient and final and formal cause of ensouled bodies (Ar. *De An.* 415b 10); *dei legein tonde ton kosmon zôion empsukhon ennoun te* – one must say that this universe is an animal with a soul and intelligent (Pl. *Tim.* 30b). Thus all living things have souls in philosophical usage; but with reference to foods vegetables are usually classed as *apsukha*: *apsukhôn men ekhomenoi pantôn, empsukhôn de t'ounantion pantôn apekhomenoi* – partaking of all inanimate foods but abstaining from all ensouled (Pl. *Laws* 782c).

enantios: in general, opposed in any way; in specialised philosophical use, contrary. Contraries may be either propositions or kinds of thing. Contrary propositions, such as 'All *A* is *B*' and 'No *A* is *B*', are distinct from contradictories, such as 'All *A* is *B*' and 'Some *A* is not *B*': *ou gar esontai oudamôs hai protaseis out'enantiai out'antikeimenai* – these propositions will in no way be either contraries or contradictories (Ar. *An. Po.* 64a 18). To any kind of thing only one other kind is contrary: *heni hekastôn tôn enantiôn hen monon est'enantion kai ou polla* – to each contrary one thing only is contrary and not many (Pl. *Prot.* 332c); this enabled Aristotle to detect the ***pollakhôs legomena***, things named ambiguously, by their having apparently two contraries: *tôi oxei en phônêi men enantion to baru, en ogkôi de to amblu· dêlon oun hoti to enantion tôi oxei pollakhôs legetai* – to the *oxu* in sound the contrary is 'deep', in a mass it is 'blunt'; so it is clear that the opposite of *oxu* [and consequently *oxu* itself] is ambiguous [which is why in English we must in one case translate *oxu* as 'high', in the other as 'sharp']. Aristotle gives a fuller analysis of the uses of *enantios* in *Met.* 1018a 20 ff.

endekhesthai: to be possible. Aristotle says that the verb may be used in wider or narrower senses of 'possible': *pollakhôs legetai to endekhesthai· kai gar to anagkaion kai to mê anagkaion kai to dunaton endekhesthai legomen* – 'to be possible' is ambiguous; for it may include the necessary or only the not necessary or only the potential (Ar. *An. Pr.* 25a 27). But usually the *endekhomena allôs ekhein* – things that may be otherwise – are contrasted with the necessary and invariable that are *mê endekhomena allôs ekhein*: *to de endekhomenon mê einai phtharton* – that which may not exist is perishable (Ar. *Met*. 1050b 12); [*auto to on*] *oudamê oudamôs alloiôsin oudemian endekhetai* – [the real] never in any way allows of any change (Pl. *Phaedo* 78d); *oute gegonen ho pas ouranos out'endekhetai phtharênai* – the whole heaven has neither come into existence nor is capable of ceasing to exist (Ar. *De Caelo* 283b 26); *esti de tekhnê pasa peri genesin kai to tekhnazein kai theôrein hopôs genêtai ti tôn endekhomenôn kai einai kai mê einai* – every craft is concerned with coming to be and contriving and thinking how to bring into existence something that can either be or not be (Ar. *E.N*. 1140a 10); *oudeis de bouleuetai peri tôn mê endekhomenôn allôs ekhein* – nobody plans about things that cannot be otherwise (Ar. *E.N*. 1139a 13).

energeia: in a general sense, activity. Plato does not use the word but, non-technically, uses the adjective *energos* once: *dikastas energous ontas* – magistrates while in office (Pl. *Laws* 674b). Technically it is usually opposed, as actuality, in a wider sense to *dunamis*, potentiality, or, in a narrower sense, as activity, to *kinêsis*, process: *esti dê energeia to huparkhein to pragma mê hôsper legomen dunamei* – actuality is the existence of a thing not in the way we call potential (Ar. *Met*. 1048a 30); *metaballei pan ek tou dunamei ontos eis to energeiaï on, hoion ek leukou dunamei eis to energeiaï leukon* – everything changes from what it is potentially to what it is actually, as from being potentially white to being actually white (Ar. *Met*. 1069b 15). The distinction between *energeia* and *kinêsis* is explained by Aristotle at *Met*. 1048b 18 ff. and further elucidated in the first four chapters of *E.N*., Book 10, Chs 1-4. An activity is complete in itself at any time, so that *horaï hama kai heôrake* – one has seen as soon as one sees (Ar. *Met*. 1048b 23); *dokei gar hê men horasis kath'hontinoun khronon teleion einai* – for sight seems to to be complete at any time (Ar. *E.N*. 1174a 14). But *ou gar hama* ... *oikodomei kai ôikodomêken* – [building is a *kinêsis*] for one has not built [e.g. a temple] as soon as one is building it (Ar. *Met*. 1048b 30). But Aristotle often speaks of *kinêsis* as a type of *energeia*: *anagkê ara oikodomêsin tên energeian einai, hê d'oikodomêsis kinêsis tis* – so the activity must be house-building; but house-building is a process (Ar. *Met*. 1066a 5).

ennoêma. See *ennoia*.

ennoia, ennoein: a thought, to think of: *ara oukhi touto dikaiôs legomen hoti anemnêsthê hou tên ennoian elaben* – do we not rightly say that when somebody thinks of something he recalls it? (Pl. *Phaedo* 73c). *ennoia* sometimes, and *ennoêma* normally, are more specialised and should be translated 'concept': *ou khôris tês tôn arithmôn ennoias katalambanetai* – it is not comprehended without the concept of number (Sextus Empiricus, *Adversus Mathematicos* 7.101); *ta genê kai ta eidê ennoêmata estin* – genera and species are concepts [not realities] (Sextus Empiricus, *Outlines of Pyrrhonism* 2.219).

entelekheia: *to de tês entelekheias onoma legetai men autou tou Aristotelous idion· sêmainei to eidos to energeiaï on* – *entelekheia* is a word that is Aristotle's own; it means the form that is actualised (Simplicius, *Physics* 278.6). Usually translated as actuality or perfection: *to onoma energeia legetai kata to ergon kai sunteinei pros tên entelekheian* – the word *energeia* is used with reference to the *ergon* [function] and it itself tends to the actuality (Ar. *Met.* 1050a 22); with reference to this passage (though he misprints *energeia* as *entelekheia*) Ross says: 'It appears that strictly speaking *energeia* means activity or actualisation, while *entelekheia* means the resulting actuality or perfection. For the most part Aristotle treats the two words as synonyms' (note to *De An.* 402a 26); *psukhê estin entelekheia hê prôtê sômatos phusikou dunamei zôên ekhontos* – soul is the first actuality of a natural body that potentially has life (Ar. *De An.* 412a 27).

enthade: generally, here; technically, in neoplatonism, in the world of becoming as opposed to *ekei*, the world of being: *hê de ekei sumphuês holotês entautha diestôsa sunekhôs posotês enulos esti* – what is there [in the world of being] a compact whole here [in the world of becoming] continually breaks apart as material quantity (Simplicius, *Physics* 774.15). *têide* is often used, like *enthade*, of the world of becoming by neoplatonists.

enulos: formed from *en*, in, and *hulê,* matter. It refers to immaterial things, especially forms and souls, that are contained in matter; the opposite is *aülos*. Not in Plato and only once in Aristotle: *ei d'houtôs ekhei, dêlon hoti ta pathê logoi enuloi eisin* – if this is so it is clear that emotions are thoughts in matter (Ar. *De An.* 403a 25); *hê enulos kai gennêtikê psukhê* – the soul engaged in matter and becoming (Plotinus 2.3.17); *ta enula eidê kai akhôrista tês hulês* –

forms that are in matter and inseparable from it (Simplicius, *Physics* 1.16); *kai to eidos de to enulon saphôs oimai paradidôsin en hois kai to aülon eidos* – and I think that he clearly teaches of the form in matter where he also does of the immaterial form (Simplicius, *Physics* 26.18). Ross, in his edition of *De Anima*, says that *enulos* there (403a 25) means 'containing a reference to matter', which would be quite different from its usual meaning.

epagein: generally, to lead on; 'leading on' is one non-technical use of the noun *epagôgê*. Philosophically, the central notion is that of leading oneself or others to some general concept or some universal truth from less general or particular cases falling under them; thus one might conclude that all animals that chew the cud have cloven hooves from observation of cows, deer, etc. The accepted translation is induction, but *epagôgê* resembles only induction by simple enumeration among methods called inductive in modern times. *epagein autous epi ta mêpô gignôskomena* – lead them on to things not yet known (Pl. *Pol.* 278a); *epagôgê hê apo tôn kath'hekasta epi to katholou ephodos* – induction is the approach to the universal from particular cases (Ar. *Top.* 105a 13); *hê epagôgê ek tôn kata meros* – induction is from the partial (Ar. *An. Po.* 81b 1); *[khrê] ei men peri arkhês tinos ho logos di'epagôgês autên pistousthai (tas gar arkhas apo tôn husterôn anagkê bebaiousthai)* – one should, if the question is about some principle, support it by induction (for first principles must be confirmed by what is posterior to them) (Simplicius, *Physics* 1185.27); *arkhai de apodeixeôs kai ta phainomena ek tês enargous aisthêseôs kai tôn kata meros kai holôs hê epagôgê kaloumenê* – for the starting points of proof are what is apparent from plain perception and from partial cases, and generally so-called induction (Simplicius, *Physics* 49.27). For a full investigation of Aristotle's usage see Ross's commentary on *Prior Analytics*, Book 2, Ch. 23.

epainetos: praiseworthy; *epainein*: to praise; *epainos*: praise. These require no comment except for Aristotle's important distinction of *timia*, things to be prized, from *epaineta*, things to be praised: *episkepsômetha peri tês eudaimonias potera tôn epainetôn esti ê mallon tôn timiôn* – let us consider whether happiness is among things to be praised or rather things to be prized (Ar. *E.N.* 1101b 10). The contrary of *epainetos* is *psektos*, blameworthy. Desire for the *kalon* is especially praiseworthy: *hai epithumiai tôn men kalôn epainetai* – desires for fine things are praiseworthy (Ar. *E.N.* 1175b 28).

ephesis: aim; *ephiesthai*: to aim. In Plato and Aristotle used of people: *to tou aristou ephiesthai* – the striving for the best (Pl. *Laws* 864b); *hê de tou telous ephesis ouk authairetos* – the aim at the goal is not self-chosen (Ar. *E.N.* 1114b 6). But later used also of the inanimate: *ho gar estin orexis en tois empsukhois, touto en tois apsukhois phusikois de ephesis* – for what is appetition in living things is nisus in natural inanimate bodies (Simplicius, *Physics* 250.22); *tên ephesin tês tou oikeiou topou katalêpseôs* – the nisus to take possession of its proper place (Simplicius, *Physics* 533.20).

epibolê: literally, throwing upon. It is an important but puzzling term in the writings of Epicurus, especially in the phrase *epibolê tês dianoias*, which seems to mean the projection of the intelligence upon something and thus attention to it. *eti te kata tas aisthêseis dei panta têrein kai haplôs kata tas parousas epibolas eite dianoias eith'hotou dêpou tôn kritêriôn* – we must keep all our investigations in accord with our perceptions, and especially with the accompanying projections of the intelligence or of any whatsoever of the instruments of judgment (Epicurus, *To Herodotus* 38); *epei to ge theôroumenon pan ê kat'epibolên lambanomenon têi dianoiaï alêthes estin* – everything that we perceive or grasp by projection of the intelligence is true (Epicurus, *To Herodotus* 62). Elsewhere with a similar meaning: *tên epibolên tês dianoias eis heterogenes* – the projection of the intelligence on the heterogeneous (Sextus Empiricus, *Adversus Mathematicos* 3.54). In a less specialised sense: *nun legei kat'allên epibolên* – he now discourses making a different approach (Simplicius, *Physics* 1258.8).

epieikeia, epieikês: in a wider sense, worthiness, worthy; *epieikês ôn tên psukhên* – being good in soul (Pl. *Symp.* 210b); *ei mê panu phusei eiê epieikês* – unless he be naturally very good (Pl. *Rep.* 538c). The contrary is *phaulos, phaulotês*, worthless(ness): *diapherousôn tôn energeiôn epeikeiaï kai phaulotêti* – the activities differing in worthiness and worthlessness (Ar. *E.N.* 1175b 24). In a narrower sense, *epieikeia* is a kind of fairness going beyond mere legality, sometimes called equity: *to epieikes dikaion men estin, ou to kata nomon de, all'epanorthôma nomimou dikaiou … hêi elleipei dia tou katholou* – the equitable is just, not however legal justice, but a correction of the legally just … where the law is deficient through its generality (Ar. *E.N.* 1137b 12).

epikhairekakia: literally, rejoicing over misfortunes, in German *Schadenfreude*. Most implausibly stated by Aristotle to be one of the defects associated with *nemesis*, righteous indignation: *nemesis de mesotês phthonou kai epikhairekakias· eisi de peri lupên kai hêdonên tas epi tois sumbainousi tois pelas ginomenas* – righteous indignation is a mean between envy and *Schadenfreude*; they are concerned with distress and pleasure over the fortunes of neighbours (Ar. *E.N.* 1108b 1).

epikheirein: in general, to attempt, to put one's hand to a task. More specifically, to argue tentatively: *hoper arti epekheiroun* – as I was recently arguing (Pl. *Theaet.* 205a). In the logic of Aristotle and works following it, an *epikheirêma* is a dialectical argument that fails to have full probative force: *esti de philosophêma men sullogismos apodeiktikos, epikheirêma de sullogismos dialektikos* – a philosophism is a demonstrative argument, an epicheirema a dialectical argument (Ar. *Top.* 162a 15).

epikheirêma. See *epikheirein*.

epipedon: originally, a floor under foot, and so something of two dimensions, a surface, a plane: *megethous de to men eph'hen grammê, to de epi duo epipedon, to de epi tria sôma* – of magnitudes the one-dimensional is a line, the two-dimensional a surface and the three-dimensional a body (Ar. *De Caelo* 268a 7). As adjective, plane: *kata suntreis epipedous gônias mian sterean gônian poiei* – where three plane angles meet they make one solid angle (Pl. *Tim.* 54e). In Plato and in geometrical contexts the *epipedon* is always a plane, but Aristotle sometimes uses it of any two-dimensional surface: *dokei epipedon ti einai kai hoion aggeion ho topos kai periekhon* – place seems to be a surface and like a vessel that contains (Ar. *Phys.* 212a 28). Compare the comment of Simplicius: *dio kai auton* [*topon*] *epipedon ekalesen, hôs tôn palaiôn pasan epiphaneian epipedon kalountôn* – so Aristotle called place also a plane, since of old they called every surface a plane (Simplicius, *Physics* 587.18).

epiphaneia: a surface. See *epipedon*.

epistêmê: knowledge; *epistasthai*: to know; *epistêtos*: known. In general, used in the same contexts as the translations are in English, by philosophers as well as others. But in strict philosophical use *epistêmê* is possible only of the unchanging and necessary, the forms in Plato and the *mê endekhomena allôs ekhein* in Aristotle, and similarly in their followers. That of which *epistêmê* is impossible is the object of *doxa*: *ep'allôi tetaktai doxa kai ep'allôi epistêmê ... epistêmê men epi tôi onti pephuke* – belief is assigned to one thing and knowledge to another ... knowledge is assigned to reality (Pl. *Rep.* 477b); *enioi gar pisteuousin ouden hêtton hois doxazousin ê heteroi hois epistantai* – some people trust their beliefs no less than others their knowledge (Ar. *E.N.* 1146b 29); *pantes gar hupolambanomen, ho epistametha mêd'endekhesthai allôs ekhein* – for we all understand that what we know is incapable of being otherwise (Ar. *E.N.* 1139b 19); *ex anagkês ara esti to epistêton, aïdion ara* – *what is known is necessary and therefore everlasting (Ar. E.N.* 1139b 23). Aristotle holds that what is *epistêton* is provable, so first principles are objects not of *epistêmê* but of *nous*: *tês arkhês tou epistêtou out'an epistêmê eiê ... leipetai noun einai tôn arkhôn* – the basic principles of knowledge are not known ... it remains that basic principles are intuited (Ar. *E.N.* 1140b 33); *kai tote legomen epistasthai hotan ta aitia gnôrisômen tôn ontôn* – only when we recognise the causes of things do we say that we have knowledge (Proclus, *Elements of Theology* 11).

epistrephein, epistrophê: to revert, reversion. These are key technical terms of neoplatonism. In neoplatonism everything comes into being by *proodos* from something that it resembles as an inferior copy, everything ultimately coming from the *hen*, the One; but being inferior it has an *orexis* to *epistrephein*, revert, to that from which it proceeds: *pan to proïon apo tinos kat'ousian epistrephetai pros ekeino aph'hou proeisin* – anything that proceeds from anything reverts in respect of its being upon that from which it proceeds (Proclus, *Elements of Theology* 31); *pasa epistrophê di'homoiotêtos apoteleitai tôn epistrephomenôn pros ho epistrephetai* – all reversion is accomplished through a likeness of the reverting things to the goal of reversion (Proclus, *Elements of Theology* 32); *psukhê de kai ho polutimêtos nous apo tou menontos proelêluthe kai epestraptai pros auto* – soul and the much-valued intuition proceeded from the unchanging and reverted to it (Simplicius, *Physics* 147.9). The whole doctrine arises from the account in the *Timaeus* of the demiurge making the sensible world in the likeness of the intelligible world, but inferior to it.

epithumia: the non-rational appetite for pleasure, particularly the simple bodily pleasures, such as eating, drinking and sex, which man shares with other animals; *epithumein*: to desire; *epithumêtikon*: concerned with appetite. *epithumia* is distinguished from other types of *orexis*, such as *boulêsis*, by its non-rationality: *to de hôi eraï te kai peinêi kai dipsêi [hê psukhê] kai peri tas allas epithumias eptoêtai alogiston te kai epithumêtikon, plêrôseôn tinôn kai hêdonôn hetairon* – that with which [the soul] lusts and hungers and thirsts and is concerned with the other appetites is non-rational and appetitive, the companion of certain fillings and pleasures (Pl. *Rep.* 439d). Parallel to Plato's distinction of three elements in the soul Aristotle distinguishes three kinds of *orexis*, which is appetition in the widest sense: *orexis men gar epithumia kai thumos kai boulêsis* – appetition is desire, and anger and rational wish (Ar. *De An.* 414b 2). According to Aristotle all animals have some *aisthêsis* – at least *haphê*, touch: *ei de aisthêsin, kai phantasian kai orexin· hopou men gar aisthêsis kai lupê kai hêdonê, hopou de tauta ex anagkês kai epithumia* – if they have sensation they also have imagination and appetition: for where there is sensation there is distress and pleasure, and where there are these there is also desire (Ar. *De An.* 413b 22).

êrema: gently; *êremaios*: gentle. Both used by Plato in a non-technical sense: *paramutheisthai auton kai peithein êrema* – encourage him and persuade him gently (Pl. *Rep.* 476e); *êremaias men lupas, êremaias de hêdonas* – mild distresses and mild pleasures (Pl. *Laws* 734a). In natural philosophy the verb *êremein* applies to anything not in motion: *anagkê ê êremein ê kineisthai pan* – everything is necessarily either at rest or in motion (Ar. *Phys.* 232a 12); *enantion gar êremia kinêsei* – for rest is the contrary of motion (Ar. *Phys.* 226b 15). But more strictly *êremia* applies only to things that may be *en kinêsei*, in motion: *ou gar pan to akinêton êremei alla to esterêmenon kinêseôs pephukos de kineisthai* – for not everything motionless is at rest, but that which is deprived of motion but naturally moves (Ar. *Phys.* 221b 12); *hôi gar hê kinêsis huparkhei, toutôi hê akinêsia êremia* – for in that to which motion belongs, its lack of motion is rest (Ar. *Phys.* 202a 5). *êremêsis kai to êremizesthai tên kinêsis dêloi tên ep'êremian* – 'coming to rest' and 'to come to rest' mean the change towards rest (Simplicius, *Physics* 1001.24). The lack of motion that is invariable is sometimes called *monê*: *tên apo kinêseôs kai êremias exêirêmenên monên* – [Xenophanes calls] that which is exempt from motion and rest immobility (Simplicius, *Physics* 23.14). The noun *monê*, immobility, should not be confused with the feminine adjective *monê*, alone.

ergon: a task, a function, or a product, so work in the widest sense. In the sense of task or function: *touto hekastou ergon ho an ê monon ti ê kallista tôn allôn apergazetai* – that is the task (function) of each thing which either it alone can perform or performs better than anything else (Pl. *Rep.* 353a); *poteron oun tektonos men kai skuteôs estin erga tina kai praxeis, anthrôpou d'ouden estin, all'argon pephuken?* – have, then, the builder and the shoemaker certain functions and pursuits, but man has none, but is without function? (Ar. *E.N.* 1097b 28). In the sense of a product: *en toutois beltiô pephuke tôn energeiôn ta erga* – in these, the works (products) are more valuable than the activities (Ar. *E.N.* 1094a 5).

eris: strife, warfare, contention in a general sense. Used philosophically by Heraclitus to denote a cosmic principle: *eidenai khrê ton polemon eonta xunon, kai dikên erin, kai ginomena panta kat'erin kai khreôn* – one should know that war is common and justice is strife, and all things are produced by strife and necessity (Heraclitus, fr. 80); cf. *Hêrakleitos to antixoun sumpheron kai ek tôn diapherontôn kallistên harmonian, kai panta kat'erin ginesthai* – Heraclitus says that it is what opposes that helps and from different notes comes the fairest tune, and all things are produced by strife (Ar. *E.N.* 1155b 4).

eristikê is derived from *eris* and used to denote unscrupulous argument for the sake of victory, in contrast to *dialektikê*, which aims at truth. The *eristikos* argues in that way. The adverb is *eristikôs*. *tên eristikên tekhnên aphôrismenos* – having set the eristic skill on one side (Pl. *Soph.* 231e); *oukoun dei peithesthai toutôi tôi eristikôi logôi* – we should not trust this eristic argument (Pl. *Meno* 81d); *hotan phainêtai sumperainesthai mê sumperainomenos, ho kaleitai eristikos sullogismos* – when [an argument] seems to prove a conclusion but does not, which is called an eristic syllogism (Ar. *Top.* 162b 3).

eskhatos: last, in all ordinary uses. It has three particular philosophical meanings. (1) The extremity of a body: *en t'autôi gar ta eskhata tou periekhontos kai tou periekhomenou* – for the extremities

61

of the surrounding bodies and the surrounded body are in the same place (Ar. *Phys.* 211b 11); *hêmeis de to tou pantos eskhaton anô legomen* – but we call the extremity of the universe above (Ar. *De Caelo* 308a 21). (2) The term that appears last in a syllogism as written by Aristotle. Thus in 'If S belongs to all M and M belongs to all P then S belongs to all P', P is the *eskhaton*: *hotan oun horoi treis houtôs ekhôsi pros allêlous hôste ton eskhaton en holôi einai tôi mesôi kai ton meson en holôi tôi prôtôi ê einai ê mê einai, anagkê tôn akrôn einai sullogismon teleion* – so when three terms are so related that the last term is wholly in the middle and the middle is wholly in or excluded from the first, the extremes must form a perfect syllogism (Ar. *An. Pr.* 25b 32). (3) In neoplatonism, the lowest and last kind of beings in the order of reality: *panta gar exêptai tôn theôn, kai ta men ex allôn, ta de ex allôn prolampetai, kai hai seirai mekhri tôn eskhatôn kathêkousi* – for all things depend on the gods, some being irradiated by one god, some by another, and the series reaches down to the last orders of being (Proclus, *Elements of Theology* 145).

ethos: habit, custom; *ethizein*: to accustom, to habituate. Sometimes an *ethos* is a mere unthinking habit: *hai mimêseis, ean ek neôn porrô diatelesôsin, eis ethê te kai phusin kathistantai* – mimicry, if it continues for a time from youth onwards, turns into a habit and becomes natural (Pl. *Rep.* 395d). But *ethizein* is often to accustom to a policy or way of life rather than to imprint a habit: *kai touto ethizein, tou Hellênikou genous pheidesthai* – to accustom [the soldiers] to spare those of Greek race (Pl. *Rep.* 469c); *hoi gar nomothetai tous politas ethizontes poiousin agathous* – for the lawgivers make the citizens good by accustomisation (Ar. *E.N.* 1103b 3). We get used to behaving well, but our actions are governed by reason not unthinking habit, according to Aristotle.

êthos: a way of life, a disposition, a character; *êthikos*: concerned with character: *pothen hama praïon kai megalothumon êthos heurêsomen?* – where might we find a disposition that is both gentle and high-spirited? (Pl. *Rep.* 375c); *diapherei d'ouden neos tên hêlikian ê to êthos nearos* – there is no difference between one who is young in years and one who is childish in character (Ar. *E.N.* 1095a 6); *peri proaireseôs hepetai dielthein· oikeiotaton gar einai dokei têi aretêi kai mallon ta êthê krinein tôn praxeôn* – it follows to discuss choice; for it seems to be very closely connected with excellence and to distinguish characters better than actions do (Ar. *E.N.* 1111b 5).

*êthikê **aretê*** is excellence of character, not moral virtue: *dittês tês aretês ousês, tês men dianoêtikês, tês de êthikês* – excellence being of two sorts, one of intelligence, the other of character (Ar. *E.N.* 1103a 14).

eudaimôn comes from *eu*, well, and *daimôn*, a divinity: *eudaimoniê ouk en boskêmasin oikei oude en khrusôi· psukhê oikêtêrion daimonos* – eudaemonia does not reside in cattle or in gold; the soul is the dwelling-place of the divinity (Democritus in Stobaeus, *Anthology* 2.7.31). Traditionally translated as 'happy', but in general use 'well off' might often do, since it can mean little more than economically prosperous. But usually in general use and always in philosophy it is the adjective denoting the life that is most worth living or the man who lives that life. ***eudaimonia*** is the state of such who live that life. These terms never refer to a temporary state of consciousness as 'happy' frequently does. *ti to pantôn akrotaton tôn praktôn agathôn· onomati men oun skhedon hupo tôn pleistôn homologeitai· tên gar eudaimonian kai hoi polloi kai hoi kharientes legousin, to de eu zên kai to eû prattein t'auton hupolambanousi tôi eudaimonein* – as to what is the highest of attainable goods, in name it is agreed upon by practically everybody; for both the many and the refined say that it is eudaemonia, and understand living well and faring well to be the same thing as being eudaemon (Ar. *E.N.* 1095a 16). One cannot be counted eudaemon if one is going to fall into misery later in life, which is why *oudena anthrôpôn eudaimonisteon heôs an zêi, kata Solôna de khreôn telos horan* – one should call no man happy while he is alive, but as Solon said, wait to see the end (Ar. *E.N.* 1100a 15). Thus *eudaimonia* is a quality of life, not an ingredient in it: *hê gar eudaimonia estin ek tinôn agathôn sugkeimenê· ou gar estin allo ti khôris toutôn hê eudaimonia, alla tauta* – for eudaemonia is composed of certain goods; for eudaemonia is not something different from these, but these (Ar. *Magna Moralia* 1184a 27). The contrary of *eudaimôn* may be *kakodaimôn*, but it is more often ***athlios***. This view of *eudaimonia* is not especially Aristotelian: *meletan oun khrê ta poiounta tên eudaimonian, ei per parousês autês panta ekhomen, apousês de panta prattomen eis to tautên ekhein* – so one ought to study the things that make eudaemonia, since when it is present we have everything and when it is absent we do everything to gain it (Epicurus, *To Menoeceus* 122).

euestô: one of the words used by Democritus as a synonym of *eudaimonia*, and literally meaning well-being: *telos d'einai tên euthumian ... kath'hên galênôs ... hê psukhê diagei ...; kalei d'autên kai euestô* – the end is to be of good heart ... through which the soul lives calmly ...; he [Democritus] also calls it well-being (Diogenes Laertius, *Lives* 9.45).

euthumia: as *euthumiê*, a synonym of *eudaimonia* in Democritus; he wrote a work called *Peri euthumiês*. The adjective is *euthumos*, cheerful, of good heart: *ho men euthumos eis erga epipheromenos dikaia kai nomima kai hupar kai onar khairei te kai errôtai kai anakêdês estin* – the man of good heart takes himself to right and lawful deeds and rejoices both awake and asleep; he is strong and free from care (Democritus in Stobaeus, *Anthology* 2.9.3). See *euestô*.

exairein: in general use, to take out or remove. The perfect passive participle *exêirêmenos* can be used in that sense, as in *kata mesên tên meizô tôn nêsôn exêirêmenos hippodromos* – a hippodrome carved out in the middle of the bigger island (Pl. *Critias* 117c). But it is the standard neoplatonic term meaning 'transcendent' and applied to such things as are *amethekta* – unmixed with the transitory world of becoming and thus *kathara*, pure: *to men gar amethekton ... exêirêmenon tôn metekhontôn, apogennaï ta metekhesthai dunamena* – for the unparticipated ... that transcends the participated, generates things that can be participated (Proclus, *Elements of Theology* 23); *têi de amiktôi pros ta en topôi onta ousiaï kai têi exêirêmenêi katharotêti oudamou estin* – but by its mode of being that is unmixed with what is in place, and by its transcendent purity, it is nowhere (Proclus, *Elements of Theology* 98); *tên apo kinêseôs kai êremias exêirêmenên monên* – its immobility that transcends motion and rest (Simplicius, *Physics* 23.14). The adverb is *exêirêmenôs*, transcendentally.

G

gê: earth, first named as one of the four basic elements, *stoikheia* in Aristotle's terminology, by Empedocles: *houtos de ta men sômatika stoikheia poiei tettara, pur kai aera kai hudôr kai gên* – he [Empedocles] makes the bodily elements four, fire and air and water and earth (Simplicius, *Physics* 25.21). Earth should be understood to include all solids, as water is all liquids. These four elements were accepted by most later philosophers: *pur kai hudôr*

kai gên kai aera phusei panta einai ... kai ta meta tauta au sômata –
[wise men] say that fire and water and earth and air all exist
naturally ... and after them bodies in their turn (Pl. *Laws* 889b);
*estin hekastou phora tis tôn haplôn sômatôn, hoion tôi puri men anô
têi de gêi katô kai pros to meson –* there is a natural locomotion for
each of the simple bodies, as upwards for fire and for the earth
downwards and towards the middle [of the universe] (Ar. *Phys.* 214b
13). *hê gê* is the earth as in English: *tên mentôi idean tês gês hoian
pepeismai einai kai tous topous autês ouden me kôluei legein –* there
is nothing to stop me saying what I believe to be the shape of the
earth and what are its regions (Pl. *Phaedo* 108d).

genesis, gignesthai. (1) Birth, being born: *prin kai genesthai hêmas*
– before we were even born (Pl. *Phaedo* 88a). (2) Becoming, to
become. Aristotle distinguishes absolute becoming (coming to be)
from becoming somehow: *phamen gar ton manthanonta gignesthai
men epistêmona, gignesthai d'haplôs ou –* for we say that he who
learns becomes learned, but not that he comes to be absolutely (Ar.
De Gen. et Cor. 318a 35). Sometimes the distinction is not heeded and
genesis covers all change: *ti to on aei, genesin de ouk ekhon, kai ti to
gignomenon men aei, on de oudepote –* what that is that ever is and
admits no becoming, and what the ever becoming that never is (Pl.
Tim. 27d); *oukoun ei men ousian anagkazei theasasthai, prosêkei, ei
de genesin, ou prosêkei –* if [a study] compels him to contemplate
being, it is suitable, if becoming, unsuitable (Pl. *Rep.* 526e). Of
absolute *gignesthai* and *genesis* the contraries are *phtheiresthai,
phthora*, cease to be, ceasing to be: *Peri geneseôs kai phthoras –* 'On
Coming to be and Ceasing to be' – is the title of a work of Aristotle.
*alloiôsis men estin hotan hupomenontos tou hupokeimenou, aisthê-
tou ontos, metaballêi en tois heautou pathesin ... hotan d'holon
metaballêi mê hupomenontos aisthêtou tinos hôs hupokeimenou tou
autou ... genesis êdê to toiouton, tou de phthora –* alteration is when a
substance that is perceptible remains, but changes its own features
... but when the whole changes without anything perceptible
remaining as a substance of the same thing, such an event is coming
to be and the ceasing to be of the former thing (Ar. *De Gen. et Cor.*
319b 10). But *hê genesis hodos estin ek tou atelous eis to enantion
teleion –* coming to be is the road from the imperfect to its contrary,
the perfect (Proclus, *Elements of Theology* 45).

genos: race, sex, genus, kind. As race: *tôi anthrôpeiôi genei –* the human race (Pl. *Symp.* 189d). As sex: *misei tou gunaikeiou genous* – through hatred of the female sex (Pl. *Rep.* 620a). As genus: *genos d'esti to kata pleionôn kai diapherontôn tôi eidei en tôi ti esti katêgoroumenon* – genus is what is predicated of many things differing in species in the category of substance (Ar. *Top.* 102a 31); *ho horismos ek genous kai diaphorôn estin* – a definition is by genus and difference (Ar. *Top.* 103b 15); *deuterai de ousiai legontai en hois eidesin hai prôtôs ousiai legomenai huparkhousi, tauta te kai ta tôn eidôn toutôn genê* – second substances are said to be the species to which those called first substances belong, they and the genera of these species (Ar. *Cat.* 2a 12). Further philosophically trivial distinctions in Aristotle, *Met.*, Book 4, Ch. 28.

gignôskein: to know, to recognise; *gnôsis*: knowledge; *gnôstos*: knowable. *tous men gar duo misthous gignôskô* – I recognise two of the rewards (Pl. *Rep.* 347a); *gnôthi sauton* – know yourself (Pl. *Prot.* 343b). In Plato, frequently contrasted with *doxa* and its cognates: *estai gnôston kai doxaston to auto, ê adunaton?* – will the same thing be the object of knowledge and belief, or is that impossible? (Pl. *Rep.* 478a). The object of *gnôsis* is *to on*, reality: *to men pantelôs on pantelôs gnôston* – the fully real is the fully knowable (Pl. *Rep.* 477a); *epi men tôi onti gnôsis ên, agnôsia d'ex anagkês epi mê onti* – knowledge was assigned to the real, so necessarily ignorance is of the unreal (Pl. *Rep.* 477a). Here, as often, it is hard to know whether *agnôsia*, like *agnoia*, is nescience or mistake, and whether the unreal is the non-existent or the false. See *einai*.

gnômê may simply be an opinion of or judgment by any one: *kata gnômên tên emên* – in my judgment (Pl. *Soph.* 225d); *met'adikou gnômês krinein tas zêmias* – to determine the penalties with unjust judgment (Pl. *Laws* 846b). In Aristotle, it is either a characteristic of the *phronimoi*, the wise, defined by him as *tou epieikous krisis orthê*, the correct judgment of the good man (Ar. *E.N.* 1143a 19), or it is the judgment or maxim delivered by such a person, a gnomic utterance such as *gnôthi seauton*, know yourself: *esti de gnômê apophansis … katholou … peri hosôn hai praxeis eisi* – a maxim is a universal proposition about practical matters (Ar. *Rhet.* 1394a 21).

gnôrimos comes from *gnôrizein*, to recognise, and has two distinct uses in philosophy. (1) In political theory, the *gnôrimoi* are the prominent or notable people, thought of as a political group.

Frequently joined with the *euporoi*, the wealthy: *Solôn ... tas d'arkhas ek tôn gnôrimôn kai tôn euporôn katestêse pasas* – Solon ... constituted all the government posts from the prominent and the wealthy (Ar. *Pol.* 1274a 18). (2) In logic and epistemology, the *gnôrimon* is what is evident, according to Aristotle in two contrasting ways: *protera d'esti kai gnôrimôtera dikhôs· ou gar t'auton proteron têi phusei kai pros hêmas proteron, oude gnôrimôteron kai hêmin gnôrimôteron. legô de pros hêmas men protera kai gnôrimôtera ta egguteron aisthêseôs, haplôs de protera kai gnôrimôtera ta porrôteron* – things are prior and more evident in two ways; for the naturally prior and the prior for us are not the same, nor the more evident and the more evident to us: I call prior and more evident to us things nearer to the senses [particulars], and prior and more evident without qualification, those furthest from them [universals] (Ar. *An. Po.* 71b 33). A completed science would start from the *haplôs gnôrima*; in trying to construct one we must work from the *gnôrima hêmin*. So, in ethics, *hêmin arkteon apo tôn hêmin gnôrimôn* – we must start from what is evident to us (Ar. *E.N.* 1095b 3).

gnôsis, gnôstos. See *gignôskein.*

grammê: a line: *megethous de to men eph'hen grammê, to de epi duo epipedon, to d'epi tria sôma* – of magnitudes the one-dimensional is the line, the two-dimensional is the plane and the three-dimensional a body (Ar. *De Caelo* 268a 7); *phasi kinêtheisan grammên epipedon poiein, stigmên de grammên* – they say a moving line makes a plane, and a point a line (Ar. *De An.* 409a 4).

H

hairesis comes from *hairein*, to take, and has the basic meaning of taking and, in philosophy, of some sort of choice: *tên hupo tôn pollôn makaristên hairesin heilesthên* – they (dual) made the choice praised by the many (Pl. *Phaed.* 256c); *pasan hairesin kai phugên epanagein ... epi tên tou sômatos hugieian* – to refer each choice and avoidance to the health of the body (Epicurus, *To Menoeceus* 128). In later writers only, a school or sect of philosophers: *kata tên dogmatikên hairesin* – according to the dogmatic school (Sextus Empiricus, *Adversus Mathematicos* 7.276); from this use comes the word 'heresy'.

hamartanein: in Homer, usually physically to miss one's mark, with a spear, etc.; from that it acquired a more general sense of making a mistake. This use is common in philosophy, and in it *oudeis **hekôn** hamartanei* – nobody makes mistakes intentionally – is, as Socrates claimed, a truism not a paradox: *kata ton akribê logon ... oudeis tôn dêmiourgôn hamartanei* – strictly speaking, a craftsman does not make mistakes (Pl. *Rep.* 340e); *eu isthi hoti **akontes** hamartanomen* – be sure that it is an unintentional mistake (Pl. *Rep.* 336e); *akrasia psegetai oukh hôs **hamartia** monon alla kai hôs kakia* – weakness of will is censured not as a mere mistake but as badness (Ar. *E.N.* 1148a 3); of injustices *ta men met'agnoias **hamartêmata** estin* – those involving ignorance are mistakes (Ar. *E.N.* 1135b 12). But the term acquired a use for unforced error, or wrong-doing; *anosiôtata hamartêmata hamartanousi* – they commit the most impious wrongs (Pl. *Gorg.* 525d).

hamartêma is defined by Aristotle as follows: *ta men met'agnoias hamartêmata estin* – [actions] done in ignorance [and therefore ***akousia***] are mistakes (Ar. *E.N.* 1135b 12). But, as in the case of ***hamartanein***, *hamartêma* acquired a sense of wrong action: *anosiôtata hamartêmata hamartanousi* – they commit the most impious wrongs (Pl. *Gorg.* 525d). In the Stoics *hamartêma* is the contrary of *katorthôma* – right-doing: *hamartêma te to para ton orthon logon prattomenon* – a fault is something done contrary to the right principle (*SVF* 500).

hamartia: basically, a mistake: *epistêmês ... ouk estin orthotês, oude gar hamartia* – knowledge cannot be correct, for it cannot be mistaken (Ar. *E.N.* 1142b 10). But, as in the case of ***hamartanein***, it can be wrong-doing: *pragmata aniata kai porrô probebêkota hamartias* – matters that are incurable and far-gone in wrongness (Pl. *Laws* 660c). *hamartia* is often the subjective state of the person who commits a ***hamartêma***.

haplôs, the adverb from ***haplous***, means 'simply' in various ways: *to d'haplôs êtoi to prôton sêmainei kath'hekaston katêgorian tou ontos, ê to katholou kai to panta periekhon* – 'simply' means either that which is first in each category of being, or the universal and that which includes everything (Ar. *De Gen. et Cor.* 317b 5); *ouk oida ... haplôs houtôs ... ei moi apokriteon estin hôs ... –* I don't know whether I should answer without qualification that ... (Pl.

Prot. 351c); *haplôs men gar oudeis apoballei hekôn* – nobody intentionally throws cargo overboard just like that [but might to save a sinking ship] (Ar. *E.N.* 1110a 9).

haplous: simple, with varying significance according to context: *êtoi haplêi diêgêsei ê dia mimêseôs* – either through simple narration [including indirect speech] or by imitation [direct speech impersonating others] (Pl. *Rep.* 392d); *tauta men hapla kai stoikheia, gên de kai pur kai hudôr kai aera suntheta* – [Anaxagoras holds that homeomeries] are simple and elements, but earth, fire, water and air are compounds (Ar. *De Gen. et Cor.* 314a 26); *hapanta ta mikta sômata ... ex hapantôn sugkeitai tôn haplôn* – all mixed bodies ... are composed of all the simple bodies (Ar. *De Gen. et Cor.* 334b 31); *oukh haploun eti touto erôtaïs* – you are no longer asking a simple [as opposed to complex] question (Pl. *Gorg.* 503a). Without qualification: *ei ... ên haploun to manian kakon einai* – if the view that madness is a bad thing was without qualification (Pl. *Phaedrus* 244a).

hêdesthai: to enjoy, to like, to be pleased, to take pleasure in. It does not mean 'have a pleasant feeling' though it may be a feeling in which one takes pleasure. It is often treated as a synonym of *khairein*. Thus both *hêdesthai* and *khairein* are frequently said to be the contrary of *lupeisthai*, to dislike, to be distressed by. Also *khairein* is often used in association with the noun *hêdonê* in preference to *hêdesthai*. Thus in Aristotle's discussion of temperance in *E.N.*, Book 3, Ch. 10 he uses both *khairein* and *hêdonê* constantly, but never *hêdesthai*. The word *hêdonê* occurs frequently in the surviving works of Epicurus, but *hêdesthai* apparently never. Plato frequently treats pleasure as a *kinêsis*, a process, which is attacked by Aristotle on the ground that, unlike a process, *hêsthênai men gar esti takheôs ... hêdesthai ou* – one may become pleased quickly, but one cannot enjoy quickly (Ar. *E.N.* 1173a 35).

hêdonê: pleasure, enjoyment, the opposite of *lupê*, dislike, distress. It often refers to pleasant feelings, since, as Aristotle says, *eilêphasi tên tou onomatos klêronomian hai sômatikai hêdonai* – the bodily pleasures have taken over the inheritance of the name (Ar. *E.N.* 1153b 33). *tote gar hêdonês khreian ekhomen, hotan ek tou mê pareinai tên hêdonên algômen· hotan de mê algômen ouketi tês hêdonês deometha. kai dia touto tên hêdonên arkhên kai telos legomen einai tou makariôs zên* – it is then that we have a need for pleasure when we are distressed by the absence of pleasure; but when we are not distressed we have no longer a need for pleasure. That is why we say that pleasure is the beginning and end of a blessed life (Epicurus, *To Menoeceus* 128). **hêdus, hêdeia, hêdu**: pleasant, enjoyable: *ou gar potoi ... oud'apolauseis paidôn kai gunaikôn ... ton hêdun gennaï bion* – it is not drinking ... nor the enjoyment of boys and women ... that make a life pleasant (Epicurus, *To Menoeceus* 132). The adverb is **hêdeôs**: *hêdeôs xunontes allêlois* – in pleasant companionship (Pl. *Rep.* 372b).

hekôn, hekousion, hekousiôs. (1) Intending, intended, intentionally: *epi tois hekousiois epainôn kai psogôn gignomenôn* – praise and blame are given to intended actions (*E.N.* 1109b 30); *ho gar di'agnoian praxas hotioun, mêden ti duskherainôn epi têi praxei, hekôn men ou peprakhen, ho ge mê êidei, oud'au akôn* – he who does something in ignorance of the facts and who is not troubled by what he does has not acted intentionally, since he did not know he was doing it, but also it is not contrary to his intention (Ar. *E.N.* 1110b 19). But (2) in some cases the correct translation must be 'willing', as in *mêdena ethelein hekonta arkhein* – nobody is willing to rule (Pl. *Rep.* 346e). The common translation 'voluntary' is best avoided. The contrary of *hekôn* is **akôn**.

hen: in general, simply the neuter singular of *heis*, one. But in neoplatonic theology and metaphysics *to hen* is the One, identical with *to agathon*, the good, from which everything else is derived and on which everything else is dependent. *to hen* is, in a way, God, but not a personal god. *pan plêthos deuteron esti tou henos* – every manifold is posterior to the One; *t'agathon tôi heni t'auton* – the Good is identical with the One; *to hen akinêtôs huphistêsin* – the One creates without changing (Proclus, *Elements of Theology* 5, 13, 26). Sometimes *to autoen*, the one itself, as in *kai pan plêthos apo tou autoenos* – every manifold is from the One itself (Proclus, *Elements of Theology* 5). Sometimes treated as indeclinable name: *hen einai tou hen parousiaï* – to be one by the presence of the One (Plotinus, 6.6.14). In *Met.*, Book 4, Ch. 6 Aristotle discusses the conditions under which a compound counts as *hen*, a unity.

henas: a henad in neoplatonic metaphysics: *ei de ex hôn to prôtôs* *hênômenon henas* – a henad if a member of the first unified group (Proclus, *Elements of Theology* 6). Once in Plato at *Philebus* 15a, where it appears to be a unit and equivalent to a *monas*.

heniaios: in neoplatonic theology, unitary, having the character of being one: *pas ho theios arithmos heniaios estin* – the whole number of the gods has the character of unity (Proclus, *Elements of Theology* 113); *hê gar henôsis kai to metron kai ho horos suggenestera tais heniaiais onta tôn theôn hupostasesi* – for unification and measure and limit are more akin to the unitary substances of the gods (Simplicius, *Physics* 638.14).

hênômenon: a unified group in neoplatonic metaphysics: *ei de mê esti plêthos monon, êtoi hênômenon estin ê henas· kai ei metekhon tou henos, hênômenon* – if it is not a mere plurality it is either a unified group or a henad; and it is a unified group if it partakes in the One (Proclus, *Elements of Theology* 6).

henôsis: in neoplatonic metaphysics, unification into a *hênômenon*: *pan agathon henôtikon esti tôn metekhontôn autou, kai pasa henôsis agathon* – every good unifies things that partake of it, and every unification is a good (Proclus, *Elements of Theology* 13).

henôtikos: unifying. See *henôsis*.

henoun: to unify. Used non-metaphysically by Aristotle: *to lian henoun zêtein tên polin* – to try to unify the city overmuch (Ar. *Pol.* 1261b 10). Used metaphysically by neoplatonics mainly in the perfect passive participle *hênômenos*. Not in Plato.

hexis. (1) In connection with the transitive use of *ekhein*, to have, *hexis* is possession: *tên tôn hoplôn hexin* – the possession of arms (Pl. *Laws* 625c); *epistêmês pou hexin phasin auto [to epistasthai] einai* – they say that [understanding] is the possession of knowledge (Pl. *Theaet.* 197b); *diapherei de isôs ou smikron en ktêsei ê en khrêsei to ariston hupolambanein, kai en hexei ê energeiaï* – perhaps it makes not a small difference whether we conceive of the greatest good as lying in owning or using, that is, in possession or activity (Ar. *E.N.* 1098b 31). (2) In connection with the intransitive use of *ekhein*, as in such phrases as *ou philosophôs ekhein* – not to be philosophically disposed (Pl. *Phaedo* 91a), *hexis* as condition or

71

disposition: *hê tôn sômatôn hexis oukh hupo hêsukhias men kai argias diollutai?* – is not the condition of bodies damaged by rest and idleness? (Pl. *Theaet.* 153b); *estin ara hê* **aretê** *hexis proairetikê* – so excellence [of character] is a disposition concerning choice (Ar. *E.N.* 1106b 36).

holos: the whole, in contrast to the *morion* or *meros*, a part: *eis to auto pheretai to holon kai to morion* – the whole and the part move to the same place (Ar. *De Caelo* 270a 4). In the neuter singular, *to holon*, it refers in physical contexts to the world as a whole: *holôs de to peirasthai ta* **hapla** *sômata skhêmatizein alogon esti, prôton men hoti sumbêsetai mê anaplêrousthai to holon* – in general it is irrational to try to give shapes to the simple bodies, first because the result will be that the world will not be filled up (Ar. *De Caelo* 306b 3). *holôs*: in general, as above: *tês kinêseôs ê tou khronou ê holôs tôn gignomenôn kai phtheiromenôn* – the motion of time or of things that come to be and pass away in general (Simplicius, *Physics* 506.6).

homoiomereia: possession of like parts; *homoiomerês*: that which is a like part or possesses like parts; from *homoios*, similar, and *meros*, a part. Anaxagoras believed in an unlimited number of *sômatikai arkhai*, primary bodies: *panta gar ta homoiomerê, hoion hudôr ê pur ê khrusos agenêta men einai kai aphtharta* – for all the like parts, such as water or fire or gold, are ungenerated and indestructible (Simplicius, *Physics* 27.5); *hapanta ta homoiomerê kathaper hudôr ê pur houtô gignesthai kai apollusthai phêsi* **sugkrisei** *kai* **diakrisei** *monon* – [Anaxagoras] says that all the things with like parts such as water and fire come into being and pass away only by conjunction and separation [of the like parts] (Ar. *Met.* 984a 13).

homônumos: in general, and very commonly in Plato, used of two persons having the same name: *ho men gar pappos te kai homônumos emoi* – my grandfather who has the same name as I (Pl. *Rep.* 330b). Used technically in Aristotle and subsequent philosophers: two different kinds of things are said to be *homônumoi*, have the same name, when we should say that the name ambiguously applies to different kinds of thing. Words are homonyms, things are *homônuma*. Those kinds of things to which the name applies in the same sense are *sunônumoi*, while words are synonyms. *to gar manthanein homônumon, to te xunienai khrômenon têi epistêmêi, kai to lambanein epistêmên – manthanein* [to learn, to understand] is homonymously named, being to understand, using knowledge, or to acquire knowledge (Ar. *Top.* 165b 32); *alla pôs dê legetai? ou gar eoike tois ge apo tukhês homônumois* – how, then, are things said [to be good]? For they do not seem like things that just chance to have the same name (Ar. *E.N.* 1096b 26). See also *parônumos* and *aph'henos*. The noun is *homônumia*: *dia to suneggus einai tên homônumian autôn lanthanei* – because the different meanings of [*dikaiosunê*] are closely connected, the ambiguity escapes notice (Ar. *E.N.* 1129a 26). The adverb is *homônumôs*: *kaleitai kleis homônumôs – kleis* is named ambiguously [since it is a key or a collar-bone] (Ar. *E.N.* 1129a 29). That which is named *homônumôs* also *pollakhôs legetai* – is named in many ways.

hoper: the same, or of the same kind. Non-technically: *skopei ei oun sundokei hoper emoi* – see whether you think the same as I (Pl. *Prot* 340b); *hoper arti elegomen* – as we were recently saying (Pl. *Rep.* 331e). Technically, explained by Aristotle: *ta men ousian sêmainonta hoper ekeino ê hoper ekeino ti sêmainei* – what signifies the substance signifies precisely what the thing is or what that thing is of which it is a part (Ar. *An. Po.* 83a 24); *hoper gar ti esti to ti ên einai* – what precisely a thing is is its essence (Ar. *Met.* 1030a 3). For a fuller account of Aristotle's use of *hoper* see Ross's note to *Met.* 1001a 26 in his edition. *hoper* does not appear in *LSJ* nor in many indices, presumably because of a preference for regarding it as two words *ho per*.

horismos: etymologically, the setting of a *horos*, a boundary. (1) Demarcation, way of distinguishing: *akribês men oun en tois toioutois ouk estin horismos, heôs tinos hoi philoi* – in such matters there is no precise way of determining how far friends can remain friends (Ar. *E.N.* 1159a 3). (2) Definition: *ho men oun horismos ti esti dêloi* – so a definition displays what a thing is (Ar. *An. Po.* 91a 1); *dêlon toinun hoti monês tês ousias estin ho horismos* – it is clear that a definition is only of substance [and not of a thing's other attributes, quality, quantity, etc.] (Ar. *Met.* 1031a 1). There is a full discussion of *horismos* in Aristotle's *Posterior Analytics*, Book 2, Ch. 3.

horizein has a basic meaning of putting a *horos*, boundary, to something, or distinguishing two or more things: *tauta ... duo hêmin hôristhô eidê en psukhêi enonta* – let these two elements in the soul be distinguished for us (Pl. *Rep.* 439e). As definition: *hoi tên hêdonên agathon horizomenoi* – those who define good as the pleasant (Pl. *Rep.* 505c); *ta metra tês* **epistrophês** *hôristai tois kata tên* **proodon** *metrois* – the measures of reversion are determined by the measures of procession (Proclus, *Elements of Theology* 39); *panta men gar ta plêthê têi heautôn phusei* **aorista** *onta dia to* **hen** *horizetai* – for all manifolds, that are of their own nature indeterminate, are made determinate by the One (Proclus, *Elements of Theology* 117).

horos. (1) Basically, a boundary, even a boundary stone: *hos d'an epergazêtai ta tou geitonos, huperbainôn tous horous* – whoever cultivates his neighbour's property, crossing over the boundaries (Pl. *Laws* 843c). (2) A standard, measure or criterion: *aristokratias horos aretê, oligarkhias ploutos* – the criterion [of eligibility to govern] in an aristocracy is excellence, in an oligarchy wealth (Ar. *Pol.* 1294a 10); *homologiaï themenoi horon eis tout'apoblepontes kai anapherontes tên skepsin poiômetha* – let us set a standard by agreement and conduct our investigation looking towards it and referring to it (Pl. *Phaedrus* 237d). (3) A term in logic: *horon de kalô eis hon dialuetai hê protasis, hoion to te katêgoroumenon kai to kath'hou katêgoreitai* – I call a term that into which a proposition is decomposed, such as the predicate and that which is given a predicate [the subject] (Ar. *An. Pr.* 24b 16); *ho men katholou tôn horôn, ho d'en merei* – one of the terms is universal [all or none], the other is particular [some] (Ar. *An. Pr.* 26a 17). The Latin from which the word 'term' is derived is *terminus*, which also means a boundary stone. (4) Very frequently, a definition: *ouk ara houtos horos esti dikaiosunês, alêthê te legein ...* – so that is not the definition of justice, to tell the truth etc. (Pl. *Rep.* 331d); *Horoi* – 'Definitions' – is the title of a spurious work ascribed to Plato, which includes: *horos· logos ek* **diaphoras** *kai* **genous** – a definition is a statement composed of difference and genus (Pl. *Def.* 414d); *esti horos logos ho to ti ên einai sêmainôn* – a definition is a statement signifying the essence (Ar. *Top.* 101b 39). In this use *horos* is a synonym of **horismos** in one of its uses.

hôs epi to polu: for the most part. Used non-technically by Plato: *lambanein en tais psukhais hôs epi to polu enantias doxas* – receive in their souls for the most part contrary opinions (Pl. *Rep.* 377b). In

74

Aristotle it is used technically in the phrase *ta hôs epi to polu* to denote the class of regularities that are not necessary and absolutely invariable: *epeidê horômen ta men aei hôsautôs gignomena, ta de hôs epi to polu, phaneron hoti oudeterou toutôn aitia hê **tukhê** legetai oude ta apo tukhês, oute tou ex **anagkês** kai aei oute tou hôs epi to polu* – since we see some things always happening in the same way, some for the most part, it is clear that neither chance nor the results of chance are said to be the explanation of either of these, neither of the necessary nor of what happens for the most part (Ar. *Phys.* 196b 10); *ta gar ginomena phusei panta ginetai ê aei hôdi ê hôs epi to polu, to de para to aei kai hôs epi to polu apo t'**automatou** kai apo tukhês* – what happens naturally all happens always thus or for the most part; what is other than always and for the most part is spontaneous and from chance (Ar. *De Gen. et Cor.* 333b 6).

hudôr: water. One of the four elements, earth, water, air and fire, recognised by most philosophers after Empedocles as constituting the sublunary region. All liquids were philosophically regarded as water, though most were recognised to be impure. Of the four bodies exhibiting some combination of hot or cold, wet or dry, water is the wet and cold: *to d'hudôr psukhron kai **hugron*** – water is cold and wet (Ar. *De Gen. et Cor.* 330b 4). Earth and water are the lower pair, air and fire the higher pair of the four elements: *pur men gar kai aêr tou pros ton **horon** pheromenou, gê de kai hudôr tou pros to meson* – fire and air belong to the pair that tends to the boundary [of the universe], earth and water to that which tends to the middle (Ar. *De Gen. et Cor.* 330b 32). *De Generatione et Corruptione*, Book 2, Ch. 3 contains an historical account of views on the elements of various philosophers. See also *aer*.

hugros: moist, wet. A characteristic of *aêr*, air, and *hudôr*, water, in Aristotle's physics: *hugron de to aoriston oikeiôi **horôi**, euoriston on, xêron de to euoriston men oikeiôi horôi, dusoriston de* – the moist has no natural boundaries, but is easily put in bounds [as in a vessel], but the dry has natural bounds but is hard to put in bounds [since it resists pressure] (Ar. *De Gen. et Cor.* 329b 30). *xêros* is the contrary of *hugros*: *legetai de xêron kai hugron pleonakhôs. antikeitai gar ... tôi hugrôi kai to xêron kai to pepêgos* – wet and dry are spoken of in more ways than one ... For both the dry and the solidified are contrary to the wet (Ar. *De Gen. et Cor.* 330a 12).

hulê: originally, wood, whether growing or timber: *hosa hulê pros ta tôn tektonôn diaponêmata parekhetai* – what wood supplies towards the constructions of builders (Pl. *Critias* 114a). In Aristotelian and neoplatonic physics, the matter that together with the form constitutes a substantial reality and which has the capacity to receive form: *hê phusis dikhôs, to te eidos kai hê hulê* – nature is twofold, form and matter (Ar. *Phys.* 194a 13); cf. Ar. *Phys.* 193a 29; *ousia hê te hulê kai to eidos kai to ek toutôn* – reality is matter and form and that which is composed of them (Ar. *Met.* 1035a 2); *legô gar hulên to prôton hupokeimenon hekastôi ex hou gignetai ti enuparkhontos mê kata sumbekêkos* – I call matter the immediate substrate of each thing from which it comes when it is present not contingently (Ar. *Phys.* 192a 31). Matter is one of the four Aristotelian causes or types of explanation: *hê hulê tôn skeuastôn ... hôs to ex hou aitia estin* – the material is the cause of artifacts as that from which they come (Ar. *Phys.* 195b 17). *hulê* is also one of the *arkhai* or basic principles of reality: *heteran tên hulên kai to hupokeimenon* – another [principle] is the matter, i.e. the substrate (Ar. *Met.* 983a 29). The adjective is *hulikos*: *peri de tês hulikês ousias* – concerning material reality (Ar. *Met.* 1044a 15).

huperbolê: excess, opposed to *elleipsis*, deficiency: *pasan tên te huperbolên kai tên elleipsin* – every excess and deficiency (Pl. *Prot.* 283c). In Aristotle's ethics *aretê* is a mean to which correspond two *kakiai*, one of *huperbolê*, one of *elleipsis*: *mesotês de duo kakiôn, tês men kath'huperbolên, tês de kat'elleipsin* – [excellence is] a mean between two faults, one of excess, the other of deficiency (Ar. *E.N.* 1107a 2); *tês men huperbolês kai tês elleipseôs phtheirousês to eu, tês de mesotêtos sôizousês* – excess and deficiency destroy the good, the mean preserves it (Ar. *E.N.* 1106b 11).

huperousios: a neoplatonic word meaning 'above being'. It is not found in Plato, but derives from his statement *ouk ousias ontos tou agathou all'eti epekeina tês ousias presbeiaï kai dunamei huperekhontos* – the Good is not a being but transcends being in dignity and power (Pl. *Rep.* 509b). A typical use of the word is *eti de, ei to prôton huperousion, hapas de theos tês tou prôtou seiras estin hêi theos, huperousios hekastos an eiê* – again, if the first principle transcend being, then, since every god *qua* god is of the order of the first principle, each must transcend being (Proclus, *Elements of Theology* 115).

huphesis: a neoplatonic word, not found in Plato, meaning 'decline' or 'deterioration': *ta de di'huphesin kai tên eis plêthos ektasin allôn deitai tôn mallon hênômenôn hina metaskhêi tôn autoenadôn ousôn* – the rest because of their decline and their extension into multiplicity require principles more unified if they are to participate in a pure henad (Proclus, *Elements of Theology* 128). See *huphienai*.

huphienai: a neoplatonic word, not used by Plato. Found mainly in perfect passive participle *hupheimenos*, declined, deteriorated: *all'hoion hupheimenê tis tou ontos hupostasis estin hê peplêthus-menê* – but that which has become manifold is like some deteriorated existence of being (Simplicius, *Physics* 102.2). See *huphesis*.

hupodokhê: non-technically, reception, as in *xenôn hupodokhês allothen* – the reception of foreigners from elsewhere (Pl. *Laws* 949e). Technically, in Plato and his commentators, the receptacle underlying all the world of becoming: *tên tou gegonotos horatou kai pantôs aisthêtou mêtera kai hupodokhên, mête gên mête aera mête pur mête hudôr legômen ... all'anoraton eidos* – let us not say that the mother and receptacle of the whole visible and generally perceptible world is either earth or air or fire or water ... but an invisible form (Pl. *Tim* 51a); *en gar Timaiôi tên hulên pasês einai geneseôs hupodokhên hoion tithênên phêsin* – in the *Timaeus* [Plato] says that matter is the receptacle of all becoming, like a nurse (Simplicius, *Physics* 539.11).

hupokeimenon: the present participle of the verb *hupokeisthai*, to underlie, meaning 'that which underlies': a person can be said to *hupokeisthai*, to be subject, to a ruler (Pl. *Gorg.* 510c). It has various special senses, including matter, logical subject and substance. (1) As matter: *tên hulên kai to hupokeimenon* – the matter, i.e. the underlying (Ar. *Met.* 983a 29); *dikhôs hupokeitai, ê tode ti on hôsper to zôion tois pathesin, ê hôs hê hulê têi entelekheiaï* – things underlie in two ways, either as a particular thing, as an animal underlies its experiences, or as the matter underlies the reality (Ar. *Met.* 1038b 5). (2) As substance: *ta gar mathêmata peri eidê estin· ou gar kath'hupokeimenou tinos* – arithmetic is about forms, for it is not concerned with any substance (Ar. *An. Po.* 79a 7); *hapanta de tauta legetai ousia hoti ou kath'hupokeimenou legetai, alla kata toutôn ta* *alla* – these are all called being, because they are not predicated of anything else, but other things are predicated of them (Ar. *Met.* 1017b 13). (3) As logical subject: *kath'hupokeimenou gar tou eidous monon to genos legetai* – of the species as subject only the genus is predicated (Ar. *Top.* 127b 3).

hupolambanein (verb) and *hupolêpsis* (noun), have a basic sense of taking over. (1) In basic sense: *en toutôi hupelabe Polemarkhos* – at that point Polemarchus took over [the discussion] (Pl. *Rep.* 544b). (2) To understand what is said: *isôs gar toi sou orthôs legontos egô ouk orthôs hupolambanô* – perhaps you are speaking correctly and I am not understanding you correctly (Pl. *Gorg.* 458e). (3) To understand or mean something by a word: *to khalepon touto isôs oukh houtô Simônidês hupelambanen* – perhaps Simonides did not understand the word 'difficult' in that way (Pl. *Prot.* 341a). (4) Frequently in Aristotle, accepting as true: *tês hupolêpseôs diaphorai epistêmê kai doxa kai phronêsis* – the varieties of acceptation are knowledge, opinion and wisdom (Ar. *De An.* 427b 25); *hê epistêmê peri tôn katholou estin hupolêpsis* – knowledge is a conception concerning universals (Ar. *E.N.* 1140b 31). The noun *hupolêpsis* is used only in a non-philosophical sense by Plato.

hupostasis has a number of non-philosophical meanings, such as 'sediment' in medical contexts. Literally, it is 'standing under', and can refer to foundations of buildings. In later philosophy, especially the neoplatonics, it is a synonym of *ousia*, being, substance, existence: *alloiôsei tên hupostasin ekeinôi parekhetai* – by alteration it provides existence to that other, *aph'heautou deuteras hupostaseis parekhomenon* – providing secondary substances from itself (Proclus, *Elements of Theology* 27); *tês phusikês hupostaseôs tês en metabolêi ousês* – the natural world that is in change (Simplicius, *Physics* 194.3); *neôteroi tôn philosophôn anti tês ousias têi lexei tês hupostaseôs ekhrêsanto* – more recent philosophers used the word *hupostasis* instead of *ousia* (Socrates, *Ecclesiastical History* 3.7).

hupothesis (noun) and *hupotithesthai* (verb), have the basic sense of setting under. Philosophically (1) proposal, intention: *hina su ta sautou kata tên hupothesin hopôs an boulêi perainêis* – so that you may do your part as you propose in the way you want (Pl. *Gorg.* 454c); *hê hupothesis tês dêmokratikês politeias eleutheria* – the aim of a democratic constitution is freedom (Ar. *Pol.* 1317a 40). (2) An hypothesis: *ei orthê hê hupothesis ên to psukhên harmonian einai* – if the hypothesis that the soul is an attunement was correct (Pl. *Phaedo* 94b); *tôi tautên tên hupothesin hupothemenôi* – to him who proposed this hypothesis (Pl. *Soph.* 244c). In Aristotle, regularly, hypothesised existence: *legô to einai ti ê mê einai ti hupothesis* – I call it an hypothesis that something exists or does not (Ar. *An. Po.* 72a 20). (3) Occasionally, the premisses of a syllogism: *tôn apodeixeôn hai hupotheseis* – the bases of demonstrations (Ar. *Met.* 1013a 16). (4) An argument based on hypotheses in the expression *ex hupotheseôs*: *ei de mê esti ta prôta eidenai oude ta ek toutôn einai epistasthai haplôs oude kuriôs all'ex hupotheseôs* – if it is not possible to know the basic premisses, then one cannot have scientific knowledge of their consequences without qualification or properly, but only hypothetically (Ar. *An. Po.* 72b 14). The expressions *ex hupotheseôs* and *kath'hupothesin* are very common in the sceptical works of Sextus Empiricus in such expressions as *kath'hupothesin sugkhôrô, ex hupotheseôs lambanô, didômi kath'hupothesin* – I admit, accept, grant, hypothetically.

I

idea comes from the same root as the Greek verb *idein* and the Latin verb *videre*, both meaning 'to see'. In its simplest, non-technical use it refers to the visual aspect of anything: *tên d'oun idean panu kalos* – very beautiful to look at (Pl. *Prot.* 315e). More abstractly, it is a type or form or species: *ê tina allên ekheis idean politeias?* – or have you any other type of constitution? (Pl. *Rep.* 544c). Technically, in Plato and his followers, it is the eternal unchanging form in the world of being: *hê tou agathou idea megiston mathêma* – the form of the good is the greatest study (Pl. *Rep.* 505a); *tas d' ... ideas noeisthai men horasthai d'ou* – the forms are thought of but not seen (Pl. *Rep.* 507b). In later neoplatonic and other theologically oriented philosophy the forms cease to be independent: Clement of Alexandria glossed the *idea* as *ennoêma tou theou* – a thought of God (Clement, *Stromateis* 5.3.16.3); see also Plotinus 3.9.1 and Philo, *De Opificio Mundi* 4, where God is said to make the eternal world of forms as a blueprint for creation. In Plato the term *idea* seems to be a synonym of *eidos*. But Aristotle used only the term *eidos* of form as a component of the *sunolon* of matter and form. Also some neoplatonic writers appear to treat *eidos* as a term covering both the *khôriston* and the *akhôriston*, but *idea* with special reference to the *khôriston*: *tên men gar hulên topon elege tôn enulôn eidôn hôs hupodokhên autôn, ta de eidê ta khôrista tês hulês êtoi tas ideas elege mê einai en topôi* – for [Plato] said that matter was the place of the enmattered forms as their receptacle, but he said that the forms that are separate from matter, or the ideas, were not in a place (Simplicius, *Physics* 545.27).

idios: that which belongs exclusively to one person or thing. Thus politically the *idion* is distinguished from the *koinon*, the public: *tôn allôn praxeôn idiôn te kai koinôn* – other activities both private and public (Pl. *Laws* 961b). It is also the exclusive: *to tês dikaiosunês idion ergon* – the exclusive (special, specific) task of justice (Pl. *Clit.* 409d). The abstract noun is *idiotês*: *kata tên idiotêta tôn praxeôn t'ounoma dikaiôs eilêphen idion* – [each science] has rightly received a special name in accordance with its special function (Pl. *Pol.* 305d). In Aristotle *idion* receives a more technical and restricted sense, being limited to that which is exclusive to a species but not part of the essence; in this use it is translated as 'property', from the Latin *proprium*: *idion d'estin ho mê dêloi men to ti ên einai, monôi d'huparkhei kai antikatêgoreitai tou pragmatos* – a property is what does not show the essence but belongs only to and is convertibly predicated of the subject matter (Ar. *Top.* 102a 18). Thus the term 'property' is here used more narrowly than in modern philosophical usage.

isos, like its contradictory *anisos*, has three basic uses. (1) Of numerical or quantitative equality: *isou ontos tou khronou hon katheudomen ôi egrêgoramen* – the time in which we sleep being equal to that in which we are awake (Pl. *Theaet.* 158d). (2) Of equality of rights and status: *bouletai hê polis ex isôn einai kai homoiôn* – a city needs to consist of equal and similar people (Ar. *Pol.* 1295b 25). (3) Of fairness: *ton mellonta dikastên ison esesthai* – him who is to become a fair judge (Pl. *Laws* 957c); *dikaios estai ho te nomimos kai ho isos. to men dikaion ara to nomimon kai to ison* – the law-abiding man and the fair man will be just. So justice is both the lawful and the fair (Ar. *E.N.* 1129a 33). The abstract noun is *isotês*. Thus (1) *khronou isotês* – equality of time (Pl. *Phaedrus* 240c); (2) *isotês philotêta apergazetai* – equality brings about friendship (Pl. *Laws* 757a). The verb *isazein*, to make equal, can be used in any of these senses.

isôs: the adverb from *isos*, can mean 'equally': *isôs tou ellatonos pleon elatton te tou meizonos* – equally is more than the less and less than the more (Pl. *Epinomis* 991a). But the term is used constantly, especially by Aristotle, to indicate an element of doubt, either because of insufficient proof or because of what Simplicius calls *philosophos eulabeia*, philosophical caution, and may be translated as 'perhaps': *touto d'estin isôs t'alêthes* – that is perhaps the truth (Pl. *Phaedo* 67a); *amphisbêtountes prostitheasin aei to isôs kai takha* – when debating people always add 'perhaps' and 'maybe' (Pl. *Apol.* 31a); *meta de tauta peri hêdonês isôs hepetai dielthein* – after that it perhaps follows to discuss pleasure (Ar. *E.N.* 1172a 16).

K

kakia: the contrary of *aretê*. It is frequently translated 'vice', as *aretê* is translated 'virtue', but 'defect', 'fault' or 'badness' is preferable. Often, but not always, with reference to human character: *aretê men ara, hôs eoiken, hugieia te tis an eiê kai kallos kai euexia psukhês, kakia de nosos te kai aiskhos kai astheneia* – so, as it seems, excellence is some health and beauty and well-being of the soul, but badness is disease and ugliness and weakness (Pl. *Rep.* 444d); *tôn peri ta êthê pheuktôn tria estin eidê, kakia, akrasia, thêriotês* – there are three types of character to be avoided, badness, weakness and brutishness (Ar. *E.N.* 1145a 16). For bodily defects: *ou monon d'hai tês psukhês kakiai hekousioi eisin, all'eniois kai hai tou sômatos* – it is not only defects of the soul that are our own fault, but in some cases those of the body (Ar. *E.N.* 1114a 22).

kakos has much the same spread of uses as the English 'bad'. (1) Of moral badness: *kakos men gar hekôn oudeis* – nobody is intentionally bad (Pl. *Tim.* 86d). (2) Of inefficiency: *kakou mageirou* – a bad cook (Pl. *Phaedrus* 265e); Aristotle notes the difference between calling somebody simply bad and calling him bad of a kind: *kakon iatron kai kakon hupokritên, hon haplôs ouk an eipoien kakon* – a bad doctor and a bad actor, whom one would not call bad without qualification (Ar. *E.N.* 1148b 8). (3) Of evils that befall people: *eleeinos ... ho ta kaka ekhôn* – he is to be pitied who suffers evils (Pl. *Laws* 731d). The adverb is *kakôs*, badly. Two common expressions are (1) *kakôs legein*, to speak evil of: *hina mê se hoi agathoi kakôs legôsin* – in order that the good may not speak evil of you (Pl. *Euthyd.* 281e); (2) *kakôs poiein*, to treat badly: *kakôs poiein tous anthrôpous* – to treat men badly (Pl. *Meno* 94e). This use must be distinguished from **kakopoiein**, to do wrong: *ei de mê, outheis hautôi aitios tou kakopoiein* – otherwise nobody will be responsible for his wrong-doing (Ar. *E.N.* 1114b 3). *kakos* is the contrary of **agathos**.

kalokagathia and **kaloskagathos** seem to be as near as Greek can get to gentlemanliness and gentleman, in the old sense of someone of gentle birth and breeding: *khalepon têi alêtheiaï megalopsukhon einai· ou gar hoion te aneu kalokagathias* – it is hard to be great-souled; for it is not possible without gentlemanliness (Ar. *E.N.* 1124a 3); *tous de pollous adunatein pros kalokagathian protrepsasthai* – to be unable to turn the generality of men into gentlemen (Ar. *E.N.* 1179b 10); *dia to mallon akolouthein paideian kai eugeneian tois euporôterois. eti de dokousin ekhein hôn heneken hoi adikoi adikousin· hothen kai kalouskagathous kai gnôrimous toutous prosagoreuousin* – because culture and good birth are found rather in the wealthy. Also they seem to possess that for which wrong-doers do wrong; which is why they call these men gentlemen and notables (Ar. *Pol.* 1293b 37); *hina hupo tôn plousiôn te kai kalôn k'agathôn legomenôn en têi polei eleutherôtheiê* – in order that [the *dêmos*] might be freed from the rich and those called gentlemen in the city (Pl. *Rep.* 569a).

kalos has a width of use which makes it difficult to find any single translation. Thus Diotima in the *Symposium* of Plato speaks of a person being led *apo tôn kalôn sômatôn epi ta kala epitêdeumata, kai apo tôn epitêduematôn epi ta kala mathêmata* – from bodies to occupations to studies all of which are called *kala* (Pl. *Symp.* 211c); *gunê ... kalê kai eueidês* – a beautiful and good-looking woman (Pl. *Crito* 44a); *to kalon telos tês aretês* – the noble is the goal of excellence (Ar. *E.N.* 1115b 12). Thus *kalos* seems to cover the aesthetic and at least some morality, and not only these. In this it is like its contrary **aiskhros**. If a single translation is needed, 'fine' is perhaps the best choice. In morality it seems to be the grand that is called *kalon*, as the mean and base is called *aiskhron*. Thus the brave man faced with death *hupomenei tou kalou heneka* – he endures for the sake of the *kalon* (Ar. *E.N.* 1115b 11); *to andreiôs kallion kai hairetôteron tou sôphronôs* – acting bravely is finer and more choiceworthy than acting temperately (Ar. *Rhet.* 1364b 35).

Similarly the English 'handsome' is used both of personal looks and of apologies. Aristotle at various places offers definitions and elucidations: *kalon men oun estin ho an di'hauto haireton on epaineton êi, ê ho an agathon on hêdu êi* – that is *kalon* which being in itself choiceworthy is praiseworthy, or what, being good, is pleasant (Ar. *Rhet.* 1366a 33); *to kalon esti to prepon* – the *kalon* is the fitting (Ar. *Top.* 102a 6). The only sign that Aristotle gives of finding ambiguity in *kalon* is: *enantion … tôi kalôi tôi men epi tou zôiou to aiskhron, tôi d'epi tês oikias to mokhthêron, hôste homônumon to kalon* – the *aiskhron* is the contrary of *kalon* in the case of animals, but *mokhthêron* in the case of a house, so that *kalon* is ambiguous (Ar. *Top.* 106a 20); *to kalon to di'opseôs ê di'akoês hêdu* – the *kalon* is what is pleasant to sight or hearing (Ar. *Top.* 146a 22); the *kalon* is distinguished from the *sumpheron*, useful, and the *hêdu*, pleasant, at *E.N.* 104b 32. Some of these definitions are offered only as examples, not as Aristotle's settled view, but they illustrate the width of coverage of the term. Plotinus shows some doubt regarding the width of coverage: *ara ge heni kai tôi autôi kalôi ta panta ê allo men en sômati to kallos, allo de en allôi?* – are all things beautiful with one and the same beauty, or is there one beauty in a body and another in something else? (Plotinus 1.6.1). The noun is *to kallos*; the adverb is *kalôs*.

karteria: distinguished from *egkrateia* by Aristotle as being endurance of distress as distinct from conquering the temptation of the pleasant: *antikeitai de tôi men akratei ho egkratês, tôi de malakôi ho karterikos· to men gar karterein estin en tôi antekhein, hê de egkrateia en tôi kratein* – the strong-willed is opposed to the weak-willed, but the enduring to the soft. For to endure consists in holding out, but strength of will in conquering (Ar. *E.N.* 1150a 32).

katalêptikê: a *phantasia*, perception or presentation is, in Stoic thought, *katalêptikê* if it is one that seizes on the perceiver as unmistakably veridical: *phantasia katalêptikê estin hê apo tou huparkhontos kai kat'auto to huparkhein enapomemagmenê kai enaposphragmenê hopoia ouk an genoito apo mê huparkhontos* – an apprehensive presentation is one caused by an existing object in accordance with that object and imaged and stamped in the subject, such as could not be derived from a non-existent object (Sextus Empiricus, *Adversus Mathematicos* 7.248). Cicero says of such presentations that they are such *quae propriam quandam haberent*

83

declarationem earum rerum quae viderentur (Cicero, *Acad. Post.* 1.41).

kataphasis: affirmation, a term introduced and defined by Aristotle: *kataphasis de estin apophansis tinos kata tinos. apophasis de estin apophansis tinos apo tinos* – an affirmation is a statement affirming one thing of another. A negation is a statement denying one thing of another (Ar. *De Int.* 17a 25). It does not occur in Plato, except in the spurious *Definitions* at 413c. The verb *kataphanai*, to affirm, is also not found in Plato's works. The noun and the verb became standard terms in philosophy.

katastêma: a specifically Epicurean word not used by Plato and Aristotle. It is defined by Simplicius as *diathesis tês psukhês* – a condition of the soul (Simplicius, *On Epictetus* 114d); *to gar eustathes sarkos katastêma kai to peri tautês piston elpisma tên akrotatên kharan kai bebaiotatên ekhei tois epilogizesthai dunamenois* – the stable condition of well-being in the body and the sure hope of its continuance holds the highest and surest joy for those who are able to calculate it (Epicurus, fr. 11). Epicurus contrasts pleasures arising from a calm condition, free from trouble, sometimes called *ataraxia* and *aponia*, but also called *katastematikai hêdonai*, with those involving *kinêsis*, change: *hê men gar ataraxia kai aponia katastêmatikai eisin hêdonai* – for freedom from trouble of soul and distress of body are pleasures of a condition (Epicurus, quoted in *Vita Epicuri* 136); *diapheretai de pros tous Kurênaïkous peri tês hêdonês. hoi men gar tên katastêmatikên ouk egkrinousi, monên de tên en kinêsei* – Epicurus differs from the Cyrenaics about pleasure; for they do not admit pleasures of condition, but only that which involves change (*Vita Epicuri* 136).

katêgorein: in Plato, usually has the common literary sense of 'accuse', but occasionally means merely 'say' or 'judge': *saphestera katêgorei hoti touto houtôs ekhei* – he clearly judges this to be the case (Pl. *Phaedo* 73c). In Aristotle and later philosophy the verb in the passive has the meaning 'to be predicated' and the participial form *to katêgoroumenon* means 'the predicate': *horon de kalô eis hon dialuetai hê protasis, hoion to te katêgoroumenon kai to kath'hou katêgoreitai* – I call a term that into which a proposition is analysed, such as the predicate and that of which it is predicated (Ar. *An. Pr.* 24b 16).

katêgoria: in Plato, has the ordinary literary meaning 'accusation': *en katêgoriaï te kai apologiaï* – in accusation and defence (Pl. *Phaedrus* 267a). In Aristotle and later philosophy it means 'category'. In the work called the *Katêgoriai* Aristotle introduces the ten categories in Ch. 4, but he does not there call them categories. But in *Topics*, Book 1, Ch. 9 he writes: *meta toinun tauta dei diorisasthai ta genê tôn katêgoriôn ... esti de tauta, ton arithmon deka, ti esti, poson, poion, pros ti, pou, pote, keisthai, ekhein, poiein, paskhein* – after that, one must distinguish the kinds of predicate ... these are, ten in number, what it is (substance), quantity, quality, relation, place, time, position, possession, action and passion (Ar. *Topics* 103b 20). Examples of all these are given in *Categories*, Ch. 4. The doctrine seems to be that each of these ten categories, or ultimate predicates, tells what sort of thing that of which it is predicated is, as being either a substance, or a quantity, or a quality, etc. These are the only two places in which Aristotle lists as many as ten categories; other lists are shorter.

katharsis: a term important in philosophy only as occurring in Aristotle's definition of tragedy: *estin oun tragôidia mimêsis praxeôs spoudaias kai teleias megethos ekhousês, hêdusmenôi logôi ... di'eleou kai phobou perainousa tên tôn toioutôn pathêmatôn katharsin* – so tragedy is a representation of some important action that is complete and sizeable, in pleasing language ... by pity and fear accomplishing purgation of such passions (Ar. *Poetics* 1449b 24). So interpreted *katharsis* is a term borrowed from medicine. Some have taken it to have the other sense of purification, as used with reference to religious ceremonies of purification. For reasons for preferring 'purgation of', rather than 'purification of' see Appendix II to the edition of the *Poetics* by D.W. Lucas, Oxford, 1968.

kathêkon: fitting. This is widely used, but is specially a Stoic term derived from the verb *kathêkein*, to be fitting. *Peri tou kathêkontos* is the title of a work by the Stoic Zeno. *kathêkonta men oun einai hosa logos hairei poiein* – such things are fitting as reason chooses (*SVF* 3.495); *tôn de kathêkontôn ta men einai phasi teleia ha dê kai katorthômata legesthai* – of the fitting some they [the Stoics] assert to be perfect and to be called perfections (*SVF* 3.494).

kath'hauto: means 'as such' or 'in itself'. It is distinguished from the *kata **sumbebêkos***, which is traditionally, but unfortunately, trans-

85

lated as *per accidens*, or contingently; a better translation might be derivatively. Thus an aircraft flies *kath'hauto*, the passengers *kata sumbebêkos*, but their flight is in no way an accidental occurrence: *eti ta men legetai kath'hauta posa, ta de kata sumbebêkos, hoion hê men grammê poson ti kath'hauto, to de mousikon kata sumbebêkos* – also some things are said to have size as such, others derivatively, as a line has size in itself but a musical thing derivatively (Ar. *Met.* 1020a 16); *esti kinoumenon to men energeiaï, to de kata sumbebêkos* – one thing moves as such, another derivatively (Ar. *Phys.* 211a 18).

katholou: universal. Both terms and propositions are said to be universal. A universal term is opposed to the particular or individual: *pas gar logos kai pasa epistêmê tôn katholou kai ou tôn eskhatôn* – for every definition and every science is of the universal and not of individuals (Ar. *Met.* 1059b 26); *kata men ton logon ta katholou protera, kata de tên aisthêsin ta kath'hekasta* – according to the rational account the universal is prior, but particulars are prior in perception (Ar. *Met.* 1018b 33). These two quotations illustrate the difficulty of translating *logos*. The universal proposition, of the forms 'All *A* is *B*' and 'No *A* is *B*', is opposed to particular propositions of the forms 'Some *A* is *B*' and 'Some *A* is not *B*', and to indeterminate propositions of the forms '*A* is *B*' and '*A* is not *B*': *legô de katholou men to panti ê mêdeni huparkhein, en merei de to tini ê mê tini huparkhein, adioriston de to huparkhein ê mê huparkhein aneu tou katholou ê kata meros* – I call belonging to all or none universal, belonging to or not belonging to some particular, and belonging or not belonging without being universal or particular indeterminate (Ar. *An. Pr.* 24a 18). The term *katholou* does not occur in Plato's works, but became a regular term of philosophy after Aristotle: *to men gar katholou hekastôi tôn sumplêrountôn auto epharmottei* – for the universal fits each of the things comprised under it (Simplicius, *Physics* 17.8).

katô: below, one of the six *diastaseis*, directions, recognised by Aristotle. Its contrary is *anô*, above. There is an absolute below in the universe: *lego d'anô men tên apo tou mesou, katô de tên epi to meson* – I call above that which is away from the middle of the universe, below that which is towards the middle (Ar. *De Caelo* 284b 30). For both Plato and Aristotle weight is the tendency to be below: *to d'enantion pathos toutois baru kai katô* – the contrary condition to these is weight and being below (Pl. *Tim.* 63d);

barutaton de to pasin huphistamenon tois katô pheromenois – the most heavy is that which is below everything that moves downwards (Ar. *De Caelo* 269b 24). Apart from this universal direction, only natural bodies have an objective above and below: *ouk en hapanti sômati to anô kai to katô kai to dexion kai aristeron kai to emprosthen kai opisthen zêtêteon, all'hosa ekhei kinêseôs arkhên en autois, empsukha onta* – one should not look for an above and below, right and left, in front and behind, in every body, but in those which have the principle of change in themselves, being alive (Ar. *De Caelo* 284b 30). Where we otherwise speak of these directions, it is relatively: *pros hêmas epanapherontes* – relating it to ourselves (Ar. *De Caelo* 285a 2).

katorthôma: a noun from the verb *katorthein*, 'to accomplish successfully'. It was used by the Stoics of the elements in what they regarded as the best life: *tôn de **kathêkontôn** ta men einai phasi teleia ha dê kai katorthômata legesthai* – [the Stoics] say that of right actions some are perfect, and these are also called perfections (*SVF* 3.494); *katorthômata men ta toiauta· phronein, sôphronein, dikaiopragein, khairein … panth'hosa kata ton orthon logon prattetai* – perfections are such things as the following: wisdom, temperance, justice, happiness … all things that are done in accordance with right reason (*SVF* 3.501).

keisthai: literally, 'to lie', is the name of one of the ten *katêgoriai* recognised by Aristotle. As such, the traditional translation is 'posture' or 'position': *keisthai de hoion anakeitai, kathêtai* – examples of posture are 'is lying', 'is sitting' (Ar. *Cat.* 2a 3). As the quotations under *katô* show, it is hard to see how this category applies to anything but living things like men. *keisthai* is omitted by Aristotle in some shorter lists of categories.

kenos: empty, void. Apart from non-technical uses, as a neuter *to kenon* is the name of alleged empty volumes of space. Aristotle, like most ancient philosophers, thought that the whole sublunar sphere was occupied by earth, air, fire and water, and all above by the aether; but some, especially Democritus, Epicurus and their followers, denied this: *eteêi atoma kai kenon* – in reality there are atoms and void (Democritus, quoted in Sextus Empiricus 7.139) Most of our knowledge of this theory is derived from Ar. *Phys.*, Book 4, Chs 6-9. If Aristotle is right, it seems that for him and the philosophers of whom he knew the *kenon* was what occurs in the *diastêmata*, intervals, between bodies, and not a continuous space part of which is occupied by bodies: *dokei dê to kenon topos einai en hôi mêden esti. toutou d'aition oti to on sôma oiontai einai, pan de sôma en topôi, kenon de en hôi topôi mêden esti sôma* – the void seems to be a place in which there is nothing. This is because they think that what is is body, but all body is in a place, but the void in the place where there is no body (Ar. *Phys.* 213b 31). But Epicurus speaks of it rather as being space that bodies may or may not occupy: *eite to kenon ên hôrismenon, ouk an eikhe ta apeira sômata hopou enestê* – if the void were limited, the infinite bodies would not have anywhere to be situated in (Epicurus, *To Herodotus* 42). Aristotle devotes Book 4, Chs 7-9 of the *Physics* to arguments designed to disprove the existence of void.

kentron: originally, a sharp-pointed goad, as in the proverb *khalepon pros kentra laktizein* – it is hard to kick against the pricks (Acts of the Apostles 26:14). From this the word came to mean the sharp-pointed central arm of a pair of compasses, among other things, and then the central point of the circle itself: *estôsan eis to kentron êgmenai hai AB* – let the lines AB be drawn to the centre (Ar. *An. Pr.* 41b 15). It was also used of the centre of a sphere: *idoi d'an tis epi tês sphairas malista tên diaphoran· ou gar t'auton takhos esti tôn te pros tôi kentrôi kai tôn ektos* – one may see this difference especially in the case of a [revolving] sphere; for the parts towards the centre do not have the same speed as those outside (Ar. *Phys.* 240b 15). Finally, it came to be used of the centre of the universe: *to katôtatô an eiê to meson tou pantos· touto d'esti to kentron kai ta toutôi plêsiazonta* – the lowest point would be the middle of the whole world; that is the central point and things close to it (Simplicius, *Physics* 605.10).

khairein: to like, to enjoy, to take pleasure. Frequently with a participle: *hoti kai hopêi khaireis onomazôn* – whatever and however you like to name it (Pl. *Symp.* 212c). Often the contrary of *lupeisthai*, to dislike or be distressed by, as is also *hêdesthai*: *en toutois dê pasin ê lupoumenous ê khairontas* – either distressed by or taking pleasure in all these things (Pl. *Rep.* 603c). Thus conjoined with *hêdonê*: *agathon einai phêsi to khairein pasi zôiois kai tên hêdonên kai terpsin kai hosa tou genous esti toutou sumphôna* – [Philebus] says that the good for all animals is enjoyment, pleasure, delight and everything conforming to that kind (Pl. *Philebus* 11b). There is a use of the verb meaning 'to say farewell' and hence an idiom where *khairetô* or *khairein ean* means 'to leave on one side': *ta ... tôn arkhaiôn peri metheisthô kai khairetô* – let us abandon and leave aside the affairs of those of old (Pl. *Laws* 886d).

khara: pleasure, enjoyment, joy – the noun from *khairein*. In Epicurus it is an active rather than *katastêmatikê*, calm, pleasure: *hê de khara kai hê euphrosunê kata kinêsin energeiai blepontai* – but joy and exultation are considered as active pleasures involving change (*Vita Epicuri* 136).

khôra: non-technically, country, or land in a non-nationalistic sense: *tês tôn plêsiôn khôras hêmin apotmêteon* – we shall have to cut off some of our neighbours' land (Pl. *Rep.* 373d). More generally, a place: *auton kath'hauton en têi hautou khôraï dunait'an idein* – would be able to see [the sun] itself in its own place (Pl. *Rep.* 516b); as hendiadys with *topos*: *eiper esti sômatos topos kai khôra* – if there is a place and situation of a body (Ar. *Phys.* 209a 7). Sometimes space, rather than place: *en tini topôi kai katekhon khôran* – in some place and occupying space (Pl. *Tim.* 52b).

khôrismos: separation. Only non-technically in Plato: *lusis kai khôrismos psukhês kai sômatos* – the freeing and separation of the soul from the body (Pl. *Phaedo* 67d). Sometimes, but rarely, the separation of a form from its matter: *tôi men gar enulôi eidei malista huparkhei to akhôriston· ho gar khôrismos toutou phthora toutou estin* – being inseparable belongs especially to the form in matter; for separation from the thing is its ceasing to be (Simplicius, *Physics* 544.23). See *khôristos*.

khôristos: separated, especially of forms on their own and not elements in a *sunolon* of form and matter. The contradictory is *akhôristos*. Not in Plato. *ho men Sôkratês ta katholou ou khôrista epoiei* – Socrates did not treat universals as separate (Ar. *Met.* 1078b 30). In the neoplatonic tradition everything in the world of being is *khôriston* from body. At least sometimes *khôristos* means 'separable' rather than 'separate': *pasa psukhê asômatos estin ousia kai khôristê sômatos* – every soul is an incorporeal substance and separable from body (Proclus, *Elements of Theology* 186). Not in

89

Plato, but *to eidêtikon aition saphôs ho Platôn paradidôsin ou to khôriston monon tês hulês alla kai to akhôriston* – but Plato clearly teaches a formal cause that is not only the one separate from matter but also the unseparated (Simplicius, *Physics* 43.14).

khôrizein: to separate: *to khôrizein hoti malista apo tou sômatos tên psukhên* – to separate as far as possible the soul from the body (Pl. *Phaedo* 67c). Especially of treating the forms as independent entities: *hoi d'ekhôrisan, kai ta toiauta tôn ontôn **ideas** prosêgoreusan* – but the others [the Platonists] separated [universals] and called them the forms of things (Ar. *Met.* 1078b 31). See *khôristos* and *akhôristos*.

khronos: time. In Plato's *Timaeus* and in neoplatonism, time is an image or copy of eternity, just as perceptible things are images or copies of the eternal forms: *eikô d'epenoei kinêton tina **aiônos** poiêsai ... touton hon dê khronon ônomakamen* – [the demiurge] designed to make a changing image of eternity ... that which we have named 'time' (Pl. *Tim.* 37d). There is a full discussion of time in Ar. *Phys.*, Book 4, Chs 10 ff. *touto gar estin ho khronos, arithmos kinêseôs kata to proteron kai husteron* – for that is time, the measure of change with regard to earlier and later (Ar. *Phys.* 219b 1). *en tôi nun khronôi* – at present (Pl. *Philebus* 35a).

kinein, kineisthai: to change, to move. See *kinêsis*.

kinêsis: traditionally translated as 'motion', but, as will be clear, 'change' or 'process' would be better, since motion, or change of place, is only one of the sorts of change the term covers; a difficulty is that Greek has too many other terms that would also naturally be translated as 'change', such as *alloiôsis* and *metabolê*. Plato recognised two sorts of *kinêsis*. (1) Motion: *ara kineisthai kaleis hotan ti khôran ek khôras metaballêi ê kai en tôi autôi strephêtai?* – do you call it change when something exchanges position for position or also twists about in the same place? (2) Other changes: *hotan de êi men en tôi autôi, gêraskêi de, ê melan ek leukou ê sklêron ek malakou gignêtai, ê tina allên alloiôsin alloiôtai, ara ouk axion heteron eidos phanai kinêseôs?* – but when something is in the same place, but grows old, or becomes black instead of white or hard instead of soft or undergoes some other alteration, is it not right to call this another kind of change? (Pl. *Theaet.* 181c-d). Aristotle accepts this, adding also change of quantity: *ei oun hai katêgoriai dièirêntai ousiaï, poiotêti, topôi, tôi poiein kai paskhein, tôi pros ti, tôi posôi, anagkê treis einai kinêseis, poiou posou topou· kat'ousian d'ou ... oude tou pros ti ... oude poiountos kai paskhontos* – if then the categories be distinguished as substance, quality, place, action and passion, relation, quantity, it is necessary that there be three changes, in quality, quantity and place; but not in substance, or in relation, or in action and passion (Ar. *Met.* 1068a 8). *genesis* – coming to be – and *phthora* – ceasing to be – are not *kinêseis* since they do not involve change in a continuing thing: *adunaton ... tên genesin kinêsin einai ... oude dê hê phthora kinêsis* – coming to be cannot be a *kinêsis* ... and nor can ceasing to be (Ar. *Met.* 1067b 30 and 37). Increase and decrease in size – *auxêsis and phthisis* – are counted as changes of place by Aristotle, and so as *kinêseis*: *tautês [kinêseôs kata topon] de to men phora, to de auxêsis kai phthisis* – of this [change of place] one sort is local motion, the other increase and decrease (Ar. *Phys.* 211a 15). It is clear that the use of 'change' as a translation restricted to *kinêsis* is artificial, but some artificiality seems inescapable, since *metabolê, alloiôsis* and *kinêsis* can all be naturally called change, while turning green, which is a *kinêsis*, is not naturally called a motion.

Aristotle also introduced a contrast between *energeia* and *kinêsis* that seems to have no connexion with the use considered above. It is developed in *Met.* 1048b 18-35 and elsewhere. It is between doings such that if someone is doing something he has done it, and those where this is not so: *hoion horaï hama kai heôrake ... all'ou manthanei kai memathêken* – one has seen as soon as one sees, but has not learnt as soon as one is learning (Ar. *Met.* 1048a 23). The former doings are *energeiai*, the latter *kinêseis*. *kinêseis* also take time and come to an end when complete – when one has learnt something, that learning ends of necessity – whereas one can look at a thing for an indefinite period. It would seem that growing bigger, for example, would be a *kinêsis* as a type of change, but an *energeia* rather than a *kinêsis*, since it has no conceptually necessary terminating point. Aristotle sometimes also treats *energeia* as a genus of which *kinêsis* is a species; for illustrative quotations see *energeia*.

kosmos: generally, good order, a near synonym of *taxis*: *mêd'en kosmôi mêd'en taxei* – neither in order nor arrangement (Pl. *Laws* 898b); *tên de taxin kai ton kosmon para phusin* – [Democritus makes] arrangement and order unnatural (Ar. *De Caelo* 301a 10). Hence, on the one hand, adornment (as in the English 'cosmetic'): *peri ton gunaikeion kosmon* – concerning female adornment (Pl. *Rep.* 373c). But also the ordered heavens, or the heavens and the universe contained therein: *ho ... pas ouranos ê kosmos ê kai allo ho ti pote onomazomenos malista an dekhoito* – the whole heaven or the cosmos or whatever else it would prefer to be called (Pl. *Tim.* 28b); *hê de tou holou sustasis esti kosmos kai ouranos* – the composition of the whole is the cosmos and the heaven (Ar. *De Caelo* 280a 21). It is sometimes hard to tell whether Aristotle is referring to the universe as a whole or to the sphere of the fixed stars that contains it when he uses the words *kosmos* and *ouranos*: *phêsin ho Alexandros dein sêmeiôsasthai hoti mekhri nun tôi tou ouranou onomati khrêsamenos epi tou kosmou pantos nun ton ouranon bouletai tên exôtatô sphairan tên tôn aplanôn legein* – Alexander says that it is necessary to have noted that up to now [*Phys.* 212b 2] Aristotle has used the word 'heaven' of the whole of the cosmos but now wishes to speak of the heaven as the outermost sphere of the fixed stars (Simplicius, *Physics* 594.17). *dei legein tonde ton kosmon zôion empsukhon ennoun* – one must say that this universe is a living, intelligent animal (Pl. *Tim.* 30b).

kouphos: light. Both Plato and Aristotle regard lightness as a natural disposition to be *anô*, above: *to anô kai to kouphon* – the above and the light (Pl. *Crat.* 423a); *haplôs men oun kouphon legomen to anô pheromenon kai pros to eskhaton ... pros allo de kouphon kai kouphoteron, hou duoin ekhontôn baros kai ton ogkon ison katô pheretai thateron phusei thatton* – we call something light without qualification which moves upwards and towards the extremity [of the universe] ... but relatively light, i.e. lighter, that than which the other of two things having weight and equal bulk moves more quickly downwards (Ar. *De Caelo* 308a 29). *kouphos* is the contrary of *barus*. For Aristotle the planets and the fixed stars have no weight or lightness, since they have no tendency to move either *anô* or *katô*.

krinein: to judge, in all senses of the word: *krineis su to megiston anthrôpois agathon einai plouton?* – do you judge (evaluate) wealth to be the greatest good for man? (Pl. *Gorg.* 452c); *ho dikastês ... krinetô* – let the juryman judge (Pl. *Laws* 925a); *to krinein to alêthes te kai mê* – to judge (distinguish) the true and false (Pl. *Theaet.* 150b).

krisis: judgment, in all senses of the word: *peri tên tôn dikaiôn krisin* – concerned with the judgment (distinction) of just acts (Pl. *Laws* 948b); *dia krisin adikon* – because of an unjust judgment (verdict) (Pl. *Apol.* 41b); *ta de toiauta en tois kath'hekasta kai en têi aisthêsei hê krisis* – such matters are particular and judgment is a matter of perception (Ar. *E.N.* 1109b 23).

kritêrion: a norm by which *krisis* and *to krinein* are to be determined, a canon of judgment. It is a notion important in both Stoic and Epicurean thought: *en toinun tôi Kanoni legôn estin ho Epikouros kritêria tês alêtheias einai tas aisthêseis kai prolêpseis kai ta pathê· hoi de Epikoureioi kai tas phantastikas epibolas tês dianoias* – in the *Canon* Epicurus says that the criteria of truth are the perceptions and concepts and the emotions; but the Epicureans add the intuitive apprehensions of the mind (*Vita Epicuri* 31); *kritêrion men legetai to te hôi krinesthai phasin huparxin kai anuparxin kai to hôi prosekhontes bioumen* – that is called the criterion by which the Stoics say existence and non-existence are judged and that by attention to which we live (Sextus Empiricus, *Outlines of Pyrrhonism* 2.14).

kuklos: a circle or something circular. A circle in argument is defined narrowly by Aristotle: *to de kuklôi kai ex allêlôn deiknusthai esti to dia tou sumperasmatos kai tou anapalin têi katêgoriaï tên heteran labonta protasin sumperanasthai tên loipên, hên elambanen en thaterôi sullogismôi* – circular or reciprocal proof is the use of the conclusion and the simple conversion of one premiss to demonstrate the other premiss which one assumed in the previous argument (Ar. *An. Pr.* 57a 17). Thus given an argument that if all *A* is *B* and all *B* is *C* then all *A* is *C*, to argue that since all *B* is *A* and all *A* is *C* then all *B* is *C* is circular.

L

lexis: in general, speech. In philosophy, *lexis* is sometimes diction as opposed to content: *kata de tên lexin … asapheian poiei to hê tôi ho logos proskeimenon kai thêlukon arthron tôi arsenikôi suntetagmenon* – as regards diction, some unclarity is caused by the '*hê*' adjoining '*ho logos*', i.e. the feminine article joined with the masculine (Simplicius, *Physics* 233.3); cf. Aspasius on *E.N.* 122.27.

logikos: basically, 'concerned with *logos* – speech', hence 'rational' or 'intellectual', as in *homoiôs de kai peri tôn logikôn aretôn* – similarly with regard to the intellectual excellences (Ar. *E.N.* 1108b 9); *noun epistêmên doxan aisthêsin ex hôn pasa tekhnê kai epistêmê kai autoi logikoi esmen* – intelligence, knowledge, belief and perception, from which comes every skill and science and through which we are rational (*SVF* 2.455). There is some difficulty in understanding the term when used of argument: *aporian ... hên logikên kalei, ê hôs ex endoxôn proïousan ê hôs ten logôi monôi to pithanon ekhousan kai ouk apo tôn pragmatôn bebaioumenên ... ê logikên legei tên koinoteran kai ou prosekhê oude idian tou prokeimenou oude ex oikeiôn arkhôn* – a problem that [Aristotle] calls logical, either because it proceeds from accepted opinions, or as having its persuasive power only in what is said and not as confirmed by the data, ... or he calls logical that which is more general and not closely connected with or special to the subject, nor derived from closely associated premisses (Simplicius, *Physics* 440.21); *to gar logikon hôs koinon antidiastellein eiôthe tôi oikeiôi kai kata tên phusin tou pragmatos kai apodeiktikôi* – [Aristotle] was accustomed to contrast the logical, as general, with the closely associated, i.e. what is concerned with the nature of the data and demonstrative (Simplicius, *Physics* 476.28); *dia logikôterôn kai akribesterôn logôn* – by more logical and more precise arguments (Ar. *Met.* 1080a 10); *proslabôn peri poia t'esti ta enthumêmata kai tinas ekhei diaphoras pros tous logikous sullogismous* – adding a knowledge of the sphere of enthymemes and their difference from logical arguments (Ar. *Rhet.* 1355a 13).

logikôs: the adverb from *logikos*. Here also, Simplicius cannot decide whether the question is one of strictness or of generality of argument: *prôton men logikôs eti epikheirei, toutesti pithanôs kai endoxôs, kai eti koinoteron pôs kai dialektikôteron* – first [Aristotle] argues logically, i.e. persuasively and from received opinion, and also more generally and dialectically (Simplicius, *Physics* 476.25).

logismos: primarily, numerical calculation: *logismoi kai ta peri arithmous hen mathêma* – calculations and numerical matters are a single study (Pl. *Laws* 817e). But also reasoning in general: *kai sômati men hêmas genesei di'aisthêseôs koinônein, dia logismou de psukhêi pros tên ontôs ousian* – in body we have a share in becoming through perception, but by reasoning in soul we share in true being

(Pl. *Soph*. 248a). Also the power of reasoning in general: *ta de megista kai kuriôtata ho logismos diôikêke* – reason has settled the greatest and most important matters (Epicurus, *Principal Doctrines* 16). The related verb is *logizesthai*, which also has both the wider and the narrower uses as to reason and to calculate.

logistikos: usually applied to matters of calculation, numbers and arithmetic; *hoi te phusei logistikoi eis panta ta mathêmata hôs epos eipein oxeis phuontai* – natural calculators are naturally quick at practically speaking all studies (Pl. *Rep*. 526b). But also more generally 'rational': *hê men oun aisthêtikê phantasia ... kai en tois allois zôiois huparkhei, hê de bouleutikê en tois logistikois* – perceptual imagination is found also in other animals, but deliberative imagination only in those that are rational (Ar. *De An*. 434a 6).

logos: the verbal noun from *legein*, 'to speak' or 'to say'; its basic meaning is 'something said'. More specialised meanings are given in *LSJ* under ten main heads, liberally subdivided, and occupy five and a half columns. Many of these meanings are to be found in philosophical writings. But one of the most important and characteristic uses in philosophy might be translated 'account' and is concerned with the giving of some account, explanation, definition of some kind of thing: *ho tou dikaiou logos* – the account, definition, of the just (Pl. *Rep*. 343a); *esti d'horos men logos ho to ti ên einai sêmainôn, apodidotai de ê logos anti onomatos ê logos anti logou* – a definition is an account signifying the essential nature; either an account is provided in place of a word or an account in place of an account (Ar. *Top*. 101b 37); *heteros gar ho kata tounoma logos autôn* – [ambiguously named things] have a different account, definition, in relation to their name (Ar. *Top*. 107a 20); *anagkê gar ê to auto einai hekateron kai hena logon amphoterôn, ê mêden einai koinon* – for either the two are identical and share a common account (definition), or have nothing in common (Proclus, *Elements of Theology* 18). Another important use is one where the best translation is perhaps 'reason': *ouden khrêma matên ginetai, alla panta ek logou te kai hup'anagkês* – nothing happens idly, but everything for a reason and from necessity (Leucippus, fr. 2); *epistêmê ... kai ho orthos logos* – knowledge and right reason (Pl. *Phaedo* 73a); *to men alogon autês einai to de logon ekhon* – one part of [the soul] is without reason, the other possesses it (Ar. *E.N.* 1102a 28).

95

lupê, lupeisthai, lupêros: opposite of *hêdonê, hêdesthai, hêdus*. *lupê* is any emotionally unfavourable reaction, and includes dislike, distress, grief and pain, but is not to be identified with any of these, and especially not with pain, though this is often given as the single translation. Andronicus, in his book *Peri Pathôn* – 'On Emotions' – lists 25 varieties of *lupê*, including *metameleia*, regret, and *oiktos*, pity. Similarly the *lupêros*, as the opposite of the *hêdus*, is the unpleasant, not specifically the painful, though pain is one among many unpleasant things. *hotan tis sterêtheis lupêthêi dia tên khreian* – when someone deprived is distressed through his need (Pl. *Philebus* 52b); *stokhasetai tou mê lupein ê sunêdonein. eoike men gar peri hêdonas kai lupas einai tas en tais homiliais ginomenas* – [the friendly man] will aim at not causing distress or at sharing pleasure. For he seems to be concerned with what is pleasant and unpleasant in social life (Ar. *E.N.* 1126b 29); *phtheirousi gar tas energeias hai oikeiai lupai, hoion ei tôi to graphein aêdes kai epilupon ê to logizesthai* – for dislike of activities destroys them, as if one finds writing disagreeable and tedious, or calculation (Ar. *E.N.* 1175b 17).

lusis: in general, and always in Plato, freeing or liberation: *lusis kai khôrismos psukhês apo sômatos* – freeing and separation of soul from body (Pl. *Phaedo* 67d). In Aristotle and his successors it also has the technical meaning of solving some *aporia* or difficulty *hê gar lusis tês aporias heuresis estin* – for the solving of the problem is a discovery (Ar. *E.N.* 1146b 6); *ean gar luêtai te ta duskherê kai kataleipêtai ta endoxa, dedeigmenon an eiê hikanôs* – for if the difficulties be dissolved and received opinion remain, the matter would be sufficiently demonstrated (Ar. *E.N.* 1145b 6).

M

maieutikê: obstetric: *hê maieutike ... tekhnê* – midwifery. Socrates maintained that he could help others to give birth to philosophical ideas, but was himself barren: *tês emês tekhnês maieutikês* – of my obstetric skill (Pl. *Theaet.* 161e). The newly born is a *maieuma* of the midwife: *son men einai hoion neogenes paidion, emon de maieuma* – that it is, so to speak, your new-born child, brought to birth by me (Pl. *Theaet.* 160e).

makarios: blessed, often conjoined with *eudaimôn*: *ho ge eu zôn makarios kai eudaimôn* – he who lives well is blessed and well-off

(Pl. *Rep.* 354a); *tina tropon zêi? athlion ê makarion?* – what sort of life does he lead? wretched or blessed? (Pl. *Rep.* 571a); *oude makarion kai eudaimona mia hêmera oud'oligos khronos* – nor does one day or a short time [make a man] blessed and well-off (Ar. *E.N.* 1098a 19). Strictly the gods are *makarioi*, men only by similitude: *tois men gar theois hapas ho bios makarios, tois d'anthrôpois eph'hoson homoiôma ti tês toiautês energeias huparkhei* – for the gods, their whole life is blessed, but for men only in so far as they exhibit some simulacrum of such activity (Ar. *E.N.* 1178b 25). *makariôs*: blessedly; *makarizein*: to count blessed; *makariotês*: blessedness. It is *makarios* that is translated 'blessed' in the Beatitudes.

mania: usually, madness in an ordinary medical sense. But, most noticably in the *Phaedrus*, it is used by Plato of what he considers to be irrational but in some way inspired: *manias de ge eidê duo, tên men hupo nosêmatôn anthrôpinôn, tên de hupo theias exallagês tôn eiôthotôn nomimôn ... tês de theias tettarôn theôn tettara merê dielomenoi, mousikên men epipnoian Apollônos thentes, Dionusou de telestikên, Mousôn d'au poiêtikên, tettartên de Aphroditês kai Erôtos* – [we say that] there are two sorts of madness, one caused by human diseases, the other by divine dispensation from customary conventions ... of the divine, we distinguished four parts caused by four gods, music being the inspiration of Apollo, initiation that of Dionysus, poetry that of the Muses, and the fourth that of Aphrodite and Eros (Pl. *Phaedrus* 265a). *mainesthai*: to be mad; *manikos*: mad.

manthanein. (1) To learn. (2) To understand. *to gar manthanein homônumon, to te xunienai khrômenon têi epistêmêi kai to lambanein epistêmên* – *manthanein* has two senses, both to understand, using knowledge, and to acquire knowledge (Ar. *Top.* 165b 32); *epi tekhnêi manthanei, hôs sophistês esomenos* – he is learning professionally, as about to become a sophist (Pl. *Protag.* 315a); *to manthanein ouk epistêmê esti lambanein toutou hou an tis manthanêi?* – is not learning the acquisition of knowledge of that which one is learning? (Pl. *Euthyd.* 277b); *ou manthaneis hôs legô? – manthanô* – do you not understand what I mean? – I understand (Pl. *Gorg.* 447d).

matên. (1) In vain, fruitlessly: *sêmeion de to matên, hoti legetai hotan mê genêtai tôi heneka allou ekeino hou heneka, hoion ei to badisai lapaxeôs heneka estin, ei de mê egeneto badisanti, matên phamen badisai kai hê badisis mataia* – an indication is the word 'fruitlessly', which is used when something is for something else that does not come about, e.g. if walking is for the sake of loosening the bowels, but this did not happen when someone walked, we say he walked fruitlessly and that the walking was fruitless (Ar. *Phys.* 197b 22). (2) Without reason, pointlessly: *hina mê matên tharrêsêis* – lest you rejoice without reason (Pl. *Theaet.* 189d); *eme de aitiaï matên* – he accuses me without good reason (Pl. *Alcib.* 1.113c).

mathêma: in its basic sense, and nearly always in Plato's works, any study which a person may *manthanein*, learn: *ta paidôn mathêmata* – the studies of children (Pl. *Tim.* 26b); *poia dê legeis mathêmata megista?* – which do you say are the most important studies? (Pl. *Rep.* 504a). But the term tended to be confined to the mathematical sciences: *eti dê toinun tois eleutherois esti tria mathêmata, logismoi men kai ta peri arithmous hen mathêma, metrikê de mêkous kai epipedou kai bathous hôs hen au deuteron, triton de tês tôn astrôn periodou* – there are still three sciences for free men, one science being calculations and the study of numbers, another the measurement of lengths, areas and solids, a third concerned with the rotation of the stars (Pl. *Laws* 812e); *ta phusikôtera tôn mathêmatôn, hoion optikê kai harmonikê kai astronomia* – the more natural of the sciences, such as optics, harmonics and astronomy (Ar. *Phys.* 194a 8).

mathêmatikos occurs only once in Plato's works, with the general sense of one who is engaged in studies: *ton de mathêmatikon ê tina allên sphodra meletên dianoiaï katergazomenon* – the student, or anyone engaged in serious intellectual activity (Pl. *Tim.* 88b). Like *mathêma*, *mathêmatikos* has subsequently usually the sense of 'mathematical' as an adjective, 'mathematician' as a noun: *mathêmatikos men pais genoit'an, sophos d'ê phusikos ou* – a child may become a mathematician, but not a sage or scientist (Ar. *E.N.* 1142a 17); *para ta aisthêta kai ta eidê ta mathêmatika tôn pragmatôn einai phêsi metaxu, diapheronta tôn men aisthêtôn tôi aïdia kai akinêta einai, tôn d'eidôn tôi ta men poll'atta homoia einai, to de eidos auto hen hekaston monon* – [Plato] said that in addition to perceptible things and forms there were mathematical entities in between, differing from sensible things by being everlasting and unchanging, and from forms by being many alike whereas each form is only one (Ar. *Met.* 987b 14). But the word continued to have also a wider sense, and Sextus Empiricus' work *Pros Mathêmatikous – Adversus Mathematicos* – for example, is a general denial of the possibility of science of all kinds.

megalopsukhia: greatness of soul; *megalopsukhos*: great-souled. Rare and dyslogistic in Plato: *hoi de euphêmotatois onomasi boulomenoi katonomazein hoi men megalopsukhous* – of those who wish to call them by the most charitable names, some call them great-souled (Pl. *Alcib.* 2.140c); *dia tên megalopsukhian – touto gar kalliston tôn en aphrosunêi ge onomatôn* – through greatness of soul – for that is the fairest of names for folly (Pl. *Alcib.* 2.150c). Aristotle uses the word favourably and makes *megalopsukhia* one of his excellences of character: *dokei dê megalopsukhos einai ho megalôn hauton axiôn axios ôn· ho gar mê kat'axian auto poiôn êlithios* – the great-souled seems to be he who estimates himself highly, being estimable; for he who does so, not being worthy, is a fool (Ar. *E.N.* 1123b 1).

megethos: size, may apply to anything in any way measurable: *tou ... megethous tês kolaseôs* – the size (severity) of the punishment (Pl. *Laws* 934b). Particularly of physical and geometrical magnitudes: *dia gar to en têi noêsei mê hupoleipein kai ho arithmos dokei apeiros einai kai ta mathêmatika megethê kai to exô tou ouranou* – because they do not give out in thought, both number and mathematical magnitudes and what is external to the heavens seem to be infinite (Ar. *Phys.* 203b 23).

mêkos: length: *diastêmata men oun ekhei tria, mêkos kai platos kai bathos* – [place] has three dimensions, length, breadth and depth, by which every body is determined (Ar. *Phys.* 209a 4); *esti de to men anô tou mêkous arkhê, to de dexion tou platous, to de emprosthen tou bathous* – the above is the basis of length, to the right of breadth, in front of depth (Ar. *De Caelo* 284a 24). Of time: *apo mêkous khronou* – from length of time (Pl. *Laws* 676a). Of speeches: *hos humin phulaxei to mêkos tôn logôn hekaterou* – who will watch over the length of the speeches of each of you (Pl. *Prot.* 338b).

meros: part, as opposed to *holos*, whole. Of time: *mekhri tritou merous hôras* – until the third part of the hour (Pl. *Laws* 784a). Of place: *en tini merei tês poleôs* – in some part of the city (Pl. *Rep.* 460c). Abstractly: *mêd'en allôi mêdeni merei aretês husterountas* –

nor being behind in any other part (aspect) of excellence (Pl. *Rep.* 484d); *en toutois gar tois logois diestêke to logon ekhon meros tês psukhês pros to alogon* – for these are the ratios in which the part of the soul that has reason stands towards the non-rational (Ar. *E.N.* 1138b 8). Adverbially *en merei*, in turn: *hekaston en merei logon peri Erôtos eipein* – each in turn to make a speech about Eros (Pl. *Symp.* 214b). *meros* appears to be a synonym of *morion*. Ar. *Met.*, Book 4, Ch. 25 discusses meanings of the term. It is clear that the Greeks used *meros* not only where we should say 'part', but also where 'aspect', 'element', 'component', etc. would be more natural than 'part'.

mesos: in the middle. Geographically: *en mesôi tês gês* – in the middle of the earth. Abstractly: *hê men hairesis houtô gignomenê meson an ekhoi monarkhikês kai dêmokratikês politeias* – such a method of selection would provide a mean between a monarchic and a democratic constitution (Pl. *Laws* 756e). As a noun in the neuter, **to meson** is the mean, numerical or non-numerical: *to ge meson ison tôn eskhatôn apekhei* – the mean is equidistant from the extremes; *isôi gar huperekhei te kai huperekhetai· touto de meson esti kata tên arithmêtikên analogian* – it exceeds and is exceeded by equal amounts; this is in accordance with arithmetical proportion (Ar. *E.N.* 1106a 34); *ei de pollakhôs legetai to meson ekhon, dioristeon to pôs meson ekhon* – if 'having a mean' has different senses, one must distinguish how a thing has a mean (Ar. *Top.* 149a 31). Abstractly: *to meson huperphanias kai aneleutherias metadiôkontes* – pursuing the mean between pride and meanness (Pl. *Critias* 112c); *hai mesai hexeis pros men tas elleipseis huperballousi pros de tas huperbolas elleipousin en te tois pathesi kai tois praxesin* – intermediate dispositions exceed in relation to the deficient and are deficient in relation to the excessive in both emotions and actions (Ar. *E.N.* 1108b 16); *ho mesos alêthês tis* – the intermediate man is truthful (Ar. *E.N.* 1108a 20). In Aristotle's philosophy of perception the *meson* is the medium between the object perceived and the perceiver: *aisthanometha ge pantôn dia tou mesou* – we perceive everything through the medium (Ar. *De An.* 423b 7): in Aristotelian logic *to meson* is the middle term in a syllogism by which the subject and predicate terms of the conclusion are linked in the premisses: *aneu mesou sullogismos ou gignetai* – there is no syllogism without a middle term (Ar. *An. Pr.* 66a 28).

mesotês: intermediacy, an abstract noun derived from *mesos*, used especially in Aristotle's doctrine of the mean: *estin ara hê aretê hexis proairetikê en mesotêti ousa têi pros hêmas* – so excellence is a disposition to choose in a mean relative to us (Ar. *E.N.* 1107b 36); *peri men oun phobous kai tharrê andreia mesotês* – so bravery is a mean state concerning fear and confidence (Ar. *E.N.* 1107a 34). Also in Aristotle's doctrine of perception a sense organ must be in a mean state in relation to what is perceived, as things, for example, feel hot and cold only to a body that is less hot and less cold: *tês aisthêseôs hoion mesotêtos tinos ousês tês en tois aisthêtois enantiôseôs* – the sense being as it were a mean state between the contraries among sense-objects (Ar. *De An.* 424a 4).

metabainein: literally, to move to another place: *metabainonta eis heteron aei topon* – continually moving to another place (Pl. *Laws* 893d). The verb in *to gar metabainon topon ek topou* – what changes one place for another – seems in Simplicius to mean the same as *metaballein* in *phamen ta merê topon ek topou metaballein* – we say that the parts change one place for another (Simplicius, *Physics* 609.8 and 632.27). By transference, *metabainei ... ek tês timarkhias eis tên oligarkhian* – it changes from timarchy into oligarchy (Pl. *Rep.* 550d); *ouk ara estin ex allou genous metabanta deixai, hoion to geômetrikon arithmêtikêi ... ex hôn men oun hê apodeixis endekhetai ta auta einai· hôn de to genos heteron, hôs per arithmêtikês kai geômetrikês, ouk esti tên arithmêtikên apodeixin epharmosai epi ta tois megethesi sumbebêkota, ei mê ta megethê arithmoi eisi* – it is not possible to demonstrate moving from another genus, e.g. into something geometrical from something arithmetical ... the elements of the proof may be the same, but where things are of a different genus, like arithmetic and geometry, one cannot fit the arithmetical demonstration to the attributes of magnitudes unless these magnitudes are numbers (Ar. *An. Pr.* 75a 37).

metaballein: to change. This appears to be a close synonym of *metabainein* in many contexts; see the quotations from Simplicius under *metabainein*, and compare *metabainei ... ek tês timarkhias eis tên oligarkhian* – it changes from timarchy into oligarchy – with *hôde malista eis oligarkhikon ek tou timokratikou ekeinou metaballei* – [a constitution] chiefly changes from that timarchic type into oligarchy in this way (Pl. *Rep.* 550d and 553a). For Aristotle's technical use see under *metabolê*.

101

metabasis: change, the verbal noun from *metabainein*: *hê metabasis ... eis ta zôia sunekhês estin* – the change [from plants] to animals is continuous (Ar. *H.A.* 588b 11); *all'ekeino men dêlon, hôs ouk estin eis allo genos metabasis, hôsper ek mêkous eis epiphaneian* – this is clear, that there cannot be a move to another genus, as from a length to a surface (Ar. *De Caelo* 268a 30).

metabolê: change: *tôn politeiôn genesis kai metabolê* – the coming into being of and change in constitutions (Pl. *Laws* 676c). In Aristotle and, under his influence, in much later philosophy, *metabolê* became the most general word for change of all kinds, the principal distinction being between substantial change, such as *genesis*, coming to be, and *phthora*, ceasing to be, on the one hand, and various types of **kinêsis** on the other: *metaballei gar aei to metaballon ê kat'ousian ê kata poion ê kata topon* – what changes always changes either in substance or in quality or in place (Ar. *Phys.* 200b 33); *hotan men oun en [logôi] êi hê metabolê genesis estai ê phthora, hotan d'en tois pathesi kai kata sumbebêkos* **alloiôsis** – when the change is in the account, it is coming or ceasing to be, but when in affections and contingently, it is alteration (Ar. *De Gen. et Cor.* 317a 259).

metalambanein: to share in, in Platonic and neoplatonic metaphysics: *êtoi holou tou eidous ê merous hekaston to metalambanon metalambanei* – each thing that has a share either shares in the whole form or a part of it (Pl. *Parm.* 131a); *auto to kreitton to meizonôs agathou meteilêphos* – the superior itself is that which has a greater share of good (Proclus, *Elements of Theology* 12). Elsewhere it frequently means 'to take instead'; *allo gar onoma meteilêphen anti tês hêdonês to agathon* – for it has taken another name, 'good', instead of 'pleasure' (Pl. *Prot.* 355c). Especially in Aristotelian logic, of substitution of problematic premisses in syllogisms: *ei gar to A kai to B tôi C endekhetai mê huparkhein ean metalêphthêi to 'endekhetai huparkhein' palin estai to prôton skhêma dia tês* **antistrophês** – if *A* and *B* may not be present in *C*, if 'may be present' be substituted there will again be the first figure by means of conversion (Ar. *An. Pr.* 39a 20). Thus if all *A* may not be *C* and all *B* may not be *C*, we may get a first figure syllogism by substituting 'all *A* may be *C*' and 'all *B* may be *C*', and then converting the latter to yield the syllogism: if all *A* may be *C* and all *C* may be *B*, then all *A* may be *B*. The noun is **metalêpsis**: *allê tis an metalêpsis khôris toutôn genoito?* – or could there be any other form of having a share except these? (Pl. *Parm*. 131a).

metamelein: to regret, in relation to past actions, as being inexpedient, mistaken or wrongful. Only in the last-mentioned case is the translation 'repent' very suitable. *ekeinois men tote metamelei hôn an eu poiêsôsin* – such men will then regret their good deeds (Pl. *Phaedrus* 231c); *oute nun moi metamelei houtôs apologisamenôi* – nor do I now regret having so conducted my defence (Pl. *Apol*. 38e). The noun is *metameleia*: *to en metameleiaï* – the deed regretted (Ar. *E.N.* 1110b 23); *metameleia te euthus tou pepragmenou gignêtai* – there is immediate repentance of the action [unpremeditated murder] (Pl. *Laws* 866e).

metapherein: to carry across, to transfer, used by Plato in a transferred sense, but not in relation to metaphor: *peri tou autou men peri houper egô te kai su nun dialegometha, peri aretês, metenênegmenon d'eis poiêsin* – on the same subject which you and I are now discussing, excellence, but transferred to the subject of poetry (Pl. *Prot*. 339a); see also Pl. *Tim*. 26c.

metaphora: metaphor, not used by Plato. *metaphora de estin onomatos allotriou epiphora ê apo tou genous epi eidos ê apo tou eidos epi to genos, ê apo tou eidous epi eidos ê kata to analogon* – metaphor is the introduction of a word belonging elsewhere, either from genus to species, or from species to genus, or from species to species, or by analogy (Ar. *Poetics* 1457b 7); examples given are *nêus de moi hêd'estêken* – my ship is standing, *muri'Odusseus esthla eorgen* – Odysseus did thousands of great deeds ['thousands' being the specific for 'very many'], *khalkôi apo psukhên arusas* – having drawn off [*vice* 'cut off'] his life with the bronze [sword], *erei toinun tên phialên aspida Dionusou* – he will call the cup the sword of Dionysus [since the cup is to Dionysus as the sword is to Ares] (Ar. *Poetics* 1457b 21). It is clear that Aristotle's use of *metaphora* is wider than our use of 'metaphor'.

metaphusika: metaphysics, does not occur in the earlier philosophers and does not appear in *LSJ*. The title of Aristotle's work on what he called *prôtê philosophia* and *theologikê, Ta meta ta phusika*, was not used by Aristotle, but is said by Jaeger to be old and used by the Peripatetics. It is thought to mean 'the work coming after the

Physics' in some catalogue. See p. xxxii of Ross's edition of the *Metaphysics*.

metaxu: 'between', in all obvious senses. The only metaphysical use in Plato is when he ascribes a state of being *metaxu ousias kai tou mê einai* – between being and not being (Pl. *Rep.* 479c) – to the objects of belief. Whether this is a state between existence and non-existence or between having and not having characteristics is not clear; see *einai*. Aristotle also frequently ascribes to Plato a doctrine of mathematical intermediates, but this doctrine does not, at least explicitly, occur in Plato's writings: *eti de para ta aisthêta kai ta eidê ta **mathêmatika** tôn pragmatôn einai phêsi metaxu, diapheronta tôn men aisthêtôn tôi aïdia kai akinêta einai, tôn d'eidôn tôi ta men poll'atta homoia einai to de eidos hen hekaston monon* – also [Plato] says that in addition to perceptible things and the forms there is a class of mathematicals, differing from perceptible things by being everlasting and unchanging and from forms by there being many of each alike, whereas there is only one form of each thing (Ar. *Met.* 987b 14). See also *Metaphysics* 991b 29, 992b 16, 997b 2, etc.

metekhein: to participate [in]. This is a key word of neoplatonism, since the lower orders of being are all said to proceed – *proienai* – from and participate in the higher: *pan plêthos metekhei pêi tou henos* – every manifold participates in unity (Proclus, *Elements of Theology* 1). *metekhomenos* is the contrary of *amethektos*: *pan to amethekton huphistêsin aph'heautou ta metekhomena, kai pasai hai metekhomenai hupostaseis eis amethektous huparxeis anateinontai* – everything unparticipated produces from itself the participated, and all participated substances are derivative from unparticipated existences (Proclus, *Elements of Theology* 23); in this usage *metekhomenos* is a synonym of *methektos*, participated: *ho methektos khronos* – participated time (Simplicius, *Physics* 784.32). Plato uses the verb in many ordinary contexts and sometimes of real existence: *ousias meteskhen* – it had a share in being (Pl. *Parm.* 143b); *metaskhon tou ontos* – having a share in reality (Pl. *Soph.* 259a). But the verb was clearly used in the Academy also of the relation of forms to particulars, as Aristotle's unfriendly comment bears witness: *to de legein **paradeigmata** einai kai metekhein autôn ta alla kenologein esti kai metaphoras legein poiêtikas* – to say that there are patterns and that other things participate in them is empty verbiage and poetic metaphor (Ar. *Met.* 1079b 24). See also *methexis* and *methektos*.

meteôrologia. See *meteôros*.

meteôrologikos. See *meteôros*.

meteôros: normally, 'up in the air': *blepôn meteôros anôthen* – in the air looking down from above (Pl. *Theaet.* 175d). In his *Meteôrologika* Aristotle describes himself as studying *ho pantes hoi proteroi meteôrologian ekaloun* – what all previous writers called meteorology; but Plato seems to use the term *meteôrologia* of abstruse physical speculation in general: *pasai hosai megalai tôn tekhnôn prosdeontai adoleskhias kai meteôrologias phuseôs peri* – all important arts need general talk and speculation about nature (Pl. *Phaedrus* 270a); *kinduneuousin hoi prôtoi ta onomata tithemenoi ou phauloi einai alla meteôrologoi kai adoleskhai tines* – it would seem that those who first assigned names were not insignificant but scientific and general speculators (Pl. *Crat.* 401b). Epicurus regularly uses *ta meteôra* to cover everything celestial: *to makarion en têi peri meteôrôn gnôsei entautha peptôkenai kai en tôi tines phuseis hai theôroumenai kata ta meteôra tauta* – the blessedness of knowledge of celestial matters lies there and in knowing the nature of the existences seen in these celestial phenomena (Epicurus, *Letter to Herodotus* 78). Aristotle gives the subject-matter of the *Meteôrologika* as *hosa sumbainei kata phusin men ataktoteran mentoi tês tou prôtou stoikheiou tôn sômatôn, peri ton geitniônta malista topon têi phoraï tôn astrôn ... hosa te theiêmen an aeros koina pathê kai hudatos· eti de gês hosa merê, kai eidê kai pathê tôn merôn* – what comes about naturally but in a less orderly way than the first element of bodies, in the region that closely adjoins the motion of the stars, ... and what we would treat as the common features of air and water, and of the various parts of the earth, and the kinds and features of its parts (Ar. *Meteor.*, Book 1, Ch. 1). Aristotle goes on to specify the causes of earthquakes and winds as included. It is clear that *ta meteôra* are far more than meteors and that *ta meteôrologika* is far more than meteorology or even events happening up in the air.

methektikos: participating. A rare word, not in Plato, used of the relation of particulars to forms: *hupotithetai hoti esti tôn ontôn ta men eidê ta de methektika tôn eidôn* – [Socrates in the *Phaedo*] assumes that of entities some are forms and others participants in the forms (Ar. *De Gen. et Cor.* 335b 12). See also Ar. *Phys.* 209b 35.

An adjective formed from *metekhein*.

methektos: participated. Not in Plato, but later used to refer to the possible relation of forms to particulars in the first place and then, in neoplatonic thought, to the relation of a being of any higher grade to one of a lower: *kata de to anagkaion kai tas doxas tas peri autôn, ei esti methekta ta eidê, tôn ousiôn anagkaion ideas einai monon* – but according to the need [of the theory] and the views held about [the forms], if the forms are participated there must be forms of substances alone (Ar. *Met.* 990b 27). As so often, it is hard to tell whether in the foregoing there is any significance in the change from *eide* to *ideai*. *oute pasai psukhai metekhousi nou tou methektou, all'hosoi noerôteroi* – nor do all souls participate in the participated intelligence, but only the more intellective (Proclus, *Elements of Theology* 111). The contrary is *amethektos*.

methexis: participation. (1) A possible relation of particulars to forms: *emoige kataphainetai hôde ekhein· ta men eidê tauta hôsper paradeigmata hestanai en têi phusei, ta de alla toutois eoikenai kai einai homoiômata, kai hê methexis hautê tois allois gignesthai tôn eidôn ouk allê tis ê eikasthênai autois* – the following seems to be the case to me [Socrates]: those forms stand in nature as patterns, and other things are like them and are likenesses of them, and this participation by other things in the forms consists simply in their being likened to them (Pl. *Parm.* 132d). Aristotle, perhaps surprisingly, ascribes this interpretation of *methexis* to Plato himself: *houtos oun ta men toiauta tôn ontôn ideas prosêgoreuse, ta d'aisthêta para tauta kai kata tauta legesthai panta· kata methexin gar einai ta polla tôn sunônumôn. tên de methexin t'ounoma monon metebalen· hoi men gar Puthagoreioi mimêsei ta onta einai tôn arithmôn, Platôn de methexei, t'ounoma metabalôn* – he [Plato] called such things forms of things, and held that perceptible things were all named in accordance with and because of them. For the many things sharing the name do so by participation. But he merely changed to the word 'participation'; for the Pythagoreans say that things are by imitation of numbers, but Plato by participation, merely changing the word (Ar. *Met.* 987b 7). (2) In neoplatonic thought, the relation of any entity of lower grade to an entity of higher grade: *ou gar an pou tois men kata methexin agathois huparkhoi to meizon agathon, tois de prôtôs agathois to elatton* – for the greater good could not belong to things that are good by participation, but the lesser to the primarily good (Proclus, *Elements of Theology* 122).

metrein: to measure: *andri mê epistamenôi metrein* – a man who does not know how to measure (Pl. *Rep.* 426d).

metrios: an adjective from *metrein*, meaning 'within measure', 'moderate', 'reasonable': *metrios khronos akmês ta eikosi etê gunaiki* – twenty years is a reasonable age for a woman to be mature (Pl. *Rep.* 460e); *ekei skia t'estin kai pneuma metrion* – there is shade there and a moderate breeze (Pl. *Phaedrus* 229d); *skopei ei soi metrios ho logos hos an phêi* ... – consider whether the argument seems reasonable to you that says ... (Pl. *Philebus* 32a); *to tên tou metriou phusin huperballon kai huperballomenon hup'autês* – what exceeds or is exceeded by what is reasonable (Pl. *Politicus* 383e); *megalopsukhou de ... pros tous mesous metrion* – it is characteristic of the great-souled to be moderate towards ordinary people (Ar. *E.N.* 1124b 29).

metriôs: reasonably, within measure: *metriôs gar moi dokeis eirêkenai* – for you seem to me to have spoken reasonably (Pl. *Politicus* 385e).

metriotês: an abstract noun from *metrios*, meaning 'moderation': *kallous kai alêtheias kai metriotêtos peri legeis?* – are you referring to beauty and truth and moderation? (Pl. *Philebus* 65b).

metron: measure: *phêsi gar pou 'pantôn khrêmatôn metron' anthrôpon einai 'tôn men ontôn hôs estin tôn de mê ontôn hôs ouk estin'* – for [Protagoras] says that man is 'the measure of all things, of things that are that they are and of things that are not that they are not' (Pl. *Theaet.* 152a); *to ... meson ta auta metra tôn eskhatôn* – the middle point which is the same distance from the extremes (Pl. *Tim.* 62d); *metra oinêra kai sitêra* – measures of wine and grain (Ar. *E.N.* 1135a 1). There is a relatively specialised use meaning 'metre' in verse (that was quantitative not accentual): *en metrôi hôs poiêtês ê aneu metrou hôs idiôtês* – in metre like a poet or in prose like a layman (Pl. *Phaedrus* 258d); *ouk hôs kata tên mimêsin poiêtas alla koinêi kata to metron prosagoreuontes* – not calling them poets as creating representations but lumping them together because of the metre (Ar. *Poetics* 1447b 14).

mimeisthai: imitate, copy, and, in relation to arts, represent:

oukoun to ge homoioun heauton allôi ê kata phônên ê kata skhêma mimeisthai estin ekeinon ôi an tis homoio? – is not making oneself like another either in voice or in posture to imitate him to whom one is like? (Pl. *Rep.* 393c); *ta men mimêsetai tên proteran politeian, ta de tên oligarkhian* – in some ways it will imitate (resemble) the previous constitution and in others oligarchy (Pl. *Rep.* 547d); *mimountai hoi mimoumenoi prattontas* – actors represent people doing things (Ar. *Poetics* 1448a 1); *pan to teleion eis apogennêseis proeisin hôn dunatai paragein, auto mimoumenon tên mian tôn holôn arkhên* – whatever is complete proceeds to generate those things that it can produce, itself imitating the one originator of the universe (Proclus, *Elements of Theology* 25). Metaphysically of the relation of becoming to being: *tôi men genesthai sunapton tois kheirosi, tôi de aei mimoumenon tên aiônion phusin* – linked to inferior things through coming to be, but imitating the eternal nature by being everlasting (Proclus, *Elements of Theology* 55).

mimêma: a copy or imitation: *touto ouk estin eti mimêma all'auto to alêthestaton ekeino* – that is not an imitation any more but the genuine article (Pl. *Pol.* 300e). Metaphysically, of the relation of becoming to being: *mimêma de **paradeigmatos** deuteron genesin ekhon kai horaton* – second, an imitation of the pattern, generated and visible (Pl. *Tim.* 48e). See *mimeisthai, mimêsis*.

mimêsis: imitation, representation: *hê … mimêsis poiêsis tis estin, eidôlôn mentoi phamen, all'ouk autôn hekastôn* – imitation is a kind of creation, but we say that it is of images and not of the things themselves (Pl. *Soph.* 265a). In Book 3 of the *Republic* Plato limits *mimêsis* in dramatic poetry to speaking in the person of a character, in contrast to *haplê diêgêsis*, simple narration, of the words of the poet, including indirect speech, but that restriction is not found later in the *Republic* or elsewhere. In *Poetics* 1447a-b Aristotle includes all that we should call the fine arts under *mimêsis*, including epic, tragedy, comedy, wind and string instruments, colours and shapes (i.e. painting and sculpture): *tautas men oun legô tas diaphoras tôn tekhnôn en hois poiountai tên mimêsin* – these I say are the differences in the arts in which there is representation (Ar. *Poetics* 1147b 28). See *mimeisthai, mimêma* and Lucas, *Aristotle Poetics*, Appendix I. Also metaphysically of the relation of forms to perceptibles: *hoi men gar Puthagoreioi mimêsei ta onta phasin einai tôn arithmôn, Platôn de **methexei**, t'ounoma* *metabalôn* – for the Pythagoreans say that things are by imitation of numbers, but Plato by participation, changing the name (Ar. *Met.* 987b 11).

mimnêskesthai: to remember. See *mnêmê* and *anamnêsis*.

mixis: mingling or mixing. In Empedocles the contrary of *diallaxis*, separation, as one of the two principles of change: *phusis oudenos estin hapantôn thnêtôn, oude tis oulomenou thanatoio teleutê alla monon mixis te diallaxis te migentôn esti, phusis d'epi tois onomazetai anthrôpoisin* – there is no birth (coming to be) of anything mortal (not divine), nor any end in destructive death (annihilation), but there is only mingling and separation of the mingled, for which men use the word 'birth' (Empedocles, fr. 8); *esti d'hê sugkrisis mixis* – combination is mingling (Ar. *De Gen. et Cor.* 322b 8). Book 1, Ch. 10 of *De Gen. et Cor.* is Aristotle's formal discussion of *mixis*, ending with the statement *hê de mixis tôn miktôn alloiôthentôn henôsis* – mingling is the unification of things mixable after alteration. The verb is *mignunai* and things mingled are *mikhthenta*. Outside physics, *hê tôn hêdonôn kai lupôn mixis* – the mingling of pleasure and distress (Pl. *Philebus* 49c); *mixin aphrodisiôn* – copulation (Pl. *Laws* 836c).

mnêmê: memory, distinguished from *anamnêsis*, recollection, as possession as opposed to recovery of awareness of the past: *phaneron hoti mnêmoneuein esti mê nun anamnêsthenta* – it is clearly possible to remember what at the moment is not recalled (Ar. *Peri Mnêmês kai Anamnêseôs* – 'Concerning memory and recollection' – 450a 31); *tou men parontos aisthêsis, tou de mellontos elpis, tou de genomenou mnêmê* – perception is of the present, expectation of the future and memory of the past (Ar. *De Mem.* 449b 27).

monas: sometimes in Plato, oneness: *oud'hôi an arithmôi ti eggenêtai, perittos estai, ouk erô hôi an perittotês all'hôi an monas* – as to what it is by whose presence in a number it will be odd, I shall not say 'oddness' but 'oneness' (Pl. *Phaedo* 105c). Usually, a unit, an individual: *ei mê monada monados hekastês tôn muriôn mêdemian allên allês diapherousan tis thêsei* – unless one postulates every single unit as in no way different from each of the countless others (Pl. *Phil.* 56e). Of Pythagoreanism: *dêlon hoti allo men estin hen*

109

*hê arkhê tôn pantôn, allo de hen to têi duadi antikeimenon, ho kai
monada kalousin* – it is clear that the One that is the originator of all
things is not the same as the one that is the contrary of the dyad,
which they [the Pythagoreans] also call a monad (Simplicius,
Physics 181.29).

monê: a verbal noun from *menein*, meaning absence of motion, rest,
remaining: *peri monês ... kai exodou tês patridos* – concerning
remaining in ... and leaving the homeland (Pl. *Laws* 856e); *poteron
gar têi entautha monêi hê ek toutou ê hê eis touto kinêsis antikeitai?* –
is motion to or from a place the contrary of rest there? (Ar. *Phys.* 229b
28). Aristotle appears to treat *monê* and *êremia* as synonyms: see
Physics 229b 28 and 230a 1. But Simplicius frequently distinguishes
them: of Parmenides' line, *aei d'en t'autôi mimnei kinoumenon ouden*
– it remains always in the same place without motion – he says: *ou
kata tên êremian tên antikeimenên têi kinêsei menein auto phêsin,
alla kata tên apo kinêseôs kai êremias exêirêmenên monên* – he
[Parmenides] does not say that it is at rest meaning the absence of
motion that is contrary to motion, but meaning the motionlessness
that is exempt from both motion and its absence (Simplicius, *Physics*
23.13). Not to be confused with the feminine adjective *monê*, single.

monoeidês: in Plato, simple, used of things that have no parts or
distinguishable natures: *ê oun allê tis ê hautê hê aitia tou monoeides
te kai ameriston auto einai* – is there some other or is this the cause of
its [the syllable's] being simple and indivisible? (Pl. *Theaet.* 205d);
tot'an tis idoi autês tên alêthê phusin, eite polueidês ê monoeidês –
then one might see its [the soul's] true nature, whether it has many
forms or is simple (Pl. *Rep.* 612a). In Epicurus the adverb *monoeidôs*
means 'each kind separately': *iris gignetai ... ê kata proskrisin idian
tou phôtos kai tou aeros, hê ta tôn khrômatôn toutôn idiômata poiêsei
eite panta eite monoeidôs* – the rainbow is caused ... or by a special
union of light and air, which will cause the special qualities of these
colours, whether all together or each kind separately (Epicurus,
Letter to Pythocles 109).

morion: a part. This seems to be a synonym of *meros*, except in such
idioms as *en merei*, in turn, to which there is no corresponding *en
moriôi*. Thus Plato speaks of a *meros aretês* – a part of excellence
(*Rep.* 484d), and says *andreia pou morion aretês hen* – bravery is no
doubt a part of excellence (*Laws* 696b).

110

morphê: basically, shape: *kata sômatos morphên* – in bodily shape (Pl. *Phaedrus* 271a); *eggona mikra tên morphên* – offspring of small shape (Ar. *Pol.* 1335a 14). But in philosophy it is commonly used, by Plato and by others, as a synonym of *idea* and *eidos*, meaning 'form' in a more general sense: *hê enantia idea ekeinêi têi morphêi hê an touto apergazêtai* – the opposite form to that character which would bring that about (Pl. *Phaedo* 104d). Aristotle frequently writes *hê morphê kai to eidos*, apparently as an hendiadys: *aition ... hôs de to hou heneka hê morphê kai to eidos* – the cause ... as that for the sake of which is the character and the form (Ar. *De Gen. et Cor.* 335b 6); *to eidos, ê hotidêpote khrê kalein tên en tôi aisthêtôi morphên* – the form, or whatever else one should call the character of the perceptible thing (Ar. *Met.* 1033b 6); *legô de tên men hulên hoion ton khalkon, tên de morphên to skhêma tês ideas, to de ek toutôn ton andrianta to sunolon* – I call matter e.g. the bronze, form the visible shape, and whole the statue composed of them (Ar. *Met.* 1029a 3).

mousikê: in its widest sense, the whole of the field of liberal studies presided over by the Muses. As such it was used of the whole of the mental side of education alongside *gumnastikê* – literally, what is done naked, the physical side of education: *hê men [paideia] epi sômati gumnastikê, hê d'epi psukhêi mousikê* – physical education for the body, mental for the soul (Pl. *Rep.* 376e); *hôs philosophias ... ousês megistês mousikês* – as philosophy ... being the greatest mental study (Pl. *Phaedo* 61a). But in a more restricted sense it is music: *oukoun kai hê mousikê peri tên tôn melôn poiêsin* – is not music also concerned with the making of songs (Pl. *Gorg.* 449d); *kai estin au mousikê peri harmonian kai rhuthmôn erôtikôn epistêmê* – further, music is knowledge about making tunes and erotic rhythms (Pl. *Symp.* 187c). The noun is *mousikos*, in both the wider and narrower uses: *andros genêsomenou philosophou ê philokalou ê mousikou tinos* – a man who is to become a philosopher, or lover of beauty, or educated (Pl. *Phaedrus* 248d); *mousikos anêr harmattomenos luran* – a musician tuning a lyre (Pl. *Rep.* 349e). The adverb is *mousikôs*: *houtoi gar hoi logoi amphoteroi ou panu mousikôs legontai· ou gar sunaïdousin oude sunarmottousin allêlois* – this pair of statements does not seem to be very musically stated; for they do not go together in harmony (Pl. *Prot.* 333a).

N

neikos: a poetical word, meaning strife, used by Empedocles of one of his principles of change: *allote men philotêti sunerkhomen'eis hen hapanta, allote d'au dikh'hekasta phoreumena neikeos ekhthei* – sometimes coming together all into one through love, sometimes being borne asunder by the enmity of strife (Empedocles, fr. 17 in Simplicius, *Physics* 158.1). But Aristotle, in criticism of Empedocles, objected: *pollakhou goun autôi hê men philia diakrinei, to de neikos sugkrinei* – at least in many places he [Empedocles] has love separating and strife bringing together (Ar. *Met.* 985a 24).

nemesis: anger or resentment at wrong-doing, particularly that involving self-assertion, or undeserved prosperity. The *nemesêtikos* is he who is so angry, he who deserves censure is *nemesêtos*, and the verb is *nemesan*: *nemesôsi te malista au tois eis orphana kai êrema hubrizousi* – they will be especially angry with those who abuse orphans and waifs (Pl. *Laws* 927c); *oude nemesêton heneka toutou hupêretein kai douleuein kai erastêi kai panti anthrôpôi* – nor can one blame him who for this [gaining wisdom] serves and slaves for a lover or any man (Pl. *Euthyd.* 282b); *nemesis de mesotês phthonou kai epikhairekakias, eisi de peri lupên kai hêdonên tas epi tois sumbainousi tois pelas ginomenois· ho men gar nemesêtikos lupeitai epi tois anaxiôs eu prattousin* – righteous indignation is a mean between envy and rejoicing in the misfortune of others, and these are concerned with the distress and pleasure that come to neighbours; for the righteously indignant is distressed about unworthy people faring well (Ar. *E.N.* 1108b 1).

noein: like *noêma, noeros, noêsis, noêtos* and *nous*, has shades of meaning varying from the everyday use to the highly technical. The verb may refer to any kind of thought at one extreme and to only the highest intellectual intuition at the other. Non-technically: *tôi onti khrusea khalkeiôn diameibesthai noeis* – in fact you are thinking of exchanging gold for bronze (Pl. *Symp.* 219a); *to tês psukhês hôde noei* – think of the state of the soul in this way (Pl. *Rep.* 508d); *to gar auto noein estin te kai einai* – it is the same thing for thought and for being [here the verbs are datives; the translation 'thought and being are the same thing' is implausible, the meaning is that only what is can be thought of] (Parmenides, fr.

2). Technically, of intellectual intuition: *tas d'au ideas noeisthai men horasthai d'ou* – the forms are intelligible but invisible (Pl. *Rep.* 507b).

noêma: a thought or concept: *ta men oun onomata auta kai ta rhêmata eoike tôi aneu suntheseôs kai diaireseôs noêmati* – nouns and verbs by themselves are like a concept without combination and separation (Ar. *De Int.* 16a 14); *mê tôn eidôn hekaston toutôn êi noêma* – perhaps each of these forms is a thought [and not an independent reality] (Pl. *Parm.* 132b). There was a saying *hama noêmati sumbainein* – to be as quick as thought: *hê genesis tôn eidôlôn hama têi noêmati sumbainei* – images come to be as quickly as thought (Epicurus, *Letter to Herodotus* 48); *hama têi noêmati touto sumbainein* – that happens as quickly as thought (Sextus Empiricus, *Adversus Mathematicos* 5.56).

noeros: commonly translated 'intellectual', but since it is always used of that which thinks and not of the subject-matter, 'intellective', used by Dodds, is better: *aisthêtikôteron kai noerôteron to leptoteron haima* – thinner blood is more perceptive and more intellective (Ar. *Part. An.* 648a 3); *tas noeras ousias pantôs exêirêsthai sômatos kai têi ousiaï kai têi energeiaï eirêtai kalôs* – it is well said [by Philoponus] that intellective beings altogether transcend the body in both essence and in activity (Simplicius, *Physics* 1198.28); *noes hoi men ousiai autoteleis, hoi de noerai tines teleiotêtes* – some intellects are self-complete substances, others are intellective perfections (Proclus, *Elements of Theology* 64; *nous* does not occur in the plural, as here, in Plato or Aristotle). See *nous* and *noein*.

noêsis: thought, in wider and narrower senses: *to de zên horizontai tois zôiois dunamei aisthêseôs, anthrôpois d'aisthêseôs ê noêseôs* – life is defined for animals as capacity for perception and for men of perception or thought (Ar. *E.N.* 1170a 16); *areskei oun … kalein … sunamphotera d'ekeina [epistêmê* and *dianoia] noêsin* – it is satisfactory to call science and reasoning, taken together, thought (Pl. *Rep.* 533e); *oute doxa estin autôn oute epistêmê kai dianoia oute noêsis* – there is neither opinion nor science with reasoning nor intellection of them [gods] (Proclus, *Elements of Theology* 123). For Proclus *noêsis* is pure intuitive apprehension, whereas *epistêmê kai dianoia* is discursive. See *noein, noêtos* and *nous*.

113

noêtos: that which is the object of *noêsis*, thought, specifically that which can be thought of but not perceived, the intelligible: *noêta atta kai asômata eidê biazomenoi tên alêthinên ousian einai* – forcing [them to admit] that certain intelligible and incorporeal forms are the true reality (Pl. *Soph.* 246b); *dunamei pôs esti ta noêta ho nous* – potentially in a way, intuitive reason is its objects (Ar. *De An.* 429b 30); *ê aisthêta ta onta ê noêta* – what is is either perceptible or intelligible (Ar. *De An.* 427a 26).

nomikos: legal: *en toioutois êthesi tethraphthe nomikois su te kai hode* – you and he were both brought up in legal institutions of this kind (Pl. *Laws* 625a). In Aristotle, legal as opposed to moral or natural: *tou de politikou dikaiou to men phusikon esti to de nomikon, phusikon men to pantakhou tên autên ekhon dunamin, kai ou tôi dokein ê mê, nomikon de ho ex arkhês men ouden diapherei houtôs ê allôs, hotan de thôntai, diapherei* – of civil justice, part is natural, part positive; the natural is what has everywhere the same force and is not a matter of opinion, the positive is what initially may run in this or that way, indifferently, but, when it is laid down, matters (Ar. *E.N.* 1134b 18).

nomimos. (1) He who is obedient to law and custom: *paronomos ... doxei gegonenai ek nomimou* – he will seem to have become a law-breaker instead of law-abiding (Pl. *Rep* 539a); *dikaios estai ho te nomimos kai ho isos* – the just man will be [ambiguously] both the law-abiding man and the fair man (Ar. *E.N.* 1129a 33). (2) In neuter plural, the accepted beliefs: *ta tôn pollôn nomima kalou te peri kai tôn allôn* – the accepted beliefs of the many about beauty and the rest (Pl. *Rep.* 479d).

nomizein: to believe. This has no technical use, but it is important to distinguish two uses. (1) To believe that something is the case: *kai autos ara nomizô einai theous* – I too believe that there are gods (Pl. *Apol* 26c). (2) Especially in the present participle passive, *ta nomizomena* are recognised rules, procedures, etc.: *aïsantas ton theon kai t'alla ta nomizomena* – having sung a hymn and carried out the other observances [libations, etc.] (Pl. *Symp.* 176a); *ti oun allo nomos eiê, ô Sôkrates, all'ê ta nomizomena?* – what else is law, Socrates, than the observances? (Pl. *Minos* 313d).

nomos has a wide variety of connected uses, referring to written law, customary law, custom in general, convention: *tithemenous de toioutous nomous, kai tous agraphous kai tous gegrammenous* – having laid down such laws, both unwritten and written (Ar. *Pol.* 1319b 40); *tithetai … tous nomous hekastê hê arkhê pros to hautêi sumpheron* – each government makes the laws in its own interest (Pl. *Rep.* 338e); *makhesthai khrê ton dêmon huper tou nomou hôsper teikheos* – the people should fight for the law as for their city wall (Heraclitus, fr. 44); *ho … nomos turannos ôn tôn anthrôpôn polla para tên phusin biazetai* – custom that is a tyrant over men makes them do many things contrary to nature (Pl. *Protagoras* 337d); *doxêi de monon kai nomôi aiskhron* – disgraceful only by opinion and convention (Pl. *Rep.* 364a); *ta de kala kai ta dikaia pollên ekhei diaphoran kai planên hôste dokein nomôi monon einai, phusei de mê* – what is fine and just permits of much difference and variety, so as to seem merely conventional and not natural (Ar. *E.N.* 1094b 14); *… nomôi khroiê, eteêi de atoma kai kenon –* … colour is by convention; really there are atoms and the void (Democritus, fr. 9).

nous, plural *noes*. (1) Intelligence in general: *haplôs men gar oudeis apoballetai hekôn, epi sôtêriaï d'hautou kai tôn loipôn hapantes noun ekhontes* – no one simply jettisons his cargo intentionally, but to save themselves and their crew all intelligent men would (Ar. *E.N.* 1110a 9). (2) Immediate awareness, intuition: *ho nous tôn eskhatôn ep'amphotera, kai gar tôn prôtôn horôn kai tôn eskhatôn nous esti kai ou logos* – intuition is of the extremes in both directions; for intuition, not discursive reason, is both of the basic terms and of particulars (Ar. *E.N.* 1143b 5). (3) Intuitive intellect, intuitive reason, concerned with *noêta* only: *to men gar epistêton apodeikton … leipetai noun einai tôn arkhôn* – scientific knowledge is demonstrated … so it remains that intuitive reason is of basic principles (Ar. *E.N.* 1140b 35, 1141a 7). Plato also distinguished *nous* from *dianoia* – discursive reason: *dianoian de kalein moi dokeis tên tôn geômetrikôn te kai tê tôn toioutôn hexin all'ou noun, hôs metaxu ti doxês te kai nou tên dianoian ousan* – you seem to me to call the condition of geometers and the like *dianoia* rather than *nous*, treating *dianoia* as being between opinion and intuitive reason (Pl. *Rep.* 511d). Aristotle regards *nous* as independent of the body and thus immune from destruction on the death of the body: *ho de nous eoiken eggignesthai ousia tis ousa kai ou phtheiresthai* – intuitive reason seems to enter into us as a substance and not to

115

perish (Ar. *De An.* 408b 18). Aristotle, like Plato, does not use *nous* in the plural; such phrases as *ho theos kai ho nous* (Ar. *E.N.* 1096a 24) may be plausibly translated as 'god, i.e. intuitive reason', which is unitary and a divine element present in all men; *phaneron hoti kai orekton pasi nous kai proeisi panta apo nou, kai pas ho kosmos apo nou tên ousian ekhei* – it is clear that reason is the goal of all things and that everything proceeds from reason and that the whole universe has its being from reason (Proclus, *Elements of Theology* 34).

nun: now. This has a variety of uses. (1) *hên su nun legeis* – which you now speak of (Pl. *Phaedo* 77a). (2) *kathaper nun eipes* – as you just said (Pl. *Soph.* 241d). (3) *nun de epeidê ouk etheleis* – but as it is, since you are unwilling (Pl. *Prot.* 335c). (4) As adjective: *kata ton nun dê logon* – according to the present argument (Pl. *Soph.* 256c). (5) *ouranon nun ou ton kosmon legei* – [Aristotle] is not calling the universe the heavens at this point (Simplicius, *Physics* 594.7). (6) With article, as a noun: *to de nun ou meros ... ho de khronos ou dokei sugkeisthai ek tôn nun* – an instant is not a part [of time] ... time does not seem to be composed of instants (Ar. *Phys.* 218a 6); *peri tou nun ... tou te kuriôs kai tou en platei legomenou* – concerning the present ... both in its strict sense [as an instant] and in a wide sense (Simplicius, *Physics* 747.33).

O

oikonomia: everything concerned with the running of a household, which Aristotle in the *Politics* divides into the relation of master and slave, of husband and wife and of parent and child, adding money-making as a fourth ingredient only. The *oikonomos* runs a household and the *oikonomikos* is the person skilled in so doing. *oikonomia hetera andros kai gunaikos· tou men gar ktasthai tês de phulattein ergon* – household management is different for a man and a woman; for his job is to obtain and hers to guard (Ar. *Pol.* 1277b 24). It is belittled by Plato; his guardians are to keep to themselves; otherwise *oikonomoi te kai geôrgoi anti phulakôn esontai* – they will be housekeepers and farmers instead of guardians (Pl. *Rep.* 417a). *Oikonomikos* is the title of an interesting little work by Xenophon on managing a household.

oligarkhia: called by Plato *tên apo timêmatôn ... politeian en hêi*

hoi men plousioi arkhousin, penêti d'ou metestin arkhês – a constitution based on rateable property in which the rich rule, and the poor
man has no share in rule (Pl. *Rep.* 550c). Aristotle distinguishes
different forms of oligarchy, e.g. *heteron eidos oligarkhias hotan pais
anti patros eisiêi* – another variety of oligarchy is when son enters
[government] to replace father (Ar. *Pol.* 1292b 4); *tên gar aristo-
kratian tês oligarkhias eidos titheasi* – they treat aristocracy as a
form of oligarchy (Ar. *Pol.* 1290a 16).

on: *to on*, in the widest sense, is everything that is and, as such, is
contrasted with *to mê on*, that which is not; in a narrower use *to on*,
sometimes called for clarity *to ontôs on*, the really real, is unchanging and imperishable and eternal, and is contrasted with the
gignomenon that is changing and perishable. In the dispute between
Parmenides and the atomists it is hard to doubt that *to mê on* as the
non-existent is confused with empty space: *oute gar an gnoiês to ge
mê on· ou gar anuston* – you cannot know that which is not; it is
impossible (Parmenides, fr. 2); *ouden gar estin ê estai allo parex tou
eontos* – nothing other than what is either is or will be (Parmenides,
fr. 8). But Simplicius reports Leucippus as saying *ouden mallon to on
ê to mê on huparkhein* – there is that which is no more than that
which is not (Simplicius, *Physics* 28.12); here *to mê on* seems to be
the *kenon*, void; cf. the **den** of Democritus. In the narrower use, *to
men pantelôs on pantelôs gnôston* – the completely real is completely
knowable (Pl. *Rep.* 477a); *ei gar panta ta onta tou agathou ephietai,
dêlon hoti to prôtôs agathon epekeina esti tôn ontôn* – for if everything
that is aims at the good, it is clear that the primary good transcends
things that are (Proclus, *Elements of Theology* 8); *to gar houtôs on
proteron têi phusei tou gignomenou esti* – that which is in this
[narrow] way is prior in its nature to the becoming (Simplicius,
Physics 1337.4).

onar: with an article, 'a dream': *akoue dê ... t'emon onar* – listen to
my dream (Pl. *Charm.* 173a). Adverbially, it means 'dreaming' and is
contrasted with *hupar*, awake. Plato consistently uses the distinction between *onar* and *hupar* as a metaphor for the distinction
between living in awareness only of the world of *genesis*, change, and
the philosopher's awareness of *to ontôs on*, true reality: *onar ê hupar
dokei soi zên?* – does he seem to you to live a dreaming or waking life?
(Pl. *Rep.* 476c); *horômen hôs oneirôttousi men peri* **to on**, *hupar de
adunaton autais idein heôs an ...* – we see how they dream about

117

reality and cannot be awake and see until … (Pl. *Rep.* 533c).

onoma: in a wide sense, a word: *emoi gar dokei tais men tou sômatos taxesin onoma einai hugieinon* – for it seems to me that the word for bodily regimes is 'healthy' (Pl. *Gorg.* 504d); *onoma ara estin … mimêma phônês ekeinou ho mimeitai kai onomazei ho mimoumenos têi phônêi ho an mimêtai* – a word is a vocal representation of that which he who vocally represents represents and names what he represents (Pl. *Crat.* 423b). But it is most commonly used of a noun as distinct from a verb. Of a proper name: *autôi poteron Kratulos têi alêtheiaï onoma* – whether Cratylus is really his name (Pl. *Crat.* 383b). Of nouns in general: *lexô toinun soi logon suntheis pragma praxei di'onomatos kai rhêmatos …'Theaitêtos kathêtai'* – I will make a statement to you by joining together a thing and an action by means of a noun and a verb … 'Theaetetus is sitting' (Pl. *Soph.* 262e); *onoma men oun esti phônê sêmantikê kata sunthêkên aneu khronou, hês mêden meros esti sêmantikon kekhôrismenon* – a noun is a spoken sound with conventional significance, without time [unlike the *rhêma*, verb, which is tensed], of which no part is separately significant (Ar. *De Int.* 16a 19). Rather surprisingly, Aristotle adds *to de Philônos ê Philôni kai hosa tosauta ouk onomata alla ptôseis onomatos* – 'of Philo' and 'to Philo' and the like are not nouns but cases of nouns (Ar. *De Int.* 16b 1). Later writers distinguished the proper name as *kurion onoma* from the common noun as *prosêgorikon onoma*.

organon: an instrument, tool or organ: *organa hosa peri geôrgian* – instruments used in farming (Pl. *Rep.* 370d); *ho men di'organôn ekêlei anthrôpous* – [Marsyas] soothed people with musical instruments (Pl. *Symp.* 215c); *organa de kai ta tôn phutôn merê, alla pantelôs hapla* – the parts of plants are also organs, but extremely simple (Ar. *De An.* 412b 1). The logical works of Aristotle are known collectively as *To Organon* – 'The Instrument' [of accurate thought] – though there is no Aristotelian authority for the name: *he logikê pragmateia organou khôran ekhei en philosophiaï* – logical matters have the place of a tool in philosophy (Alexander of Aphrodisias, *Topics* 74.29).

orthos: right, upright, in a variety of uses. (1) Physically upright: *hestôs orthos* – standing upright (Pl. *Laws* 665e). (2) Geometrically: *mian men orthên ekhontos hekaterou gônian, tas de oxeias* –

[triangles] each having one right angle and the others acute (Pl. *Tim.* 53d). (3) Ethically upright: *ho orthos nomothetês* – the upright lawgiver (Pl. *Laws* 660a). (4) Correct, right as not mistaken: *to de meson estin hôs ho orthos logos legei* – but the mean is as the correct account (reason) says (Ar. *E.N.* 1138b 20). The noun *orthotês* is used mainly in this last way: *onomatos orthotês estin hautê hêtis endeixetai hoion esti to pragma* – the rightness of a name is such that the name will display the nature of the object (Pl. *Crat.* 428e); *dêlon hoti orthotês tis hê euboulia estin* – it is clear that good deliberation is a way of being correct (Ar. *E.N.* 1142b 8).

ouranos: in a basic sense, the heavens (though always in the singular in classical Greek). But Aristotle, from whom derives most discussion of the heavens, knowingly uses the term in different senses. In *Peri Ouranou – De Caelo* – 'On the Heavens' – he writes: *hena men tropon ouranon legomen tên ousian tên tês eskhatês tou pantos periphoras ... allon d'au tropon to sunekhes sôma têi eskhatêi periphoraï tou pantos en hôi selênê kai hêlios kai enia tôn astrôn ... eti de allôs legomen ouranon to periekhomenon sôma hupo tês eskhatês periphoras· to gar holon kai to pan eiôthamen legein ouranon* – in one way we call the substance of the outermost periphery of the whole the heavens ... but in another way the body that is continuous with the outermost periphery of the whole, in which is the moon and the sun and some of the stars ... and still in another way we so call the body that is contained by the outermost periphery; for we are accustomed to call the all and the whole the heavens (Ar. *De Caelo* 278b 11, 16, 18). This could cause difficulties: *ho men Alexandros ouranon legesthai nun phêsi ou tôn aplanôn sphairan oude to theion sôma monon alla ton kosmon panta* – Alexander says that what is called the heavens now is not the sphere of the fixed stars [first sense], nor only the divine body [sense two] but the whole universe [sense three] (Simplicius, *Physics* 593.7). It is clear from the above that both *to pan* and *ho kosmos* are used as synonyms of each other and of *ouranos*. The adjective is *ouranios*: *ouranion theôn genos* – the heavenly race of gods (Pl. *Tim.* 39e).

ousia: an abstract noun connected with the verb *einai* (present participle feminine *ousa*). Non-technically, possessions: *tên hautou labonta ousian apienai* – to go away taking his own goods with him (Pl. *Laws* 850b). Philosophically, nature, essence, substance, being:

ê hekastôi tôn onomatôn toutôn hupokeitai tis idios ousia – whether some special nature underlies each of these words [i.e. has each a specific sense] (Pl. *Prot.* 349b 9; *geneseôs kai ousias peri* – concerning becoming and being (Pl. *Soph.* 232c); *pros tên ontôs ousian hên aei kata t'auta hôsautôs ekhein phate* – in relation to the true being which you say always remains in every way the same (Pl. *Soph.* 248a). Aristotle in the *Categories* distinguishes two sorts of *ousia*, substance: *tôn kata mêdemian sumplokên legomenôn hekaston ê ousian sêmainei ê poson ê poion ...* – each uncombined term signifies either substance [what it is] or quantity [how large] or quality [of what sort] ... (Ar. *Cat.* 1b 25); *ousia d'estin hê kuriôtata te kai prôtôs kai malista legomenê hê mête kath'hupokeimenou tinos legetai, mêt'en hupokeimenôi tini estin, hoion ho tis anthrôpos ê ho tis hippos. deuterai d'ousiai legontai en hois eidesin hai prôtôs ousiai legomenai huparkhousi, tauta te kai ta tôn eidôn toutôn genê* – the what is basically, primarily and especially called substance is that which is neither predicated of a subject nor is in a subject, such as a particular man or a particular horse. Those things are called second substances that are the species in which occur the first substances and those that are the genera of these species (Ar. *Cat.* 2a 11). But Aristotle also says *oute to katholou ousia oute to genos* – neither the universal nor the genus is substance (Ar. *Met.* 1042a 21), and this is repeated more elaborately at *Met.* 1035b 29.

oxus has a set of connected uses. It can be used of an acute accent, an acute pain, an acute angle: *mian men orthên ekhontos hekaterou gônian, tas de oxeias* – each [triangle] having one right and two acute angles (Pl. *Tim.* 53d); acute senses: *opsis ... hêmin oxutatê tôn dia tôn sômatôn erkhetai aisthêseôn* – sight is the sharpest of the bodily senses (Pl. *Phaedrus* 250d); a hasty person: *Pôlos de hode neos tis esti kai oxus* – Polus here is young and hasty (Pl. *Gorg.* 463e); a vivid pleasure: *oxuteran ekheis eipein hêdonên tês peri ta aphrodisia* – can you mention a more vivid pleasure than that of sex (Pl. *Rep.* 403a); quick learners: *hoi te oxeis ... kai agkhinoi* – the sharp and quick-witted (Pl. *Theaet.* 144a). Of a high note: *hôs hoion te oxutatên kai barutatên khordên poiein* – to make the string as high or as low as possible (Pl. *Phaedrus* 268d). Aristotle noted that *oxus* was used in different senses: *tôi oxei en phônêi men enantion to baru, en ogkôi de to amblu* – in sound the low is the contrary to the *oxus* [high], in masses the blunt [as opposed to sharp] (Ar. *Top.* 106a 13).

P

paideia: education. The traditional education was in *mousikê* (chiefly literature and song) and *gumnastikê*: *tis oun hê paideia? ê khalepon heurein beltiô tês hupo tou pollou khronou hêurêmenês? estin de pou hê men epi sômasi gumnastikê, hê de epi psukhêi mousikê* – What education shall we give them? Is it not difficult to find a better than that found over the ages? That is gymnastic for the body and arts for the mind (Pl. *Rep.* 376e). It is the education received rather than the process, which is *paideusis*: *paideusis paideias paradosis* – education is the handing on of culture (Pl. *Def.* 416); *hekastos de krinei kalôs ha gignôskei kai toutôn estin agathos kritês, kath'hekaston men ara ho pepaideumenos, haplôs d'ho peri pan pepaideumenos* – each man judges well on matters he understands, and is a good judge on those matters, on special topics the expert and generally the man of universal education (Ar. *E.N.* 1094b 27).

pan: *to pan* is the totality of things, or the universe. Aristotle tends to use *ouranos, kosmos* and *to pan* as interchangeable: *para de to pan kai holon ouden estin exô tou pantos, kai dia touto en tôi ouranôi panta, ho gar ouranos to pan isôs* – there is nothing outside the totality beyond the totality and the whole, and therefore everything is within the heavens, for the heavens are perhaps the totality (Ar. *Phys.* 212a 16); *poteron noun aition kai phusin einai … toude tou pantos* – whether intelligence is the cause and nature … of this totality [the universe] (Ar. *Phys.* 198a 13).

paradeigma: either an exemplar, a paradigm, after which other things of the same name are so called, or an example or illustration. (1) Exemplar, paradigm: *en ouranôi isôs paradeigma anakeitai tôi boulomenôi horan* – perhaps a paradigm [of the perfect city] is laid up in heaven for him who wishes to see it (Pl. *Rep.* 592b); *ta … eidê tauta hôsper paradeigmata hestanai en têi phusei* – that these forms stand in nature as something like paradigms (Pl. *Parm.* 132d). (2) Example, illustration: *prosêkei … paradeigmati tois allois gignesthai hina alloi horôntes paskhonta ha an paskhêi phoboumenoi beltious gignôntai* – it is fitting that he should become an example to others in order that others may see him suffering what he suffers and in fear become better (Pl. *Gorg.* 525b); *paradeigma*

121

ton amphorea oinou parathemenos – using the jar of wine as an illustration (Simplicius, *Physics* 555.12); *smikron labe paradeigma kai panta eisêi ha boulomai* – take a small illustration and you will understand all that I mean (Pl. *Theaet.* 154c).

paradoxos: basically, what is contrary to accepted opinion. It may, however, be accepted by the speaker: *ededoikê houtô paradoxon logon legein* – I [Socrates] was afraid to present an account so contrary to opinion [but will now do so] (Pl. *Rep.* 472a). It may be merely surprising: *kaitoi erôtikou ontos kai akratous ou paradoxon tên mousikên spoudazesthai* – since he was amorous and lacked self-control it is not surprising that [Achilles] was fond of music (Sextus Empiricus, *Adversus Mathematicos* 6.25). But sometimes an unacceptable paradox: *thesis estin hupolêpsis paradoxos tôn gnôrimôn kata philosophian hoion ouk estin antilegein* – a thesis is a paradoxical opinion of well-known philosophers, such as that contradiction is impossible [as Antisthenes said] (Ar. *Top.* 104b 19). Later philosophers introduced *paradoxologein*, to utter paradoxes, and *paradoxologia* – the uttering of paradoxes: *saphesteron epênegke paradeigma paradoxologias kai hama oikeioteron ho Aristotelês eipôn 'ê hôs ei tis hena anthrôpon to on legoi' ... esti de kai allos tropos ho mê monon apophantikôs paradoxologôn alla kai sullogizesthai dokôn ... hoioi tines eisin hoi sophistikoi paralogismoi* – Aristotle added a clearer example of a paradox saying 'or if someone said that an individual man was reality' ... but there is also another kind where the propounding of the paradox does not merely make a statement but also seems to argue ... like some of the sophistic fallacies (Simplicius, *Physics* 50.24).

paragein has a variety of uses in classical Greek. (1) To bring forward, to instance: *martura paragomenos tên tôn thêriôn phusin* – bringing forward as evidence the nature of wild beasts (Pl. *Laws* 836c); *hôs en tragôidiaï paragomena prosôpa* – like characters brought on in a tragedy (Simplicius, *Physics* 1015.10). (2) To lead astray: *mête hêmas pseudesi paragein en logôi ê en ergôi* – nor lead us astray with falsehoods in word or in deed (Pl. *Rep.* 383a). (3) Of verbal derivation: *oud' ... ho andrias xulon alla paragetai xulinos kai khalkous all'ou khalkos* – and the statue is not wood but is derivatively called wooden, and not bronze but brazen (Ar. *Met.* 1033a 17). But in neoplatonic philosophy the verb *paragein* is used technically of the creation or production of some lower grade of

122

reality by a higher grade and the higher grade was said to be *paraktikos*, productive or creative, an adjective not used by Plato and Aristotle: *pan to paraktikon allou kreitton esti tês tou paragomenou phuseôs* — everything productive of another is superior to the nature of that which is produced (Proclus, *Elements of Theology* 7); *to de heauton paragon heautôi tou einai paraktikon huparkhon* — that which creates itself being creative of its own existence (Proclus, *Elements of Theology* 40); *homologôn ta amesôs hupo theou paragomena hoion einai kai ton kosmon nomizei mête dia geneseôs mête dia khronikês **parataseôs** huphistasthai* — agreeing that the things directly created by god, as he [Philoponus] believes is the case even with the universe, exist neither through coming to be nor through [in the course of] temporal duration (Simplicius, *Physics* 1146.17).

paraktikos. See *paragein*.

paralogismos: a faulty argument, but not necessarily through formal defects. It may be through such material faults as ambiguity: *tôn de exô tês lexeôs paralogismôn eidê estin hepta* — there are seven types of faulty argument that arise apart from diction [i.e. what are traditionally called material fallacies] (Ar. *S.E.* 166b 21). The maker of such arguments is *paralogistikos*: *ou gar estai paralogistikos ex hôrismenou tinos genous arkhôn, alla peri pan genos estai ho eristikos* — the eristic man [who aims at victory, not truth] will not argue fallaciously from some limited kind of premises, but in all areas (Ar. *S.E.* 172b 3). To use fallacious arguments is *paralogizesthai*: *khrêsimon de kai pros to mê paralogisthênai kai pros to paralogisasthai* — [awareness of ambiguity] is useful both in order not to suffer from fallacies and also in order to use them (Ar. *Top.* 108a 26). A fallacious argument is *paralogos*: *sumbainei amphoterôs atopon kai paralogon* — the result in both cases is absurd and fallacious (Ar. *De An.* 411a 14). None of these terms is found in Plato's works.

paranomein: to act contrary to *nomos*: *paranomounta kai adikounta* — acting lawlessly and wrongly (Pl. *Rep.* 338e). He who so acts is *paranomos*, lawless, and is the contrary of the *nomimos* or *ennomos*: *paranomos ... doxei gegonenai ek nomimou* — he will seem to have become lawless from being law-abiding (Pl. *Rep.* 539a); *to paranomon kai ennomon* — the legal and illegal (Pl. *Pol.*

302e); *dokei dê ho te paranomos* **adikos** *einai kai ho pleonektês kai anisos* – both the lawless man and the grasping and unfair man seem to be unjust (Ar. *E.N.* 1129a 32).

paratasis: extension, usually in time as duration, but sometimes spatial. The word does not occur in Plato, but became very common in later, especially neoplatonic, philosophy. It is a noun from *parateinein*, to stretch alongside, or simply to stretch out: *para tên dotheisan autou grammên parateinanta* – stretching it out alongside the given line (Pl. *Meno* 87a). The verb is used of literary works: *para dunamin parateinontes ton muthon* – stretching out the story beyond their capability (Ar. *Poetics* 1451b 38). *paratasis* as of temporal duration: *oukh hama ara holon estin, en tôi skidnamenôi tês khronikês parataseôs on* – it is not a simultaneous whole, being in the dispersal of temporal duration (Proclus, *Elements of Theology* 50); *ou gar dunametha têi aïdiôi paratasei sumparateinein tên noêsin* – we cannot extend our thought through everlasting duration (Simplicius, *Physics* 461.25); *paratasis khronikê* and *paratasis en khronôi* are very common expressions in later philosophy, both meaning 'temporal duration'. Spatially: *tôn triôn toutôn hex gignesthai parataseis ... anô kai katô ... en aristeraï kai en dexiaï ... prosô kai opisthô* – from these three [dimensions] six directions result – above and below, to right and to left and in front and behind (Sextus Empiricus, *Adversus Mathematicos* 3.19). These directions are called *diastaseis* by Aristotle.

parônumos: is used strictly of a term that is formed from another by giving it a new termination: *parônuma de legetai hosa apo tinos diapheronta têi ptôsei tên kata t'ounoma prosêgorian ekhei, hoion apo tês grammatikês ho grammatikos kai apo tês andreias ho andreios* – things are paronyms [derivatively named] that get their name from some other by having a different termination, as a grammarian from 'grammar' and a brave man from 'bravery' (Ar. *Cat.* 1a 12); *poiotêtes men eisin hai eirêmenai, poia de ta kata tautas parônumôs legomena ê hopôsoun allôs ap'autôn. epi men oun tôn pleistôn kai skhedon epi pantôn parônumôs legetai, hoion apo tês leukotês leukos kai ...* – qualities are those listed; things have a quality that are named from them paronymously or in some other way. In most and virtually all cases they are named paronymously, as white from whiteness and ... (Ar. *Cat.* 10a 28). Plato uses the noun *parônumion*, a derived name, in this way of the sophist:

mimêtês d'ôn tou sophou dêlon hoti parônumion autou ti lêpsetai – being an imitator of the wise it is clear that he will take a name derived from him (Pl. *Soph*. 268c). But Plato also uses the term *parônumion* of a term used in a derivative sense: *anagkaion ge mên kai toutois [dikaion, ison] parônumioisi pote proskhrêsthai polin hapasan –* it is however necessary for every state to treat even these [the just and the fair] in a derivative way (Pl. *Laws* 757d). The words *parônumos* and *parônumôs* do not occur in Plato. See also **sunô-numos, homônumos.**

parousia: presence, derived from the verb **pareinai**, which is used non-technically by Plato: *ep'auto ge toi touto paresmen –* it is for that precisely that we are present (Pl. *Gorg*. 447b); *hê nun parousa hêmera –* the present day (Pl. *Laws* 683c). *parousia* is one of the terms used by Plato of the relation of immanent form to particular: *ouk allo ti poiei auto kalon ê hê ekeinou tou kalou eite parousia eite koinônia ê ... –* nothing makes it fine other than the presence or communion or ... of that fine itself (Pl. *Phaedo* 100d); *dikaiosunês hexei kai parousiaï toiautên autôn hekastên gignesthai –* by the possession and presence of justice each of [the souls] becomes such (Pl. *Soph*. 247a); *auto d'einai to agathon hôi huparkhei to te prôtôi einai tôn agathôn kai to aitiôi têi parousiaï tois allois tou agatha einai –* [the Platonists say that] it is the good itself that is both the first of all goods and the cause by its presence of other things being good (Ar. *E.E*. 1217b 3). In neoplatonism the presence of any higher reality: *hupomenei tên tou **henos** parousian ouk onta **hoper** hen –* they are subject to the presence of the One, not being themselves one unqualified (Proclus, *Elements of Theology* 3).

paskhein: the opposite both of *poiein*, to do, to make, and of *prattein*, to act. According to context it can be translated 'undergo', 'suffer', 'experience', and often 'X *paskhei* Y' is best translated as 'Y happens to X': *hoion an poiêi to poioun toiouton to paskhon paskhein –* that to which it happens undergoes the same as what that which is active does (Pl. *Gorg. 476c); en hêi mêden sumballetai ho prattôn ê ho paskhôn –* where the agent, or rather he to whom it happens, contributes nothing (Ar. *E.N*. 1110a 2); *ê allo hêdu paskhonta autôi tôi sômati –* or experiencing some other pleasure in the body itself (Pl. *Prot*. 337c). Often of suffering evils: *dikaiotat'an hotioun paskhoi –* he would justly suffer anything whatsoever (Pl. *Pol*. 128d). Abstractly and atemporally: *hoion kai hê trias peponthe –* as is the case with the number three (Pl. *Phaedo* 103c). See also ***pathos*** and ***pathêma***.

pathêma appears to be a synonym for most, though not all, uses of ***pathos***. Thus *eleos* and *phobos*, called *pathê* in *E.N.*, are called *pathêmata* in Ar. *Poetics* 1449b 27, and *hêdonês hêttasthai*, being overcome by pleasure, is called by Plato a *pathêma* at *Prot.* 353a and a *pathos* at *Prot.* 352a. Plato frequently writes *pathêma ê poiêma* – suffering or doing – as at *Soph.* 248b.

pathos: the internal accusative of ***paskhein***. It is what happens to anything that undergoes, suffers, or experiences anything: *pathos legetai hena men tropon poiotês kath'hên alloiousthai endekhetai, hoion to leukon kai to melan ... kai hosa toiauta· hena de hai toutôn energeiai kai alloiôseis êdê, eti toutôn mallon hai blaberai alloiôseis kai kinêseis, kai malista hai lupêrai blabai· eti ta megethê tôn sumphorôn kai lupêrôn pathê legetai* – a *pathos* is (1) a quality by which it is possible to be changed, such as white and black and the like; (2) the actual occurrence of such changes; (3) of these, in particular, harmful alterations and changes, especially harms that distress; (4) also extremes of misfortune and distress are called *pathê* (Ar. *Met.* 1022b 15). *geômetria peri ta sumbebêkota pathê tois megethesi* – geometry [is] about the features that may characterise magnitudes (Ar. *Rhet.* 1355b 29); *erôtômenos to hosion hoti pot'estin, tên men ousian moi autou ou boulesthai dêlôsai, pathos de to peri autou legein, hoti peponthe* – when asked what the holy is you seem not to wish to reveal to me its essence but to tell me of one of the qualities that it has [being loved by the gods] (Pl. *Euth.* 11a); *ho estin autois to pathos ho phasin hupo tôn hêdonôn hêttasthai* – what this experience is that they call being overcome by pleasures (Pl. *Prot.* 352a); *prosaptein hekastôi tôn* **hamartêmatôn** *tên axian tou pathous te kai praxeôs* – to attach to each offence the penalty merited by the wrong as suffered and committed (Pl. *Laws* 876d); *skopôn kai ta peri ton ouranon te kai gên pathê* – examining also the things that happen to the heavens and the earth (Pl. *Phaedo* 96c). In psychological matters the *pathê* are what were traditionally called the passions of the soul, but which might be better called emotions: *legô de pathê men epithumian orgên phobon tharsos phthonon kharan philian misos pothon zêlon eleon, holôs hois hepetai hêdonê ê lupê* – I call emotions appetite, anger, fear, confidence, envy, joy, friendliness, hatred, longing, emulation, pity and, in general, what is accompanied by pleasure or distress (Ar. *E.N.* 1105b 22). *pathos* also has a semi-technical use in literary criticism: *duo men oun tou muthou merê taut'esti, peripeteia kai anagnôrisis· triton de pathos ... pathos de esti praxis phthartikê ê odunêra* – these, reversal and recognition, are two elements in the plot; suffering is a third ... suffering is some action that is destructive or painful (Ar. *Poetics* 1452b 9); cf. *Poetics* 1453b 18.

peira: a test: *megistê ... peira dialektikês phuseôs kai mê* – the greatest test of what is and what is not a dialectical nature (Pl. *Rep.* 537c); *tês alêtheias kai hêmôn autôn peiran lambanontes* – making a test of truth and of ourselves (Pl. *Prot.* 348a). See *peirasthai, peirastikê*.

peirasthai has its usual meanings of try, attempt, etc., in philosophy. But the use meaning 'to test' is relevant to the technical term *peirastikê*: *peirômetha ara ti legeis* – let us test whether you are right (Pl. *Phaedo* 95b).

peirastikê: probing, testing: *esti dê tôn en tôi dialegesthai logôn tettara genê, didaskalioi kai dialektikoi kai peirastikoi kai eristikoi ... peirastikoi d'hoi ek tôn dokountôn tôi apokrinomenôi kai anagkaiôn eidenai tôi prospoioumenôi ekhein tên epistêmên* – in question-and-answer discussions there are four kinds, didactic, dialectical, peirastic and eristic ... the peirastic are those starting from the opinions of the answerer that are needed to be known by one who pretends to have knowledge (Ar. *S.E.* 165a 38); *hê gar peirastikê esti dialektikê tis kai theôrei ou ton eidota alla ton agnoounta kai prospoioumenon* – peirastic is a type of dialectic and examines not him who knows but the ignorant who claims knowledge (Ar. *S.E.* 171b 4). Diogenes Laertius tells us that such dialogues as Plato's *Euthyphro* were classified as peirastic (Diogenes Laertius, *Lives of the Philosophers* 3.58). *peirastikos* means 'testing': see *peira, peirasthai*.

perainein: to bound or limit; *peras*: a limit or boundary: *hotan mêden êi peras tou kakou* – when there is no limit to evil (Pl. *Phaedrus* 254b); *to gar kakon tou apeirou hôs hoi Puthagoreioi eikazon, to de agathon tou peperasmenou* – for evil is of the unlimited, as the Pythagoreans speculated, but the good is of that which is bounded (Ar. *E.N.* 1106b 29). Of a spatial limit: *to tou periekhontos peras akinêton prôton, tout'esti ho topos* – the immediate motionless limit of the container, that is place (Ar. *Phys.* 212a 20); *meros gar pôs hê epiphaneia hê men hôs peras tou peperasmenou sômatos* – for the surface is a sort of part, in one way as the limit of the bounded body (Simplicius, *Physics* 610.9).

peras. See *perainein*.

periekhein: to surround or contain: *to ge periekhon peras an eiê* – what contains should be a limit (Pl. *Parm.* 145a). The term is important for its role in Aristotle's definition of *topos*, place: *to tou periekhontos peras akinêton prôton, tout'estin ho topos* – so that the immediate motionless boundary of the container, that is place (Ar. *Phys.* 212a 20). Simplicius found difficulties in this definition: *kata poion oun sêmainomenon periokhês periekhein legomen ton topon* – in what sense of containment are we saying that place contains? (Simplicius, *Physics* 604.17). The noun is *periokhê*, as in the above quotation.

periokhê: containment, as in the quotations under *periekhein*. It may also mean 'compass' as in *hê ektos periokhê* – the external compass [of a body] (Ar. *Col.* 797b 22). Also *kosmos esti periokhê tis ouranou* – a universe is a circumscribed area of the heavens (Epicurus 2.88). Epicurus allowed many universes at different areas of the heavens.

perittos (adjective); *perittôs* (adverb). There are three distinct uses. (1) Excessive: *hê perittê hautê epimeleia tou sômatos* – that excessive care of the body (Pl. *Rep.* 407b). (2) Elegant: *kompsôs men eirêtai kai perittôs* – it is cleverly and elegantly expressed (Ar. *De Caelo* 290b 14). (3) Odd, as opposed to even: *ei en têi tou perittou kai artiou hairesei hêmin ên hê sôtêria* – if our safety rested on our selection of odd and even (Pl. *Prot.* 356e).

phainein. See *phainesthai*.

phainesthai has two closely connected uses that can only be distinguished by reference to context. On the one hand, it is to appear with an implicit contrast with being the case. On the other, it is to be plain to see, literally or metaphorically. This holds also of the verbal noun *to phainomenon*, which is what is apparent. The

English verb 'appear' and the adjective 'apparent' exhibit the same ambiguity. The sense of transitively making visible or intransitively becoming visible are regular in the active verb **phainein**: *takh'an empodion genomenon auto phêneiê to zêtoumenon* – perhaps the thing we are seeking would appear right before us (Pl. *Theat.* 200e). *hoi dikhade dioikhthentes phainontai endothen agalmata ekhontes theôn* – [Silenuses] that, when opened up, can be seen to contain statues of gods (Pl. *Symp.* 215b); *hôs g'emoi phainetai* – as it seems to me at least (Pl. *Prot.* 324d). The same contrast in *ta phainomena*: *houtos men oun ho logos amphisbêtai tois phainomenois enargôs* – this statement [that there is no weakness of will] is plainly at odds with the phenomena (Ar. *E.N.* 1145b 27); *hê de boulêsis ... dokei de tois men t'agathou einai, tois de tou phainomenou agathou* – wish ... seems to some to be for the good and to others to be for the apparently good (Ar. *E.N.* 1113a 15); *eoike d'ho te logos tois phainomenois marturein kai ta phainomena tôi logôi* – the argument seems to support observation, and observation the argument (Ar. *De Caelo* 270b 3). A translation of *ta phainomena* as 'the apparent facts' often seems best to preserve the ambiguity.

phanai (1st person singular present is *phêmi*): usually to assert or affirm, not merely to say something; also *ou phanai* is not to fail to say something but to deny: *phanai te kai aparneisthai* – to assert and to deny (Pl. *Theaet.* 165a); *ho d'ouk ephê* – but he denied it (Pl. *Prot.* 317d). But also of other speech acts: *poiôn, phaien an isôs, hêdonôn* – 'of which pleasures?' they may say (Pl. *Philebus* 63c).

phantasia, phantasma: imagination, mental image. Sometimes used neutrally of immaterial phenomena, usually mental, sometimes, particularly in Plato, pejoratively of mere imagination and its figments. Neutrally: *dianoia te kai doxa kai phantasia ... tauta ge pseudê te kai alêthê panth'hêmôn en tais psukhais eggignetai* – thought, opinion and imagination ... all these enter into our souls both true and false (Pl. *Soph.* 263d); *phantasia gar heteron kai aisthêseôs kai dianoias, hautê te ou gignetai aneu aisthêseôs kai aneu tautês ouk estin hupolêpsis* – imagination is different from both perception and thinking, and imagination does not occur without perception, and without imagination there is no conception (Ar. *De An.* 427b 14); *oudepote noei aneu phantasmatos hê psukhê* – the soul never thinks without a mental image (Ar. *De*

An. 431a 16). Pejoratively: *phantasmatos ê alêtheias ousa mimêsis* – being a copy of a phantom or a reality (Pl. *Rep.* 598b). Of a non-mental image: *ta en tois hudasi phantasmata* – images in water (Pl. *Rep.* 510a). But in contrast with that: *paraplêsia sumbainei ta phantasmata tois en tois hudasin eidôlois* – mental images are akin to images in water (Ar. *De Divin.* 464b 9).

philein, philêsis, philêtos, philia, philos. *philein* is to like or love a person or thing, without sexual implications: *philêsis* is the love, liking or affection felt for a person or thing that is *philêtos*, its object. *philos*, as an adjective, is of anything that is liked or loved, but as a noun it is of a person; the personal relationship of *philoi* is *philia*. *dokei gar ou pan phileisthai alla to philêton· touto d'einai agathon ê hêdu ê khrêsimon ... triôn d'ontôn di'ha philousin, epi men têi tôn apsukhôn philêsei ou legetai philia* – not everything seems to be loved, but only the lovable, and that seems to be the good, the pleasant and the useful ... there being three reasons for loving, the love for the inanimate is not called friendship (Ar. *E.N.* 1155b 18); *tria dê ta tês philias eidê, isarithma tois philêtois* – there are three types of friendship, equal in number to the lovable [true friendship, business friendship and partnership in pleasure] (Ar. *E.N.* 1156a 7); *isotês philotêta apergazetai* – equality brings about amity (Pl. *Laws* 757a). In the philosophy of Empedocles *philotês* is the principle opposed to *neikos*, strife, that brings about union of elements: *allote men philotêti sunerkhomen'eis hen hapanta, allote d'au dikh'hekasta phoreumena neikeos ekhthei* – sometimes coming together in one in friendship, at others being carried apart by the enmity of strife (Empedocles in Simplicius, *Physics* 158.7). Though used in the above translations, 'love' is clearly not always the right word: a business associate is a *philos* and thus *philêtos*, but not as such loved and lovable.

philosophia, philosophos: philosophy, philosopher. Pythagoras is said to have coined the term *philosophos*: *hoi men andrapodôdeis, ephê, phuontai doxês kai pleonexias thêratai, hoi de philosophoi tês alêtheias* – he [Pythagoras] said that the slavish naturally pursue glory and riches, but philosophers the truth (Diogenes Laertius 8.8); *philosophia ktêsis epistêmês* – philosophy is the acquisition of knowledge (Pl. *Euthyd.* 258d); *to ge philomathes kai philosophon t'auton* – the love of learning and love of wisdom are the same (Pl. *Rep.* 376b); *theôn oudeis philosophei oud'epithumei sophos* *genesthai· esti gar* – none of the gods is a lover of wisdom or desires to become wise; for he is (Pl. *Symp.* 203e); *ei de esti tis ousia akinêtos hautê protera kai philosophia prôtê* – if there is some changeless substance, that is prior and [the subject matter of] first philosophy (Ar. *Met.* 1026a 29). Aristotle always called metaphysics either *prôtê philosophia* or *theologikê: treis an eien philosophiai theôrêtikai, mathêmatikê, phusikê, theologikê* – there would be three branches of theoretical philosophy, mathematical, natural and theological (Ar. *Met.* 1026a 18). The translation 'love of wisdom' is conventional; 'love of knowledge' or, better, 'love of understanding' would be more accurate. 'Wisdom' is, in standard English, applied to practical matters (wise plans, precautions, policies, investors, parents, etc.), whereas *sophia* is theoretical. *philosophos* is also used as an adjective, philosophical: *meta philosophôn logôn* – using philosophical arguments (Pl. *Phaedrus* 257b).

pheresthai. See *phora*.

phobeisthai, phobos, phoberos: to fear, fear, fearful. Like 'fear' in English, *phobos* and *phobeisthai* are used in Greek both with regard to the merely *kakon* and with regard to the *phoberon*. Thus we say 'I fear (am afraid) he is not at home', a state of affairs not normally terrifying, and 'he is afraid to go out at night', which he presumably does find terrifying. (1) Fear of the *kakon*: *prosdokian tina legô kakou touto eite phobon eite deos kaleite* – I call that a certain expectation of evil, whether you name it fear or dread (Pl. *Prot.* 358d); *ton phobon horizontai prosdokian kakou* – men define fear as expectation of evil (Ar. *E.N.* 1159a 9); *mallon de kai phobêsometha mê ti miasma êi pros hieron ta toiauta apo tôn oikeiôn pherein* – we shall rather be afraid that there should be some pollution in bringing such things taken from relations to a holy place (Pl. *Rep.* 470a). (2) Fear of the *phoberon*: *orthai hai trikhes histantai hupo phobou* – their hair stands on end through terror (Pl. *Ion* 535c); *ho de tôi phobeisthai huperballôn deilos* – the excessively fearful man is a coward (Ar. *E.N.* 1115b 34); *phoboumetha dêlon hoti ta phobera* – we are manifestly afraid of the frightening (Ar. *E.N.* 1115a 8). The opposite of *phobos* is said to be *tharros: tharros kai phobon, aphrone xumboulô* – confidence and fear, a pair of unwise counsellors (Pl. *Tim.* 69d).

phora: carrying; *pheresthai*: to be carried. In non-philosophical uses:

dia phoras psêphôn aph'hierôn pheronta – by bringing the votes from sacred places (Pl. *Laws* 948d); metaphorically: *apo de thaumastês … elpidos ôikhomên pheromenos* – I went, carried away by a remarkable hope (Pl. *Phaedo* 98b). In technical use with regard to mechanics *phora* is local motion, and *pheresthai* is to be moved, or move, locally: *tên tôn astrôn phoran* – the motion of the stars (Pl. *Gorg.* 451c); in widest use in Aristotle: *pasa de kinêsis hosê kata topon, hên kaloumen phoran, ê eutheia ê kuklôi ê ek toutôn miktê* – every change of place, which we call local motion, is either in a straight line or in a circle or is a mixture of the two (Ar. *De Caelo* 268b 17). But elsewhere restrictions are imposed: *legetai ge tauta pheresthai mona kuriôs hotan mê eph'hautois êi to stênai tois metaballousi ton topon kai hosa mê auta hauta kinei kata topon* – only those things are properly said to be moved locally where it is not in the power of the things that change their place to be stationary, i.e. those things that do not move themselves from place to place (Ar. *Phys.* 226a 35); this restriction is disregarded at times: *hapan dê to pheromenon ê huph'heautou kinêtai ê hup'allou* (Ar. *Phys.* 243a 11). A similar restriction is imposed in the *Topics*: *outh'hê kata topon metabolê pasa phora. hê gar badisis ou dokei phora einai. skhedon gar hê phora epi tôn akousiôs topon ek topou metaballontôn legetai, kathaper epi tôn apsukhôn sumbainei* – Nor is all change of place locomotion. For walking does not seem to be locomotion. 'Locomotion' is used, roughly, when things move involuntarily from place to place, as is the case with inanimate objects (Ar. *Top.* 122b 32). Simplicius reports a quite different restriction suggested by Alexander of Aphrodisias: *dio ou kata phoran alla kata periphoran hê kinêsis* – therefore the motion [of the heavens] is not locomotion but peripheral motion (Simplicius, *Physics* 593.20).

phronêsis: basically, thought or understanding: *tou logou d'eontos xunou, zôousin hoi polloi hôs idian ekhontes phronêsin* – though reason is common to all, men live as though they had a private understanding (Heraclitus, fr. 2). The word is normally used by both Plato and Aristotle of practical wisdom, sagacity, prudence, as is the adjective *phronimos*: *phronimos eis hupodêmatôn ergasian* – an intelligent cobbler (Pl. *Alcib.* 1.125a); *phronimos te kai agathos ho adikos* – the unjust man is wise and good (Pl. *Rep.* 349d); *kallistês tês phronêseôs hê peri tas tôn poleôn te kai oikêseôn diakosmêseis* – the fairest wisdom is that concerned with the ordering of cities and habitations (Pl. *Symp.* 209a); *dokei dê phronimou einai to dunasthai kalôs bouleuesthai peri ta hautôi agatha kai sumpheronta* – it seems to be a mark of the practically wise man that he is able to deliberate well about what is to his advantage (Ar *E.N.* 1140a 25); *phronêsis d'estin aretê dianoias kath'hên eu bouleuesthai dunantai peri agathôn kai kakôn tôn eirêmenôn eis eudaimonian* – wisdom is an excellence of the intelligence by which men are able to deliberate well about the aforementioned goods and evils with a view to well-being (Ar. *Rhet.* 1366b 20). This is subsequently the usual use: *philosophias timiôteron huparkhei phronêsis ... didaskousa hôs ouk estin hêdeôs zên aneu tou phronimôs* – wisdom is to be more highly valued than philosophy ... since it teaches us that one cannot live pleasantly unless one lives wisely (Epicurus, *To Menoeceus* 132). But both Plato and Aristotle occasionally use *phronêsis* of theoretical excellence, where we would expect **sophia**: *houtô dê gegenêmenos pros to logôi kai phronêsei perilêpton kai kata t'auta ekhon dedêmiourgêtai* – having thus come about, [the world of forms] was constructed to be grasped by reason and wisdom, and to be unchanging (Pl. *Tim.* 29a); *ho men philosophos bouletai peri phronêsin einai kai tên theôrian tên peri tên alêtheian* – the philosopher wishes to be concerned with thought and the contemplation concerning the truth (Ar. *E.E.* 1215b 1); *hoi men gar tên phronêsin megiston einai phasin agathon, hoi de tên aretên, hoi de tên hêdonên* – some say that *phronêsis* is the greatest good, others that it is excellence of character, and others that it is pleasure (Ar. *E.E.* 1214a 32). *phronêsis* is closer to the English 'wisdom' than is *sophia*.

phthora: destruction or ceasing to be. In philosophy it refers to the ceasing to exist of a substance, the contrary being **genesis**, which is the coming into existence of a substance. In Aristotle both are usually distinct from change of all kinds in a continuing substance, though in *Physics* 3.1 *kinêsis* seems exceptionally to include substantial change. *genomenôi panti phthora estin* – everything that has come to be ceases to be (Pl. *Rep.* 546a); *peri geneseôs kai phthoras tên aitian diapragmateuesthai* – to work out the cause of coming to be and ceasing to be (Pl. *Phaedo* 95e). *Peri geneseôs kai phthoras* is the title of a work of Aristotle's, whose Latin title is *De generatione et corruptione*, which has a misleading sound to English speakers. Aristotle's basic problems are how there can be any coming into existence and ceasing to exist if matter is everlasting, and how they can be distinguished from mere *alloiôsis*, alteration.

phuein: to generate, give birth to: *hosa gê phuei* – the fruits of the earth (Pl. *Rep.* 621a). In the perfect form, ***pephukenai***, it means 'to be naturally' or 'it is the nature of': *pephuken hê pterou dunamis to embrithes anô agein* – it is the nature of the wing to carry the heavy upwards (Pl. *Phaedrus* 246d); *ou gar phusei hekastôi pephukenai onoma ouden oudeni* – no name belongs naturally to anything whatsoever (Pl. *Crat.* 384d); *pephuke de ek gnôrimôterôn hêmin hê hodos kai saphesterôn epi ta saphestera têi phusei kai gnôrimôtera* – the route is naturally from things that are more obvious and clearer to us to things that are clear and more obvious in their nature (Ar. *Phys.* 184a 16).

phusikos: concerned with ***phusis***, nature; *dedeiktai proteron en tois phusikois* – it was previously demonstrated in the *Physics* [as Aristotle's basic work on nature is misleadingly called]; *kathaper tôn phusikôn kaloumenôn phêsi tis* – as one of the so-called students of nature says (Epicurus, *To Pythocles* 90); *tên tôn allôn phusikôn problêmatôn katharsin* – the clearing up of the remaining problems about nature (Epicurus, *To Pythocles* 86). Not in Plato. *ho phusikos* is a student of nature or a natural scientist, rather than specifically a physicist.

phusiologein, phusiologia, phusiologos: to treat of nature (***phusis***), the treatment of nature, he who treats of nature: *peri pantôn phusiologountes* – treating of nature in general (Ar. *Met.* 988b 26); *tois neôsti phusiologias gnêsiou geuomenois* – for those who are newly tasting genuine natural science (Epicurus, *To Pythocles* 85); *enioi tôn phusiologôn hen hupothemenoi to on* – some natural scientists who suppose that reality is unitary (Ar. *Met.* 986b 14). Aristotle frequently calls the pre-Socratic philosophers *phusiologoi*. None of these words occur in Plato.

phusis: either the nature of something – *phusis tinos* – or, absolutely, nature as opposed to the conventional, artificial, etc. With genitive: *kai gunaikos ara kai andros hê autê phusis eis phulakên poleôs* – surely the nature of both women and men is the same for guarding the city (Pl. *Rep.* 456a); *metekhein tês tou philokhrêmatou phuseôs* – to share the nature of the acquisitive (Pl. *Rep.* 549b); *tên tôn blepharôn phusis* – the nature of eyelids (Pl. *Tim.* 45b). Absolutely: *peri hou saphesteron en tois peri phuseôs eirêkamen* – as we have said more clearly in the book on nature [one

of Aristotle's names for what we call the *Physics*, or a part thereof]
(Ar. *Phys.* 986b 30); *hôs ousês tês phuseôs arkhês tinos kai aitias tou
kineisthai kai êremein* – as nature's being some principle and cause
of change and rest (Ar. *Phys.* 192b 21). In various contrasts: *ha
phusei men ouk esti kala nomôi de* – that are not fine by nature, but
by convention (Pl. *Gorg.* 482e); *ê phusei ê tekhnêi* – either by nature
or by art (Pl. *Rep.* 381a); *pephuke de ek tôn gnôrimôterôn hêmin hê
hodos kai saphesterôn epi ta saphestera têi phusei kai gnôrimôtera* –
the route is from things that are more obvious and clear to us to those
that are naturally clearer and more obvious (Ar. *Phys.* 184a 16).
Plato usually uses the word of the nature of a thing, but *peri phuseôs
kai tôn meteôrôn astronomika tina dierôtan* – to discuss certain
astronomical issues about nature and celestial phenomena (Pl. *Prot.*
315c). There is a general discussion of the concept of *phusis* in Ar.
Met., Book 4, Ch. 4.

pistis has two meanings in addition to various non-philosophical
uses. (1) Belief: *du'eston tô peri theôn agonte eis pistin* – there are two
things leading to belief about the gods (Pl. *Laws* 966d); *tên te apistian
kai tên pistin* – disbelief and belief (Ar. *Phys.* 213a 15). *pistis* is the
name given by Socrates to the third segment of the line in the
Republic: *tôi tritôi … pistin apodos* – give [the name] belief to the
third [segment] (Pl. *Rep.* 511e). (2) A less than demonstrative proof:
hikanê de pistis kai ek tês epagôgês – the proof from induction is
sufficient (Ar. *An. Po.* 90b 14); *tôn de pisteôn hai men atekhnoi eisin,
hai d'entekhnoi* – of proofs [in law courts] some are non-technical,
others are technical [depending on the resources of rhetoric] (Ar.
Rhet. 1355b 35).

platos: breadth: *diastêmata men oun ekhei tria, mêkos kai platos
kai bathos* – it [place] has three dimensions, length and breadth and
depth (Ar. *Phys.* 209a 5). For the adverb *plateôs*, see *platus*.

platus: broad. It has a figurative as well as a physical use. Physically: *platutaton ton tou kheilous kuklon ekhein* – to have the circle of
the rim widest (Pl. *Rep.* 616e). Figuratively: *peri tou nun … tou te
kuriôs kai tou en platei legomenou* – concerning the 'now' … both in
its strict and in its broad senses (Simplicius, *Physics* 747.30). The
adverb *plateôs* is also used figuratively.

pleonakhôs: in various ways or senses: *epei de to auto pleonakhôs legetai* – since 'the same' is used in various ways (Ar. *An. Po.* 89a 28); *dêlon d'hoti pleonakhôs tou philotoioutou legomenou ouk epi to auto pheromen aei to philotimon* – since 'the lover of so-and-so' is used in various senses, it is clear that we do not always use 'lover of honour' in the same way (Ar. *E.N.* 1125b 14). Not in Plato.

pleonektein, pleonektês, pleonexia: to be greedy, greedy, greediness: *dokei dê ho te paranomos adikos einai kai ho pleonektês* – both the lawless man and the greedy seem to be wrong-doers (Ar. *E.N.* 1129a 32); *pleonektei kai autos ê kharitos ê timôrias* – he himself is greedy for favour or revenge (Ar. *E.N.* 1137a 1); *ep'autophôrôi oun laboimen an ton dikaion tôi adikôi eis t'auton ionta dia tên pleonexian* – we would catch the just man in the act, becoming the same as the unjust through greed (Pl. *Rep.* 359c).

plêrês: full. Ordinarily as in English: *tên khôran plêrê naupêgêsimôn xulôn* – the country full of wood fit for ship-building (Pl. *Laws* 706b); *odunês plêrês* – full of pain (Pl. *Theaet.* 210). Also a technical term of the early atomists: *Leukippos de kai ho hetairos autou Dêmokritos stoikheia men to plêres kai to kenon einai phasi* – Leucippus and his colleague Democritus say that the elements are the full and the void (Ar. *Met.* 985b 5); *arkhas etheto to plêres kai to kenon, hôn to men on to de mê on ekalei* – [Democritus] posited as principles the full and the void, of which he called the first that which is, and the other that which is not (Simplicius, *Physics* 28.16). Aristotle discusses and attacks this theory in *Physics*, Book 4, Chs 6-9.

plêthos: multitude, manifold. Ordinarily as in English: *hê tou plêthous arkhê* – the rule of the mob (Pl. *Pol.* 291d); *plêthos apeiron tôn ontôn* – an unlimited multitude of existents (Pl. *Parm.* 144a). In neoplatonism, a manifold, as opposed to the unitary and simple: *pan plêthos metekhei pêi tou henos* – every manifold participates in a way in the one (Proclus, *Elements of Theology* 1); *pôs oun diakrisis kai plêthos ephanê?* – how then did separation and the manifold appear? (Damascius, *First Principles* 2 Ruelle).

poiein, poiêma, poiêsis, poiêtês, poiêtikos: to make, a thing made, making, a maker, concerned with making. (1) In their widest use these terms are used of any doing or making, like Latin *facere* and French *faire*. (2) In a narrower use they are used of making as

136

distinguished from doing. (3) In their narrowest use they are used specifically of poetry and its composition. (1) *eite poiêmatôn eite pathêmatôn* – whether things done or things suffered (Pl. *Rep.* 437b); *ê oukh houtô poieis pros tous kalous?* – or is not that how you behave to the good-looking? (Pl. *Rep.* 474d). (2) *tou d'endekhomenou allôs ekhein esti ti kai poiêton kai prakton· heteron d'esti poiêsis kai praxis* – in the sphere of the variable there is the made and the done: but making and doing are different (Ar. *E.N.* 1140a 1); *klinês poiêtês* – the maker of a bed (Pl. *Rep.* 597d); *poiêtên kai patera toude tou pantos* – the maker and father of this universe (Pl. *Tim.* 28c); *hai hupo pasais tais tekhnais ergasia poiêseis eisi kai hoi toutôn dêmiourgoi pantes poiêtai ... apo de pasês tês poiêseôs hen morion aphoristhen to peri tên mousikên kai ta metra tôi tou holou onomati prosagoreuetai* – the works of all skills are creations and the workmen who make them are all creators ... but from all creation one part, cut off, which is concerned with music and metre is called by the name that belongs to all (Pl. *Symp.* 205c); *poiêtikên ... pasan ephamen einai dunamin hêtis an aitia gignêtai tois mê ousin husteron gignesthai* – we said that the whole of making was a power which can cause that which is not to come subsequently to be (Pl. *Soph.* 265b). (3) *peri ... tôn poiêmatôn hôn pepoiêkas* – concerning the poems you have composed (Pl. *Phaedo* 60c); *poiein eis ta paidika* – compose poems to my boy-love (Pl. *Lysis* 205a); *peri poiêtikês autês te kai tôn eidôn autês* – concerning poetry itself and its species (Ar. *Poetics* 1447a 8): *poiêtikê* is in the feminine because *tekhnê* is understood. *poiêsis* is either the composing of the poem, as in *hê tês tragôidias poiêsis* – the composition of tragedy (Pl. *Gorg.* 502b), or the poem itself, as in *peri hôn Homêros tên poiêsin pepoiken* – about which Homer composed his poetry (Pl. *Ion* 531d). In classical Scottish usage a poet was called a maker (rhyming with 'hacker').

poios, poiotês: of what sort, 'of-what-sort-ness' i.e. quality. The word *poiotês* was apparently coined by Plato: *to de poioun poion ti all'ou poiotêta. isôs oun hê 'poiotês' hama allokoton te phainetai onoma kai ou manthaneis athroon legomenon* – what acts is something of a sort and not a quality. Perhaps 'quality' seems a disagreeable word that you do not understand used out of context (Pl. *Theaet.* 182a); *poiotêta de legô kath'hên poioi tines einai legontai· esti de hê poiotês tôn **pleonakhôs** legomenôn* – I call a quality that through which things are called of a sort; but 'quality' has many senses (Ar. *Cat.* 8b 25). *poion*, or *poiotês*, is one of the ten

137

categories listed by Aristotle in his *Categories*. For the list see *Cat.* 1b 25 ff. There is a general discussion of *poiotês* in Ar. *Met.*, Book 4, Ch. 14. In the quotation from the *Theaetetus* above, the *OCT* has *hathroon*, presumably as a misprint.

polis: (1) A city as opposed to countryside and villages. (2) A city-state, including countryside and villages. (1) *peritheousi tois Dionusiois oute tôn kata poleis oute tôn kata kômas apoleipomenoi* – they run around, not missing any Dionysia either in the cities or in the villages (Pl. *Rep.* 475d). (2) *hê ek pleionôn kômôn koinônia teleios polis* – the complete city is a community of several villages (Ar. *Pol.* 1252b 27; *ta tês poleôs dunatôtatos ... kai prattein kai legein* – most capable of acting and speaking on affairs of state (Pl. *Prot.* 319a).

politeia: generally, the constitution of any *polis*: *to skhêma tês politeias* – the form of the constitution (Pl. *Rep.* 501a); *hosai de to spheteron monon tôn arkhontôn hêmartêmenai pasai kai parekbaseis tôn orthôn politeiôn* – those [that look to the interest] of the rulers alone are flawed departures from the correct constitutions (Ar. *Pol.* 1279a 19). But Aristotle also called his preferred form of government *politeia*, or constitutional government: *têi kaloumenêi politeiaï* – so-called polity (Ar. *Pol.* 1295a 33).

politês (fem. *politis*): a full member of a *polis*: *hê gar polis politôn ti plêthos estin* – for the state is a collection of citizens (Ar. *Pol.* 1274b 41); *pantas tous politas kai tas politidas* – all the citizens, male and female (Pl. *Laws* 814c). Various qualifications for citizenship are discussed by Aristotle in *Pol.* 1275a 1 ff.

politeuesthai: to conduct the affairs of the city, or for them to be conducted: *suggignôskousin hêmin te kai ekeinois hosoi hêmôn eggus politeuontai* – they forgive us and those who conduct their civic affairs like us (Pl. *Rep.* 568b); *hontina pote tropon oiei dein politeuesthai en hêmin* – in what way you think that we should conduct our political affairs (Pl. *Gorg.* 515b).

politikos: concerned with running a city, whether a person, a life, a skill or a book: *politikos· epistêmôn poleôs kataskeuês* – a statesman: one who is knowledgable about the structure of the state (pseudo-Pl. *Def.* 415c); *Politikos* – 'the Statesman' – is the title of a Platonic dialogue; *Politika* – 'the Politics' – is the title of a work of Aristotle; *treis gar eisi malista hoi proukhontes, ho te nun eirêmenos, kai ho politikos kai tritos ho theôrêtikos* – there are three most prominent [ways of life], the one just mentioned [pleasure], that concerned with the state, and thirdly the contemplative (Ar. *E.N.* 1095b 17); *edoxe … hêmin hê politikê kai hê basilikê tekhnê hê autê* – it seemed to us that the skills of a statesman and of a king were the same (Pl. *Euthyd.* 291c).

pollakhôs: in many ways: *to men hamartanein pollakhôs estin … to de katorthoun monakhôs* – one can be wrong in many ways … but right only in one (Ar. *E.N.* 1106b 29); *pollakhôs to **poiein** legetai* – 'make' has many senses (Ar. *E.N.* 1136b 29); *to on legetai pollakhôs kathaper dielometha proteron en tois peri tou posakhôs* – 'being' has many senses, as we earlier distinguished them in the discussion of how many senses [various terms had] (Ar. *Met.* 1028a 10). Not in Plato, but he uses *pollakhêi*, which normally means 'in many places or parts', also as *pollakhôs* is used: *geloion gar an eiê pollakhêi* – for it would be laughable in many ways (Pl. *Theaet.* 158e).

ponêria, like the adjective ***ponêros***, is hard to distinguish from ***kakia***, *mokhthêria* and *aiskhos*. Etymologically, and in early Greek, it is connected with *ponos*, harsh and grievous labour. In Plato, at least, if we are to attempt to refine on 'bad', perhaps 'ill-condition(ed)' is as good as any other translation; it should be noted that he always contrasts *ponêros* with *khrêstos*, not with *agathos*: *peri tôn khrêstôn sitiôn kai ponêrôn* – concerning healthy and unhealthy foods (Pl. *Gorg.* 464d); *ê khrêston auto genesthai ê ponêron* – it [the body] becomes healthy or diseased (Pl. *Prot.* 313a); *hê sômatos ponêria nosos ousa* – the ill-condition of the body being disease (Pl. *Rep.* 609c); *khôleia de podôn oukhi ponêria?* – is not lameness of the feet an ill-condition? (Pl. *Hip. Min.* 374c). For other examples of *ponêria* as disease, see *Hip. Min.* 374d, *Prot.* 326c, *Tim.* 86d. *ponêras doxas kai khrêstas* – sound and unsound opinions (Pl. *Philebus* 40e). *hoi ponêroi kai akhrêstoi* (Pl. *Laws* 950b) seems to be a hendiadys, meaning 'worthless people'. Aristotle treats *ponêros* as a close synonym of *mokhthêros*; he says that *oudeis hekôn ponêros* – no one is intentionally bad – is false, since *hê de mokhthêria hekousion* – wickedness is intentional – is true (Ar. *E.N.* 1113b 15).

posos as an interrogative means 'how big', 'how much': *posôn an eiê podôn to holon?* – how many feet is the whole? (Pl. *Meno* 82c); *posou*

139

didaskei? – what are his tuition fees? (Pl. *Apol.* 20b). Aristotle uses the interrogative as the name of the category of quantity (Ar. *Cat.* 1b 26). In the neuter singular *to poson* can be a particular quantity: *poson ti gar on, hoposon an êi tosouton holon anagkaion auto einai* – for since it is a quantity, of whatever size it may be it must be a whole of that size (Pl. *Soph.* 245d). See *posotês*.

posotês: quantity. Not used by Plato, though he coined *poiotês*. Not used by Aristotle in the *Categories*, where the name of the category of quantity is *poson*, but in the plural *ta de alla legetai onta tôi tou houtôs ontos ta men posotêtes einai ta de poiotêtes ...* – but the others are called existences by being quantities or qualities [etc.] of that which exists in this way [as a substance] (Ar. *Met.* 1028a 18). Later: *hoi de toutou agnoountes, tên posotêta tou khronou akribes* – those who do not know the exact time (Sextus Empiricus, *Adversus Mathematicos* 5.58). See *posos*.

pothein, pothos: to long (longing) for the absent, like Latin *desiderium*: *kai mên pothos au kaleitai* [*ho himeros*] *sêmainôn ou parontos einai alla tou allothi pou ontos kai apontos* – and [yearning] is also called longing, signifying that it is of what is not present but is somewhere else and absent (Pl. *Crat.* 420a). But Andronicus distinguishes it from *himeros*: *himeros de epithumia philou apontos homilias· pothos de epithumia kata erôta apontos* – yearning is a desire for the companionship of an absent friend: longing is an erotic desire for the absent (Andronicus, *Peri pathôn* 4, in *SVF* 3.397). Thus Plato speaks of *pothou kentron* – the spur of longing – and of *tas en têi neotêti hêdonas pothountes* – longing for the pleasures of youth (Pl. *Rep.* 573a and 329a). But also in abstract: *eti pothei, ephê, hê apokrisis erôtêsin toiande* – the answer, [Diotima] said, presupposes a [missing] question of the following sort (Pl. *Symp.* 204d).

praktikos, praktos, prattein, praxis have a wide variety of uses, all concerned with the sphere of action. Distinguished from speech: *ta prakhthenta kai lekhthenta* – things done and said (Pl. *Phaedrus* 241a). Distinguished from being acted on: *mêden sumballetai ho prattôn ê ho paskhôn* – nothing is contributed by the agent or, rather, him to whom it happens (Ar. *E.N.* 1110a 2). Distinguished from making: *poiêsis kai praxis heteron* – making and doing are a different matter (Ar. *E.N.* 1140a 16). But *prattein* may be either to act or to fare, as in *epistêmonôs an prattontes eu an prattoimen kai eudaimonoimen* – if we acted intelligently we should fare well and be well off (Pl. *Charm.* 173d). Compare *to de eu zên kai to eu prattein t'auton hupolambanousi tôi eudaimonein* – they take living well and faring well to be the same thing as well-being (Ar. *E.N.* 1095a 19). Here the common translation of *eu prattein* as 'do well' is wrong, unless 'do well' is used as in 'he is doing well in his profession'; compare *nomôi ou touto melei, hopôs hen ti genos en polei diapherontôs eu praxei* – it is not the concern of the law to ensure that one class in the state should fare especially well (Pl. *Rep.* 519e). *praxis* is concerned with particulars: *prakta ta kath'hekasta* – things done are particular, *praktikos ho phronimos* – the wise man is concerned with action (Ar. *E.N.* 1147a 3, 1146a 8). There is an idiomatic use of *prattesthai* in which it means 'to make a monetary charge': *ei tinos akêkoate hôs egô paideuein epikheirô anthrôpous kai khrêmata prattomai* – if you have heard from somebody that I try to educate people and charge a fee (Pl. *Apol.* 19d).

proagein: to bring forward, to lead on, to persuade, in non-technical use. The only philosophical use of importance is of the perfect passive participle *proêgmenon*. The *proêgmenon* in Stoic philosophy is that which though not good, being *adiaphoron*, indifferent, like wealth and health, is none the less preferred. The contrary is the *apoproêgmenon*, which is undesirable but not, in Stoic ethics, a *kakon*, bad: *proêgmenon … ho adiaphoron on eklegometha* – the preferred … that which though indifferent we select (Zeno in *SVF* 1.48).

proaireisthai: to choose; *proairesis*: choice; *proairetikê*: involving choice; *proairetos*: chosen: *ar'ouk en hekastêi têi proairesei proairoumetha tine hô orthôs ekhei kaleisthai amphotera* – do we not in each choice choose a pair that can be correctly called 'both'? (Pl. *Parm.* 143c); *tous te gar bebaiotatous kai tous andreiotatous proaireteon* – for we should choose the most reliable and the bravest (Pl. *Rep.* 535a). There is a study of *proairesis* in *E.N.*, Book 3, Ch. 2; the following quotations are all from that work: *hê proairesis dê hekousion men phainetai, ou t'auton de, all'epi pleon to hekousion* – choice seems to be intentional, but not the same as it, since the intended is wider (1111b 7); *to de hekousion ou pan proaireton* – but not all the intended is chosen (1112a 14); *kai proairesei men epithumia enantioutai* – and appetite opposes choice (1111b 16); *proelomenoi men hosa probouleusamenoi* – having chosen what we had planned in advance (1135b 10); *estin ara hê **aretê** hexis proairetikê* – excellence [of character] is a disposition to choose (1106b 36); ***praxeôs** men oun arkhê proairesis* – so choice is a source of action (1139a 31).

problêma: a verbal noun from *proballein*, to throw in front, used physically in that way by Plato: *tên de sarka probolên men kaumatôn, problêma de kheimônôn* – [the demiurge made] flesh as a shield against heat and a protection against the cold (Pl. *Tim.* 74b). Generally in philosophy a problem, as in English: *problêmasi ara ... khrômenoi hôsper geômetrian houtô kai astronomian metimen* – we approach astronomy as we do geometry, with problems (Pl. *Rep.* 530a). Aristotle has a narrower, technical use: *diapherei de to problêma kai hê **protasis** tôi tropôi. houtô men gar rhêthentos 'ara to "zôion pezon dipoun" horismos estin anthrôpou?' ... protasis gignetai· ean de 'poteron to "zôion pezon dipoun" horismos estin anthrôpou ê ou', problêma gignetai* – a problem and a proposition differ in their form. Thus, if one says 'Is "two-footed animal" the definition of a man?' ... we have a proposition: but if one says 'Is "two-footed animal" the definition of a man or is it not?', we have a problem (Ar. *Top.* 101b 29).

proêgmenon: preferred. See *proagein*.

proienai: non-technically, to proceed or go on: *proïthi ge eti eis t'oumprosthen* – keep going on forwards, then (Pl. *Gorg.* 497a); *proïontos de êdê tou khronou* – as time is already getting on (Pl. *Phaedrus* 255a). There is an important technical use in neoplatonism, where *proienai* is always translated 'proceed', in which lower orders of being are said to proceed from higher. The following quotations from Proclus' *Elements of Theology* give the bare gist of the doctrine: *panta ta onta proeisin apo mias aitias tês prôtês* – all existences proceed from the single first cause (21); *pasa taxis apo monados arkhomenê proeisin eis **plêthos*** – every order proceeds from a monad to a manifold (24); *pan to apo tinos **paragomenon** amesôs menei te en tôi paragonti kai proeisin ap'autou* – everything produced from something remains immediately in the producer and proceeds from it (33). Also: *akolouthon epi toutois an eiê zêtein ei proeisi ti ap'ekeinou eis ta met'auto kai* *hotioun* – it follows to examine whether anything whatever proceeds from it [the one] into that which is after it (Damascius, *First Principles* 1.66 Ruelle). But Plotinus also uses *proienai* non-technically: *esti de kai proiousi pros to anô apo tês aisthêseôs kai epitêdeumata kala kai praxeis* – for those who proceed upwards from perception there are fine occupations and actions (Plotinus 1.6.1).

proödos: procession, used by neoplatonists as a noun correlative with *proienai*: *tis houtôs esti opsimathês hôs agnoein hoti kata tên aph'henos proödon apo tês **aïdiou** ousias hê genetê **proeisin*** – who is so uninformed as not to know that in the procession from the one created substance proceeds from the everlasting? (Simplicius, *Physics* 1133.9). Not in Plato.

propeteia: impetuosity, impulsiveness; *propetês*: impetuous, impulsive, unreflecting; *propetôs*, impulsively, without thinking. *akrasias de to men propeteia to de astheneia* – one sort of acrasia is impetuosity, the other weakness (Ar. *E.N.* 1150b 19); *malista d'hoi oxeis kai melagkholikoi tên propetê akrasian eisin akrateis* – the keen and excitable are especially liable to the impetuous form of acrasia (Ar. *E.N.* 1150b 25); *mê propetôs apokrinomenoi ptaisômen* – lest we stumble by answering without thought (Pl. *Phil.* 45a).

pros hen: in relation to a single thing. Aristotle, in addition to *sunônuma* – things of the same sort with a single name – and *homônuma* – things of a different sort with the same name, recognises things that, though different, share the same name because they contribute to a single central case: *oude gar iatrikon sôma kai ergon kai skeuos legetai oute homônumôs oute kath'hen alla pros hen* – nor are the patient, the treatment and the implement called medical either homonymously or as the same, but as contributing to the one end (Ar. *Met.* 1030b 2); *all'ara ge tôi **aph'henos einai** ê pros hen hapanta suntelein?* – or [are good things so called] through having a single source or all contributing to one end? (Ar. *E.N.* 1096b 27). *aph'henos* and *pros hen* seem to be the same phenomenon differently viewed, as being dependent on or contributing to a central case.

pros ti: the name given by Aristotle to the category of relation in his list of *katêgoriai*: *tôn kata mêdemian sumplokên legomenôn hekaston êtoi ousian sêmainei ê poson ê poion ê pros ti ê ...* – each

143

uncombined term signifies either a substance or a quantity or a quality or a relation or ... (Ar. *Cat.* 1b 25); *pros ti de ta toiauta legetai hosa auta haper estin heterôn einai legetai, ê hopôsoun allôs pros heteron* – such things are said to be relative that are said to be what they are by being of other things, or in some way related to something else (Ar. *Cat.* 6a 37).

protasis: a proposition. Not in Plato. *protasis men oun esti logos kataphatikos ê apophatikos tinos kata tinos* – a proposition, then, is an utterance that affirms or denies something of something (Ar. *An. Pr.* 24a 16). '*A* is *B*' is an assertoric proposition, but propositions may also be apodeictic or problematic: *antistrephousi hai kata to endekhesthai protaseis* – problematic propositions are convertible (Ar. *An. Pr.* 33b 2). A problematic proposition is such as *endekhetai anthrôpon genesthai leukon* – it is possible for a man to become white (Ar. *An. Pr.* 30b 37). Aristotle also calls interrogatives propositions: *ara ge to zôion genos tou anthrôpou? protasis gignetai* – 'Is "animal" the genus of man?' is a proposition (Ar. *Top.* 101b 29). In logical contexts *protasis* often refers to a premiss: *ek pseudôn d'alêthes esti* **sullogizesthai** *kai amphoterôn tôn protaseôn pseudôn ontôn kai tês mias* – it is possible to draw a true conclusion from falsehoods, both when both premisses are false and when one is (Ar. *An. Pr.* 53b 26).

pseudês: false, mistaken; **pseudomai**: to be mistaken; **pseudos**: a falsehood, a mistake. In a suitable context the falsehood may be deliberate and so a lie, but this is rarely the case in philosophy: *amathian ara to toionde legete, to pseudê ekhein doxan kai epseusthai peri tôn pragmatôn tôn pollou axiôn?* – do you say that ignorance is like this – to have a false belief and to be mistaken about matters of importance? (Pl. *Prot.* 358c); *to gar ta mê onta doxazein ê legein tout'esti pou to pseudos* – to think or say what is not is presumably what a falsehood [mistake] is (Pl. *Soph.* 260c). Something may also be called *pseudês* if it is deceptive or spurious: *poteron* **alêtheis** *tautas tas lupas te kai hêdonas ê pseudeis einai lexomen?* – shall we say that such forms of distress are genuine or bogus? (Pl. *Philebus* 36c).

psukhê: usually translated 'soul'; it is better to stick to this dummy translation than to use such substitutes as 'mind', which in some contexts (the mind of a vegetable) may be absurd. A minimum statement to which all philosophers would have agreed is *hê psukhê de touto hôi zômen* – soul is that in virtue of which we are alive (Ar. *De An.* 414a 12). Anything that is alive has a soul: *kath'hekaston zêtêteon tis hekastou psukhê, hoion tis phutou kai tis anthrôpou ê thêriou* – we must examine each kind to find what kind of soul it has, e.g. a plant or a man or a wild animal (Ar. *De An.* 414b 32); *eis thêriou bion anthrôpinê psukhê aphikneitai* – a man's soul takes over the life of a beast [in reincarnation] (Pl. *Phaedrus* 249b). The soul is sometimes thought to be a separate entity in the body and immortal: *ex anagkês agenêton kai athanaton psukhê an eiê* – it is necessary that the soul be uncreated and immortal (Pl. *Phaedrus* 246a); *pasa psukhê asômatos estin ousia kai khôristê* – every soul is an incorporeal substance and separable (Proclus, *Elements of Theology* 186). Or the soul is regarded as separate but mortal: *hê psukhê sôma esti leptomeres par'holon to athroisma paresparmenon ... dialuomenou tou holou athroismatos hê psukhê diaspeiretai* – the soul is a body with fine parts that is spread throughout the structure ... when the whole structure is dissolved the soul is dispersed (Epicurus, *To Herodotus* 63 and 66). Or the soul is regarded as neither a separate entity nor immortal: *ei oun tugkhanei hê psukhê ousa harmonia tis dêlon hoti hotan khalasthêi to sôma hêmôn ametrôs ... tên men psukhên anagkê euthus huparkhei apolôlenai* – if then the soul turns out to be some attunement [of the body], it is clear that when our body is unduly relaxed ... it is necessary that the soul should perish at once (Pl. *Phaedo* 86c). Aristotle's influential view is that *anagkaion ara tên psukhên ousian einai hôs eidos sômatos phusikou dunamei zôên ekhontos* – so it is necessary that the soul should have its nature as the form of a natural body that is potentially alive; *ei gar ên ho ophthalmos zôion psukhê an eiê autou hê opsis* – for if the eye were an animal sight would be its soul; *hoti men oun ouk estin hê psukhê khôristê tou sômatos ... ouk adêlon* – so it is not unclear that the soul is not separable from the body (Ar. *De An.* 412a 19, 412b 17, 413a 3). There is clearly a tension in the works of such philosophers as Plato between the view of the soul as responsible for all manifestations of life, including anger and appetite in the *Republic*, and also including animal life, and the view that it is a rational, directive entity, temporarily lodged in a body, from whose appetites it longs to be free, as sometimes in the *Phaedo* and the *Phaedrus*.

psukhros: cold. One of the four elementary qualities of body in Aristotle's physical theory, together with the ***thermon, hugron*** and

145

xêron – the warm, the wet and the dry: *to d'hudôr psukhron kai hugron, hê de gê psukhron kai xêron* – water is the cold and moist, earth is the cold and dry (Ar. *De Gen. et Cor.* 330b 5).

ptôsis: literally, a fall: *hôsper en ptôsei kubôn* – as in the fall of dice (Pl. *Rep.* 604c). Of words, the *ptôsis* is the termination, including such things as case, adverbs etc.: *parônuma de legetai hosa apo tinos diapheronta têi ptôsei tên kata t'ounoma prosêgorian ekhei, hoion apo tês grammatikês ho grammatikos* – paronyms are said to be things named after something but differing in termination, as a grammarian is named after grammar (Ar. *Cat.* 1a 12). Also in logic of the mood of syllogisms: *en pleiosi skhêmasi kai dia pleionôn ptôseôn* – in many figures and in many moods (Ar. *An.* Pr. 42b 30).

pur: fire. One of the four elements generally accepted after Empedocles. But Heraclitus, followed by the Stoics, had given it a pre-eminence: *kosmon tonde oute tis theôn oute anthrôpôn epoiêsen, all'ên aei kai estin kai estai, pur aeizôon, haptomenon metra kai aposbennumenon metra* – the universe was made by no god or man, but always was, is and will be, an everlasting fire kindling and being quenched in turn (Heraclitus in Clement, *Strômateis* 5.104.1). In Aristotle's universe the four elements are all in the sublunar sphere, fire being the outermost, and all move naturally to their proper place: *ei gar estin hekastou phora tis tôn haplôn sômatôn phusei, hoion tôi puri men anô ...* – for if there is some natural local motion of each of the simple bodies, as upwards for fire ... (Ar. *Phys.* 214b 13). *to men gar pur thermon kai xêron* – for fire is hot and dry (Ar. *De Gen. et Cor.* 330b 2): this distinguishes it from the other elements, *aêr, gê* and *hudôr*, that are either cold or moist, or both.

R

rhein: to flow: *potamous ... ex tôn hupsêlôn rheontas* – rivers flowing from high places (Pl. *Laws* 682c); *ton rheonta khronon* – the time that flows (Simplicius, *Physics* 1163.2). Importantly, of the doctrine attributed to the Pythagoreans, Heraclitus and Cratylus by Plato, and to Plato also by Aristotle, that everything is in a continual state of flux, which is clearly the genesis of the neoplatonic, and perhaps Platonic, doctrine that the perceptible world is one of *genesis* – becoming – in contrast with the world of being: *hôs iontôn hapantôn aei kai rheontôn* – that everything is in process and flowing (Pl. *Crat.* 439c); *ek neou te gar sunêthês genomenos prôton Kratulôi kai tais Hêrakleiteiois doxais, hôs hapantôn tôn aisthêtôn aei rheontôn … tauta men kai husteron houtôs hupelaben* – for [Plato] having become familiar when still young with Cratylus and the Heraclitean opinions, that all perceptible things were in everlasting flux … he continued to hold this opinion on this matter (Ar. *Met.* 987a 32).

rhêma: basically, any verbal expression exceeding a word (*onoma*): *tou kallous tôn onomatôn kai rhêmatôn* – the beauty of the words and expressions (Pl. *Symp.* 189b); *hina anti rhêmatos [Dii philos] onoma [Diphilos] genêtai* – in order that instead of an expression [loved by Zeus] we may have a name [Diphilus] (Pl. *Crat.* 399c); *all'oistha … hou moi dokei einai to rhêma to phanai dikaion einai tous philous ôphelein tous d'ekhthrous blaptein?* – do you know to whom I attribute the statement that it is just to help friends and harm enemies? (Pl. *Rep.* 336a). Sometimes, words as opposed to thought: *ean tis rhêmati hamartêi* – if someone makes a verbal slip (Pl. *Gorg.* 489b); *mêdeis oun pros to rhêma blepôn enantiousthai nomizetô tous philosophous* – so let nobody, looking at the words, think that the philosophers are disagreeing (Simplicius, *Physics* 1155.20). *rhêma* also has a more specific sense in which it is a verb and *onoma* a noun: *rhêma de esti to prossêmainon khronon, hou meros ouden sêmainei khôris, kai estin aei tôn kath'heterou legomenôn sêmeion. legô d'hoti prossêmainei khronon hoion hugieia men onoma, to de hugiainei rhêma· … to de oukh hugiainei … estô aoriston rhêma· … to hugiainen ê to hugianei ou rhêma, alla **ptôsis** rhêmatos* – a verb is that which also indicates time, of which no part is independently meaningful, and which alaways means something that is said of something else. I say that it also indicates time, as, for example, 'health' is a noun but 'is healthy' is a verb; … but let us call 'is not healthy' an indefinite verb; … 'was healthy' or 'will be healthy' is not a verb but a declension of a verb (Ar. *De Int.* 16b 6); *suntheis pragma praxei di'onomatos kai rhêmatos* – combining deed with doing by means of a noun and verb (Pl. *Soph.* 262e).

rhêtôr: an orator; *rhêtorikê*: rhetoric; *rhêtorikos*: versed in rhetoric: *hoi rhêtores hotan legôsin en tôi dêmôi* – the orators when they speak in public (Pl. *Euthyd.* 284b); *hê rhêtorikê an eiê tekhnê psukhagôgia tis dia logôn* – rhetoric is an art of influencing souls by means of words (Pl. *Phaedrus* 261a). Aristotle, like many others of his time, wrote a textbook on the art of rhetoric, giving the definition *estô dê hê rhêtorikê dunamis peri hekaston tou theôrêsai to endekhomenon pithanon* – let us say that rhetoric is the power to see that which is capable of persuading on each matter (Ar. *Rhet.* 1355b 25). *rhêtorikôs gar me epikheireis elegkhein* – you are trying to refute me in rhetorical fashion (Pl. *Gorg.* 471e). *hê rhêtorikê* is feminine because *tekhnê* is understood.

rhusmos: an Ionic version of *rhuthmos*, used by Democritus to mean 'shape'; he wrote a book called *Peri tôn diapherontôn rhusmôn* – 'On different shapes' (Democritus, fr. 5). *diapherein gar phasin to on rhusmôi kai **diathigêi** kai **tropêi** monon ... toutôn de ho men rhusmos skhêma estin* – for they [the atomists] say that what is differs only in rhythm and touch and turning ... of these rhythm is shape (Ar. *Met.* 985b 15).

rhuthmos: in philosophy, rhythm: *têi tês kinêseôs taxei rhuthmos onoma eiê* – the name for the ordering of change is rhythm (Pl. *Laws* 665a); *to melos ek triôn esti sugkeimenon, logou te kai harmonias kai rhuthmou* – song is composed of three elements, words, melody and rhythm (Pl. *Rep.* 398d); *k'an tais eirêmenais tekhnais hapasai men poiountai tên mimêsin en rhuthmôi kai logôi kai harmoniaï, toutois d'ê khôris ê memigmenois· hoion harmoniaï men kai rhuthmôi khrômenai monon hê te aulêtikê kai hê kitharistikê ... autôi de tôi rhuthmôi khôris harmonias hê tôn orkhêstôn* – in the aforesaid arts all achieve representation in rhythm, words and melody, using them all together or separately: e.g. oboe-playing and harping use melody and rhythm alone ... while the art of dancing employs just rhythm on its own (Ar. *Poetics* 1447a 21). See *rhusmos*.

S

sêmainein: to signify, to show, to mean. Of a person: *mê sêmênantos sou hoti boulei auto tethnanai* – if you have not signified that you wish it to be dead (Pl. *Phaedo* 62c). Of an argument: *hôs ho logos sêmainei* – as the argument shows (Pl. *Gorg.* 511b). Of a word: *ho gar anax kai ho hektôr skhedon ti t'auton sêmainei* – for 'ruler' and 'holder' mean more or less the same (Pl. *Crat.* 393a). Absolutely: [*onoma dipoun*] *to men ek sêmainontos kai*

asêmou plên ouk en onomati sêmainontos kai asêmou – one sort of
[dysyllabic name] consists of a meaningful and a meaningless
component, except that within the name they are not meaningful
and meaningless (Ar. *Poetics* 1457a 31).

sêmeiousthai: to be a sign; *sêmeion*: a sign: *to eiôthos sêmeion to
daimonion* – the usual divine sign (Pl. *Theages* 129b); *hekastôi tôn
ontôn sêmeion te kai onoma poiôn* – making a sign and name for
each thing that is (Pl. *Crat.* 427c); *hoion ho kêros tou daktulou aneu
tou sidêrou kai tou khrousou dekhetai to sêmeion* – as the wax
receives the sign on the ring without the iron and the gold (Ar. *De
An.* 424a 19). In addition to these and other non-technical uses
there are three that are technical. (1) In Aristotle's logic:
*enthumêma de esti **sullogismos** ex eikotôn ê sêmeiôn ... sêmeion
bouletai einai **protasis** apodeiktikê ê anagkaia ê endoxos ... ean men
oun hê mia lekhthêi protasis, sêmeion gignetai monon, ean de kai hê
hetera proslêphthêi, sullogismos* – an enthymeme is an argument
from probabilities or from signs ... a sign is the sort of probative
proposition that is either necessary or commonly received ... if the
one premiss is stated we have merely a sign, if the other is added, a
syllogism (Ar. *An. Pr.* 70a 10) [thus 'the ambitious are generous, so
Pittacus is generous' would be an enthymeme, which would become
a syllogism if 'Pittacus is ambitious' were added]. Aristotle does not
always use *sêmeion* in this way: thus in *De Anima* (421a 18) the
alleged fact that people with an acute sense of touch are cleverer
than those without it is given as a *sêmeion* that it is because of a
good sense of touch that men are more intelligent than other
animals. (2) In later, notably Epicurean and Stoic, philosophy, a
sêmeion is some perceptible state of affairs that is used as a sign of
the imperceptible: *sêmeia d'epi tôn en tois meteôrois sunteloumenôn
pherein tôn par'hêmin tina phainomenôn, ha theôreitai hêi
huparkhei, kai ou ta en meteôrois phainomena* – we have signs of
the happenings in the heavens from some of the phenomena here
about us, such that we can see how they come about, as is not the
case with heavenly phenomena (Epicurus, *To Pythocles* 87); *kapnon
idontes sêmeioutai pur* – when we have seen smoke, that is a sign of
fire (Sextus Empiricus, *Outlines of Pyrrhonism* 2.102). (3) A point in
space: *ou gar hê autê estin hê apo tou A lambanomenê periphereia
kai hê apo tou B kai tou G kai tôn allôn hekastou sêmeiôn* – for the
circumference beginning from A is not the same as that from B and
that from G and from the other points of each (Ar. *Phys.* 240b 1); a

point in time: *eti ti mallon epi tôide tôi sêmeiôi aei on proteron ephtharê ê mê on apeiron egeneto* – still more, does something everlasting before cease to exist at this moment or, not having existed, become endless? (Ar. *De Caelo* 283a 11).

skepsis: enquiry, investigation; *skeptesthai*: to enquire, to investigate; *skeptikos*: concerned with or inclined to investigation, with special reference to the sceptical philosophers: *apetês men mestê hê dia tôn ommatôn skepsis* – investigation using the eyes is full of illusion (Pl. *Phaedo* 83a); *peri gar toi tou megistou hê skepsis* – our investigation is concerning the most important matter (Pl. *Rep.* 578c); *kai eu mala skepsamenos apokrinou* – consider well before you reply (Pl. *Gorg.* 496c). *hê skeptikê agôgê* – the sceptical procedure – was directed by the Sceptics against the alleged dogmatism without grounds of e.g. Platonism and Stoicism. They advocated *skepsis* – undogmatic investigation – and *epokhê* – suspension of judgment: *apoleipetai ta hupo tôn stôikôn pros tous apo tês skepseôs legomena para meros kai hupo tôn skeptikôn pros ekeinous legesthai* – it remains for the attacks by the Stoics on the Sceptics to be made in their turn by the Sceptics on the Stoics (Sextus Empiricus, *Adversus Mathematicos* 7.433); *hoi apo tês skepseôs* was used as a synonym for *hoi skeptikoi*. *skepsis* never means 'disbelief'.

skhêma: shape, form: *estô … hêmin touto skhêma ho monon tôn ontôn tugkhanei khrômati aei hepomenon* – let … shape be for us that which alone among what is always follows on colour (Pl. *Meno* 75b); *tên autên tou skhêmatos morphên* – shape is the same as form (Ar. *Part. An.* 640b 34). In transferred senses: *basileias skhêma* – the characteristic form of a kingdom (Ar. *E.N.* 1160b 25); *ta tês kômôidias skhêmata* – the forms of comedy (Ar. *Poetics* 1448b 36); *muthou skhêma ekhon* – having the form of a myth (Pl. *Tim.* 22c). Logically, the figures of the syllogism: *esti de kai anagein pantas tous sullogismous eis tous en tôi prôtôi skhêmati katholou sullogismous* – it is also possible to reduce all syllogisms to the universal syllogisms in the first figure (Ar. *An. Pr.* 29b 1). *skhêma* and the verb *skhêmatizesthai* are also used of a false appearance: *prothura men kai skhêma … aretês* – a façade and appearance of excellence (Pl. *Rep.* 365c); *oukh hupo skhêmatizesthai tou erôntos all'alêthôs touto peponthotos* – not a pretending lover but one who really experiences it (Pl. *Phaedrus* 255a).

skopos: a target, goal or end aimed at, to which one looks (the root is as in *skopein*, to look at). The central case of the bowman aiming at his target is never lost from view: *houtos emoige dokei ho skopos einai pros hon bleponta dei zên* – this seems to me to be the target with an eye on which one ought to live (Pl. *Gorg.* 507d); *hoion toxotên hienta parallaxai tou skopou kai hamartein* – like an archer to shoot and pass the target and miss it (Pl. *Theaet.* 194a); *esti tis skopos pros hon apoblepôn ho ton logon ekhôn epiteinei kai aniêsin* – there is a certain target with an eye on which he who understands [literally] tightens and relaxes his bow-string, i.e. adjusts his activities (Ar. *E.N.* 1138b 22).

sôma: in Homer, always a dead body of man or animal. In philosophy the term is extended to include, first, living bodies and then all three-dimensional solids. (1) As opposed to *psukhê*: *to sôma estin hêmin sêma* – our body is a tomb (Pl. *Gorg.* 493a); *hai kata to sôma hêdonai* – bodily pleasures (Pl. *Rep.* 328d); *pantôn sômatôn epekeina estin hê psukhês ousia* – the nature of the soul is superior to all bodies (Proclus, *Elements of Theology* 20). (2) Of physical objects in general: *ei gar esti sômatos logos epipedôi hôrismenon, ouk an eiê sôma apeiron* – if the account of a body is that which is bounded by a surface, there will not be an infinite body (Ar. *Phys.* 204b 5); *mêkos kai platos kai bathos, hois horizetai sôma pan* – length, breadth and depth, by which every body is defined (Ar. *Phys.* 209a 4). (3) Mathematical solid: *mêkos de grammê, platos de epiphaneia, bathos de sôma* – a line has length, a surface breadth and a body depth (Ar. *Met.* 1020a 13).

sômatikos: bodily (as opposed to *psukhikos* – psychical) or corporeal (as opposed to *asômatos* – incorporeal): *ta d'egkômia tôn ergôn kai tôn sômatikôn kai tôn psukhikôn* – encomia are for deeds, whether physical or psychical (Ar. *E.N.* 1101b 33); *dieirêsthôsan dê hai psukhikai kai hai sômatikai* [*hêdonai*] – the psychic pleasures must be distinguished from the bodily (Ar. *E.N.* 1117b 28); *diapherontai de peri tôn arkhôn ... malista men hoi sômatikas poiountes tois asômatous* – those who make the first principles corporeal differ especially from those who make them incorporeal (Ar. *De An.* 404b 30).

sophia: skill, intellectual excellence; *sophos*: skilful, excellent in intelligence. These terms are often translated as 'wisdom' and 'wise', but, except in translated phrases such as 'the seven wise men', 'wisdom' and 'wise', have, in English, a practical reference (see *phronêsis*), whereas *sophia* and *sophos* are usually theoretical in reference. Generally, and sometimes in philosophy, the terms are applied to skill in a craft: *entautha men oun outhen allo sêmainontes tên sophian ê hoti aretê tekhnês estin* – in such contexts we mean nothing by *sophia* other than excellence in a skill (Ar. *E.N.* 1141a 11); *oukoun hê êniokheia sophia estin* – surely driving is a skill (Pl. *Laches* 123d). Of philosophical insight: *eiê an hê sophia nous kai epistêmê* – intellectual excellence is intuitive and discursive understanding (Ar. *E.N.* 1141a 17); *Anaxagoran kai Thalên kai tous toioutous sophous men phronimous d'ou phasin einai, hotan idôsin agnoountas ta sumpheronta heautois* – men call Anaxagoras and Thales and the like intellectually excellent but not wise, when they see that they do not know what is to their advantage (Ar. *E.N.* 1141b 3).

sophistês: a sophist. Originally simply a man of high scientific attainments – the seven wise men were called *sophistai*. Those who taught professionally were the purveyors of higher education in fifth-century Greece. Plato disapproved of their taking payment for teaching and philosophically thought that they did not truly know about what they taught. Some, like Protagoras and Gorgias in the dialogues named after them, are treated with a certain respect, even if defeated in argument; others, like Thrasymachus in the *Republic* and Polus in the *Gorgias*, are presumptuous fools; still others, like those in the *Euthydemus*, are tricksters with words, arguing for victory. These last came to be regarded, unjustly, as typical, as the word 'sophistical' suggests: *ouk an aiskhunoio eis tous Hellênas sauton sophistên parekhôn?* – would you not be ashamed to present yourself to the Greeks as a sophist? (Pl. *Prot.* 312a); *neôn kai plousiôn emmisthos thêreutês* – [the sophist is] one who preys for money on the young and the rich (Pl. *Soph.* 231d). Neutrally: *kalousi ... tautên diametron hoi sophistai* – the professors call this line a diameter (Pl. *Meno* 85b). See *sophistikos*.

sophistikos: neutrally, of a sophist; pejoratively, sophistical. Pejoratively: *peri de tôn sophistikôn elegkhôn kai tôn phainomenôn men elegkhôn, ontôn de paralogismôn all ouk elegkhôn* – concerning sophistical arguments and apparent arguments that are paralogisms and not arguments (Ar. *S.E.* 164a 20); *esti gar hê sophistikê phainomenê sophia ousa d'ou, kai ho sophistês khrêmatistês, apo phainomenês sophias all'ouk ousês* – for the sophistic art is an apparent and not a real intellectual excellence and the sophist is a businessman called from his apparent but unreal intellectual excellence (Ar. *S.E.* 165a 22). Neutrally: *tên sophistikên tekhnên* – the art of the sophist (Pl. *Prot*. 310d). See *sophistês*.

sôphrôn: temperate; *sôphronein*: to be temperate; *sôphronôs*: temperately; *sôphrosunê*: temperance. These are standard, but dummy, translations; the use of the terms can be found from the following quotations. (1) *ho men mainetai, ho de sôphronei* – the one is mad, the other of sound mind (Pl. *Phaedrus* 244a); this use is uncommon in philosophy. (2) *hê sôphrosunê ... to peri tês epithumias mê eptoêsthai all'oligôrôs ekhein kai kosmiôs* – temperance is to be unconcerned about appetite, but to treat it with sober contempt (Pl. *Phaedo* 68c); *mesotês esti peri hêdonas hê sôphrosunê ... peri de tas sômatikas eiê an hê sôphrosunê, ou pasas de oude tautas ... peri tas toiautas d'hêdonas hê sôphrosunê kai he akolasia hôn kai ta loipa zôia koinônei ... hautai d'eisin haphê kai geusis* – temperance is a mean concerning pleasures ... but temperance is concerned with the bodily pleasures, and not all of these ... but temperance and intemperance are about those pleasures that are shared with other animals ... and these are [the pleasures of] touch and taste (Ar. *E.N.* 1179b 25, 1118a 1, 1118a 23). So *sôphrosunê* is a mean state with regard to such pleasures as those of eating, drinking and sex.

sphaira: non-technically, a ball: *hôsper sphairan ekdexamenos ton logon*: taking over the argument like a ball [thrown from one person to another] (Pl. *Euthyd*. 277b); *eukuklou sphairês enaligkion ogkôi* – [reality is] like the bulk of a well-rounded ball (Parmenides in Simplicius, *Physics* 146.16). Technically, a sphere. (1) Mathematically: *proteron an eiê tôn skhêmatôn ho kuklos· hôsautôs de kai sphaira tôn stereôn* – first among [plane] figures is the circle: similarly the sphere among solids (Ar. *De Caelo* 286b 24). (2) Astronomically: *tou ... pantos ouranou sphairoeidous ontos* – the whole heaven being spherical (Pl. *Tim*. 62d); *hê aplanês sphaira ... tôn planômenôn sphairôn ... tês tou Kronou sphairas* – the sphere of the fixed stars ... the planetary spheres ... the sphere of Saturn (Simplicius, *Physics* 588.7, 589.30, 589.18). It appears from *De Caelo* 287a 4 ff. that Aristotle conceived of the outermost sphere of

153

the fixed stars as occupying the whole volume of space from its outer surface to the sphere of Saturn, which occupied the next volume of space, and so on through the rest of the spheres until finally the sublunary sphere was the volume from the moon to the earth's surface: *ta de katô haptetai tês epanô sphairas* – for what is below touches the sphere above (*De Caelo* 287a 8). But Simplicius, and apparently others, believed that each sphere was solid to the centre so as to interpenetrate, as is clear from Simplicius, *Physics* 643.18 ff. There were eight generally recognised spheres, those of the fixed stars, the sun, the moon, and the five known planets, *Kronos* (Saturn), *Zeus* (Jupiter), *Arês* (Mars), *Aphroditê* (Venus), *Hermês* (Mercury).

stasis: etymologically related to *histanai*, to stand, this has a variety of meanings. (1) Status, position: *en têi kallioni stasei einai* – to be in the better position (Pl. *Phaedrus* 253d). (2) As contrary of *kinêsis*, unchangingness: *hê de stasis apophasis tou ienai bouletai einai* – being stationary is the negation of going (Pl. *Crat.* 426d); *toutôn men gar hekaston en heautôi arkhên ekhei kinêseôs kai staseôs* – each of these [natural objects] has the principle of changing or not changing in itself (Ar. *Phys.* 192b 14); *polloi oun kai ou mia hê kinêsis hôn estin êremia metaxu, hôste ei tis kinêsis stasei dialambanetai ou mia oude sunekhês* – there are many changes and not one when rest intervenes, so that if some change is interrupted by a pause it is not single nor continuous (Ar. *Phys.* 228b 4). This last quotation raises the question whether *stasis* and *êremia* are synonyms. They appear to be so in Aristotle, but Simplicius says *all'ou pasa stasis êremia estin, all'hê meta kinêsin* – but not all changelessness is rest, but only that after change (*Physics* 264.26). Plotinus also applies the term *stasis* to changelessness in the intelligible world in *Enneads* 6.3.27. (3) Politically, civil strife: *epi ... têi tou oikeiou ekhthraï stasis keklêtai* – the name 'stasis' is given to enmity with one's own people (Pl. *Rep.* 470b); *hê de penia stasin empoiei kai kakourgian* – poverty breeds civil strife and crime (Ar. *Pol.* 1265b 12).

stereos: hard, solid. (1) Non-technically: *hairêsesthai kusi polemein stereois kai iskhnois* – to be about to choose to fight against hard and lean dogs (Pl. *Rep.* 422d); *touto ... êdê stereôteron ... kai ouketi rhaïdion ekhein hoti tis eipêi* – that ... is already harder ... and it is no longer easy to know what one should say (Pl. *Rep.* 348e). (2)

Technically (a) mathematically: *trigôna de isopleura sunistamena tettara kata treis epipedous mian sterean gônian poiei* – four isosceles triangles adjoining each other in three planes make one solid angle; (b) physically: *kai gar epipeda kai sterea ekhei ta phusika sômata kai mêkê kai stigmas peri hôn skopei ho mathêmatikos* – for natural bodies contain planes and solids and the lengths and points that the mathematician studies (Ar. *Phys.* 193b 23).

sterêsis: privation, lack, etymologically connected with *steresthai*: to lack, be deprived of: *eiper sterometha epistêmês* – if we are deprived of understanding (Pl. *Theaet.* 196e). Apart from obvious non-technical uses, as in *sterêsis de estin aisthêseôs ho thanatos* – death is the privation of perception (Epicurus, *To Menoeceus* 124), *sterêsis*, together with *hule*, matter, and *eidos*, form, is one of the three primitive concepts used by Aristotle for explaining *kinêsis*, change. Thus, to use his example, when a non-musical man becomes musical, the man who is, in this context, the *hupokeimenon* (substrate) gains the *eidos* of musicality instead of *sterêsis*, being the sort of thing that has the *dunamis* (potentiality) to become musical. *phamen gignesthai men mêthen haplôs ek mê ontos, pôs mentoi gignesthai ek mê ontos hoion kata sumbebêkos, ek gar tês sterêseôs* – we say that nothing comes to exist simply out of the non-existent, but comes into being in a qualified way, for it does so from privation (Ar. *Phys.* 191b 13); *hêmeis gar tên hulên kai sterêsin heteron phamen einai* – for we say that matter and privation are different (Ar. *Phys.* 192a 3).

stoa: a porch. From their practice of meeting in the *stoa poikilê*, the decorated porch, at Athens, certain philosophers centred on Zeno became known as the *Stôïkoi* or simply the *Stoa* or, very commonly, *hoi apo tês stoas* – those from the porch. In English, the Stoics used to be known as the Porch at one time. *hoi apo tês stoas ekhontai têsde tês diaireseôs* – those from the porch adopt this division [of the parts of philosophy] (Sextus Empiricus, *Adversus Mathematicos* 7.16); *eien d'an kai hoi Stôïkoi tautês tês doxês* – this [the conflagration] would be the opinion of the Stoics (Simplicius, *Physics* 480.28).

stoikheion: a primitive element in any kind of system. (1) A letter of the alphabet: *stoikheion phônês phônê asunthetos* – a letter is an uncompounded sound in a sound [a syllable] (pseudo-Pl. *Def.* 414e); *eikositessarôn toinun stoikheiôn ontôn tês eggrammatou phônês* –

155

there being twenty-four letters of written sound (Sextus Empiricus, *Adversus Mathematicos* 1.100). (2) In nature: *legomen arkhas auta tithemenoi stoikheia tou pantos* – we call them principles, positing them as elements of the universe (Pl. *Tim.* 48b); *ta hôs en hulês eidei legomena stoikheia tettara prôtos eipen* – [Empedocles] first stated the four elements of the material sort (Ar. *Met.* 985a 32). (3) In demonstration: *hai gar prôtai apodeixeis kai en pleiosin apodeixesin enuparkhousai, hautai stoikheia tôn apodeixeôn legontai* – for the primitive proofs that occur in many proofs are called the elements of proofs (Ar. *Met.* 1014a 26). The *Stoikheia* – 'Elements' – of Euclid and other geometers are so called in this last use.

suggignôskein: to pardon. See *suggnômê*.

suggnômê: frequently, pardon or forgiveness, as *suggignôskein* is to pardon or forgive and *suggnômonikos* is forgiving: *tôn ... akousiôn suggnômên ekhein* – to pardon the unintended (Pl. *Phaedrus* 233c); *epi men tois hekousiois epainôn kai psogôn gignomenôn, epi de tois akousiois suggnômê* – praise and blame being bestowed on the intended, but pardon for the contrary to intention (Ar. *E.N.* 1109b 32); *suggignôske moi* – forgive me (Pl. *Phaedrus* 230d). But sometimes it is rather understanding of what might seem at first sight to require censure or forgiveness, but in the circumstances is proper: *hê de suggnômê gnômê esti kritikê tou epieikous orthê* – understanding is the correct critical judgment of the equitable man (Ar. *E.N.* 1143a 23); *epieikes kai suggnômon* – equitable and understanding (Pl. *Laws* 757d); *ho epeidan idêis te kai akousêis tina suggnômên hexeis hoti eikotôs ara ôknoun te kai ededoikê houtô paradoxon logon legein* – when you see and hear it you will gain a certain understanding that I reasonably hesitated and feared to say something so paradoxical (Pl. *Rep.* 472a).

sugkrinein: to combine; *sugkrisis*: combination. Mainly used in natural philosophy in accounts of the nature of change: *hoi men sugkrinesthai kai diakrinesthai ta atoma sômata kai ta tettara stoikheia legontes, Anaxagoras de ekkrinesthai tas homoiomereias apo tou migmatos legôn* – some saying that the atoms [Democritus] and the four elements [Empedocles] were combined and separated, but Anaxagoras that the homeomeries were extruded from the mixture (Simplicius, *Physics* 1120.20); *sugkrinetai gar kai diakrinetai kai ta anaisthêta sômata* – for imperceptible bodies also are combined and separated (Simplicius, *Physics* 1095.4); *ta men sugkrinonta, ta de diakrinonta* – combining some things and separating others (Pl. *Tim.* 67d); *puknôsis de kai manôsis sugkrisis kai diakrisis* – condensation and rarefaction are combination and separation (Ar. *Phys.* 260b 11). But *sugkrisis* is also comparison: *tên amphoin poioumenos sugkrisin* – making a comparison of the two (Simplicius, *Physics* 35.14).

sullogismos: argument; *sullogistikos*: argumentative; *sullogizesthai*: to argue. Generally applicable to any ratiocination; *drôsi tauta agnoountes autôn hekasta, ou sullogizontai* – they do these things being ignorant of these matters, and do not take thought (Pl. *Laws* 670c); *sullogisai dê koinêi met'emou ti hêmin sumbainei ek tôn hômologoumenôn* – think out with me where we stand on the basis of what we have agreed on (Pl. *Gorg.* 498c). In a narrower use, the syllogism as in Aristotle's logical works: *estai sullogistikê men protasis haplôs kataphasis ê apophasis tinos kata tinos, sullogismos de esti logos en hôi tithentôn tinôn heteron ti tôn keimenôn ex anagkês sumbainei* – a simple syllogistic premiss is an affirmation or negation of something of something else, and a syllogism is an utterance in which, certain things being posited, something other than the posited necessarily results (Ar. *An. Pr.* 24a 28); *pas sullogismos estin dia triôn horôn monon, toutou d'ontos dêlon hôs kai ek duo protaseôn kai ou pleionôn* – every syllogism contains only three terms, and, this being so, it is clear that it contains two premisses and not more (Ar. *An. Pr.* 42a 31). Aristotle also recognised practical syllogisms of which the conclusion was a decision to act or the act itself and the premisses were of the general form 'An *A* is needed and this is an *A*'; *hoi gar sullogismoi tôn praktôn arkhên ekhontes eisin epeidê toionde to telos kai to ariston* – practical syllogisms have the major premiss: 'a thing of this kind is the goal and the best' (Ar. *E.N.* 1144a 31).

sumbainein: to come about, to follow, to result. See *sumbebêkos*.

sumbebêkos is the perfect participle of *sumbainein*. Non-technically, in Plato: *ta emoi sumbebêkota* – the things that happened to me (Pl. *Apol.* 32a). In Aristotle it is a technical term, traditionally and unsatisfactorily transliterated as 'accident' from the Latin *'accidens'*, which is something that happens and not an accident. *sumbebêkota* are features of a thing that do not belong to it necessarily or from the thing's own nature (*kath'hauto*), but which simply happen to be present as a matter of fact. *sumbebêkota* are present *kata sumbebêkos* and not *kath'hauto*: *kath'hauta d'hosa huparkhei te en tôi ti estin, hoion trigônôi grammê ... kai hosois tôn huparkhontôn autois auta en tôi logôi enuparkhousi tôi ti esti dêlounti, hoion to euthu huparkhei grammêi kai to peripheres ... hosa de mêdeterôs huparkhei sumbebêkota hoion to mousikon ê leukon tôi zôiôi* – 'as such' are what belong to the definition, as a line is part of the definition of a triangle ... and to such things as themselves figure in the definition of the things that belong to them, as straight and circular belong to a line ... but such things as belong in neither of these ways are happenings, such as the presence of musicality or whiteness in an animal (Ar. *An. Po.* 73a 34); *to sumbebêkos gar endekhetai mê huparkhein* – for what happens may possibly not occur (Ar. *An. Po.* 75a 19). But sometimes Aristotle uses *sumbebêkos* more generally of predicates, including the *kath'hauto*: *sumbebêkos kath'hauto* – inhering as such (Ar. *Phys.* 203b 33).

sumperasma: the conclusion of an argument, a technical term of logic not found in Plato. *ouk estai sumperasma out'anagkaion outh'huparkhon einai, mê lêphtheisês anagkaias ê huparkhousês protaseôs* – there will not be either an apodeictic [*S* is necessarily *P*] or an assertoric [*S* is *P*] conclusion unless an apodeictic or assertoric premiss is provided (Ar. *An. Pr.* 32a 13); *entautha d'ek tôn duô **protaseôn** to sumperasma gignetai hê praxis* – there [in the **sullogismos** *tôn praktôn*] the conclusion from the two premisses becomes an action (Ar. *De Motu Animalium* 701a 12).

sunagein: to collect; *sunagôgê*: the action of collecting. Non-technically: *sunaxomen tas te numphas kai tous numphious* – we shall bring together the brides and the bridegrooms (Pl. *Rep.* 459e). Also used as a technical term by Plato, particularly in the *Sophist* and the *Phaedrus*, where the contrary of *sunagôgê* is *diairesis*, division: *toutôn dê egôge autos te erastês, ô Phaidre, tôn diaireseôn kai sunagôgôn* – I am myself, Phaedrus, a lover of these divisions and collections (Pl. *Phaedrus* 266b). Collection appears to be bringing together under a single genus a variety of things which are then to be divided formally into species and sub-species: *eis mian te idean sunorônta agein ta pollakhêi diesparmena* – to survey under one form things that are scattered in many areas (Pl. *Phaedrus*

158

265d). In Aristotle and in later philosophy *sunagein* is often to draw a conclusion: *endekhetai de **sullogizesthai** kai sunagein ta men ek **sullelogismenôn** proteron, ta d'ex asullogistôn men, deomenôn de sullogismou* – it is possible to argue and draw a conclusion either from things previously argued or from things not argued for but needing argument (Ar. *Rhet.* 1357a 7); *dunaton esti ek tou te 'ei hêmera esti phôs estin' kai 'alla mên hêmera estin' sunagesthai tên epiphoran to 'phôs estin'* – it is possible from 'if it is day it is light' and 'but it is day' to conclude the consequent 'it is light' (Sextus Empiricus, *Adversus Mathematicos* 8.228). From this use of *sunagein* comes the adjective **sunaktikos**, conclusive: *tôn de logôn hoi men sunaktikoi, hoi de ou* – some arguments are conclusive, others not (Sextus Empiricus, *Adversus Mathematicos* 8.303).

sunaktikos. See *sunagein*.

sunaptein (perfect passive participle *sunêmmenos*): to join together, to unite, and, intransitively, to be connected with: *sunaptôn arthron arthrôi* – joining limb to limb (Pl. *Tim.* 75d); *hôsper ek mias koruphês sunêmmenô* – like two joined together from one head (Pl. *Phaedo* 60b); *tôi de katholou kai tôi genei kai hai ideai sunaptousin* – the ideas also unite with the universal and the genus (Ar. *Met.* 1042a 15). The most important use is of the perfect passive *sunêmmenon* to mean 'hypothetical proposition' in later writers. The usual name for the antecedent 'If *p*' is *to hêgoumenon*, and for the consequent 'then *q*' *to hepomenon* or *to lêgon*. In a hypothetical argument of the form 'If *p* then *q*, but *p*, therefore *q*' [or 'but not *q*, therefore not *p*'] the second premiss is called *hê proslêpsis*: *ei adunaton topon apeiron einai, en topôi de pan sôma, adunaton apeiron einai sôma. alla mên to hêgoumenon, to ara hepomenon. kai to men sunêmmenon kataskeuazein hôs prodêlon parêke, tên de proslêpsin tên legousan 'alla adunaton topon apeiron' tithêsi* – if it is impossible for place to be boundless and every body is in a place, it is impossible for there to be an unbounded body. But the antecedent is true, so the consequent is true. But [Aristotle] omitted setting out the hypothetical, as being utterly obvious, but he includes the further premiss that says 'but it is impossible for place to be boundless' (Simplicius, *Physics* 489.31); *en gar tois sunêmmenois tote hugiês hê kata antistrophên akolouthia hotan to antikeimenon tou hepomenou labontes epenegkômen to tou hêgoumenou antikeimenon* – for in hypotheticals the sequence by

159

conversion is sound when we take the opposite of the consequent and conclude to the opposite of the antecedent [i.e. If 'If *p* then *q*', then 'If not-*q* then not-*p*' is sound] (Simplicius, *Physics* 104.30); *tôn de en tôi sunêmmenôi axiômatôn to meta ton 'ei' ê ton 'eiper' sundesmon tetagmenon hêgoumenon te kai prôton kaleitai to de loipon lêgon te kai deuteron* – of the propositions in a hypothetical we call the one coming after the conjunction 'if' or 'if in fact' the antecedent and the first, and the other one is called the consequent and the second (Sextus Empiricus, *Adversus Mathematicos* 8.110). Sometimes the term *sunêmmenon* seems to be applied to the consequent only: *kai to men sunêmmenon alêthes dia to axiôma* – and the consequent is true because of the proposition [= antecedent] being true (Simplicius, *Physics* 171.21).

sunekheia: continuity; *sunekhôs*: continuously; *sunekhês*: continuous; from the verb *sunekhein*, to hold together. Non-technically: *polemos aei pasi dia biou sunekhês esti* – there is always a continuous war for all throughout life (Pl. *Laws* 625e); *ex onomatôn men monon sunekhôs legomenôn ouk esti pote logos* – there is never a sentence from a continuous string of nouns on their own (Pl. *Soph*. 262a). Technically, as opposed to *diêirêmenon*, discrete: *legô de sunekhes hotan t'auto genêtai kai hen to hekaterou peras hois haptontai kai sunekhontai* – I call that continuous when the boundary of each at which they touch and are held together becomes one (Ar. *Met*. 1069a 5); *dikhôs gar legetai kai to mêkos kai ho khronos apeiron, kai holôs pan to sunekhes, êtoi kata diairesin ê tois eskhatois* – both length and time, and everything whatsoever that is continuous, are called infinites in two senses, either as divisible, or at their extremities (Ar. *Phys*. 233a 24); *koinônia kai sunekheia kai tautotês* – community, continuity and identity (Proclus, *Elements of Theology* 21).

sunesis: intelligence in practical matters; *sunetos*, intelligent, is not found in Plato. *phoboumenoi … tous … pepaideumenous mê sunesei kreittous genôntai* – fearing … the educated, lest they become superior by their intelligence (Pl. *Phaedrus* 232c); *sophian men kai sunesin kai phronêsin dianoêtikas* – intellect, intelligence and wisdom are mental [excellences] (Ar. *E.N.* 1103a 5); *oute gar peri tôn aei ontôn kai akinêtôn hê sunesis estin oute peri tôn gignomenôn hotououn, alla peri hôn aporêseien an tis kai bouleusaito* – for intelligence is not concerned with the everlasting and unchanging or about anything whatsoever that changes, but concerned with things about which one may be puzzled and plan (Ar. *E.N.* 1143a 4); *esti de kai hê sunesis kai hê eusunesia kath'has legomen sunetous kai eusunetous* – there is also intelligence and good intelligence, through which we call people intelligent and of good intelligence (Ar. *E.N.* 1142b 34).

sunolos: whole. Non-technically: *khoreia ge mên orkhêsis te kai ôidê to xunolon estin* – choir-training is as a whole dancing and song (Pl. *Laws* 654b); *tês peri ta phuta xunolês tekhnês* – the whole skill regarding plants (Pl. *Pol.* 299d). The neuter substantive *to sunolon* is a technical term in Aristotle for the individual thing composed of *hulê* and *eidos*, matter and form: *zêtêteon ... poteron esti ti para to sunolon. legô de to sunolon hotan katêgorêthêi ti tês hulês* – we must examine whether there is anything beyond the composite whole. I call something a composite whole when something is predicated of matter (Ar. *Met.* 995b 32); *legô de tên men hulên hoion ton khalkon, tên de morphên to skhêma tês ideas to de ek toutôn, ton andrianta, to sunolon* – I call matter such as the bronze, and form the shape informing it, but the thing composed of these, the statue, I call the composite whole (Ar. *Met.* 1029a 3).

sunônumos. (1) Applied to things, univocal. Things are univocal if they have the same name and also the same definition, as distinguished from *homônuma*, equivocal things having the same name but different definitions, *parônuma*, things related as are the referents of nouns, verbs, etc. with the same root, such as 'race' and 'racer', things named as serving or derived from a central case, called *aph'henos* or *pros hen*, and things named *kat'analogian*, such as the foot of a man and of a mountain: *sunônuma de legetai hôn to te onoma koinon kai ho kata t'ounoma logos tês ousias ho autos, hoion zôion ho te anthrôpos kai ho bous* – things are called univocal whose name is common and the account of the essence corresponding to the name is the same, as man and an ox are both animals (Ar. *Cat.* 1a 5). Adverbially: *sunônumôs legetai* – are spoken of univocally (Ar. *Cat.* 3b 9). (2) Applied to words, synonymous as in English: *tôn d'onomatôn ... khrêsimoi ... tôi poiêtêi ... sunônumiai. legô de kuria te kai sunônuma hoion to poreuesthai kai to badizein* – synonymities of words are useful to the poet. I call genuine synonyms cases such as 'travel' and 'journey' (Ar. *Rhet.* 1404b 39); *holon gar kai pan*

161

sunônumon – 'whole' and 'all' are synonyms (Sextus Empiricus, *Adversus Mathematicos* 1.314).

T

taxis covers all kinds of arrangement in the abstract, and various concrete arrangements. Frequently, in non-technical use, a battle-line: *ton liponta taxin ê hopla apobalonta* – him who left the line of battle or threw away his arms (Pl. *Rep.* 468a). Technically, one of the three kinds of arrangement of atoms in Democritus, called by him *diathigê*: *hê de diathigê taxis ... diapherei gar ... to de AN tou NA – diathigê* is arrangement ... for AN differs from NA (Ar. *Met.* 985b 17). Also political order: *kata tên taxin tou nomou* – according to the legal constitution (Pl. *Laws* 925b). Of good order generally: *pleiston de logou aphistatai oukh hoper nomou te kai taxeôs* – is not that which is further from law and good order furthest from reason? (Pl. *Rep.* 587a). Particularly of the orderliness of nature: *ouden ge atakton tôn phusei kai kata phusin. hê gar phusis aitia pasin taxeôs* – nothing natural or in accordance with nature is disordered. For nature is the cause of orderliness for all things (Ar. *Phys.* 252a 4); *pan hoson ên horaton paralabôn oukh hêsukhian agon alla kinoumenon plêmmelôs kai ataktôs eis taxin auto êgagen ek tês ataxias* – taking over everything visible that was not at rest but changing discordantly and without order, [God] reduced it to order from disorder (Pl. *Tim.* 30a); *taxeôs edeêthê topikês* – stood in need of ordering in place (Simplicius, *Physics* 773.22).

tekhnê: art, skill, craft, as distinguished from both nature and mere *tribê*, practice; *tekhnikos* is a possessor of such skill and *tekhnêma* a product of such skill: *epei ... oudemia oute tekhnê estin hêtis ou meta logou poiêtikê hexis estin, oude toiautê hê ou tekhnê, tauton an eiê tekhnê kai hexis meta logou alêthous poiêtikê* – since there is no skill that is not a rational creative disposition, nor any such that is not a skill, skill must be a creative disposition with a true rationale (Ar. *E.N.* 1140a 6); *tôn peri ta dêmiourgika tekhnêmata diaponountôn* – those working at commercial crafts (Pl. *Laws* 846d). Particularly rhetoric: *tekhnês rhêtorikês* – the art of rhetoric (Pl. *Phaedrus* 270b); *hoi peri tous logous tekhnikoi prospoioumenoi einai* – those who claim to be skilled in the use of speech (Pl. *Phaedrus* 273a); *ouk esti tekhnê all'atekhnos tribê* – [rhetoric] is not a skill but an unskilled knack (Pl. *Phaedrus* 273a). Works on the art of rhetoric, of which Aristotle's was not the first, were called *tekhnai*: *hoi tas tekhnas tôn logôn suntithentes* – the authors of 'Arts of Speaking' (Ar. *Rhet.* 1354a 12).

tekmêrion: a sign; and *tekmairesthai*: to infer through a sign: *oistha hothen tekmairomai* – do you know what sign I rely on? (Pl. *Rep.* 433b); *apaideusias mega tekmêrion* – a clear sign of lack of education (Pl. *Rep.* 405b). The term was given a narrower sense by Aristotle, so that only those *sêmeia*, indications, that were universally reliable could be called *tekmêria*, as having milk is a sign that a woman has given birth: *tôn de sêmeiôn to men houtôs ekhei hôs tôn kath'hekaston ti pros to katholou ... to men anagkaion tekmêrion* – of indications one kind is such as a particular in relation to the universal ... that which is necessary is a sign (Ar. *Rhet.* 1357b 1); *to gar tekmêrion to eidenai poioun phasin einai* – they call that a sign that is productive of knowledge (Ar. *An. Po.* 70b 2); *dêlon hoti tekmêriôdês estin hê gnôsis hê peri tôn arkhôn, all'ouk apodeiktikê* – it is clear that the knowledge of first principles is based on signs and not on demonstration (Simplicius, *Physics* 18.28).

teleios (= *teleos*): complete; *teleiôsis*: completion; *teleiotês*: completeness; *teleioun*: to complete; *telesiourgos*: completing; *telikos*: final [of completion]; *telos*: end. A *telos* may be merely an end-point: *sunaptei têi arkhêi to telos* – it links its end to its beginning (Proclus, *Elements of Theology* 33); but it may be an end-point that is the aim of action, and thus a goal or a success: *hê men boulêsis tou telous esti mallon* – wish is rather for a success (Ar. *E.N.* 1111b 26). Similarly the *teleios* may be merely the complete or the perfect: *teleion legetai hen men hou mê estin exô to labein ... kai to kat'aretên kai to eu mê ekhon huperbolên pros to genos* – 'teleion' is (1) that of which not even one part is missing ... and (2) that which in excellence and merit has nothing exceeding it of its kind (Ar. *Met.* 1021b 12). (1) *tên telean adikian* – complete injustice (Pl. *Rep.* 384b); *eti d'en biôi teleiôi* – also in a complete life (Ar. *E.N.* 1098a 18). (2) *anendees de on teleion esti, teleion de on ekhei telos kai ouk estin ateleuton, telos de ekhon peras ekhei kai horon* – lacking nothing it is complete, and being complete it has a final point, and having a final point it has a limit and bounds [the unlimited being a bad condition for neoplatonists] (Simplicius,

163

Physics 30.11); *hêdistê hê teleiotatê* – the most perfect [perception] is the most pleasant (Ar. *E.N.* 1174b 21). So *teleioun* is not usually merely to bring to an end but rather to perfect: *teleioi de tên energeian hê hêdonê* – pleasure perfects the activity (Ar. *E.N.* 1174b 23); *teleiôtheisi tois toioutois paideiâi kai hêlikiâi* – when such men have been perfected by education and growing up (Pl. *Rep.* 487a). Similarly *teleiôsis* is making complete in the sense of perfect: *tôn eis tên teleiôsin agomenôn tês phuseôs* – of things leading to the perfection of its nature (Ar. *E.N.* 1153a 12). Similarly with *telikos, telesiourgos* and *teleiotês*: *telikos an eiê topos hôs sunektikos kai telesiourgos kai peripoiêtikos tês hekastou teleiotêtos* – place must have a goal as holding together and completing and caring for the perfection of each thing (Simplicius, *Physics* 600.32). That of the four causes which Aristotle called *to hou heneka* – that for the sake of which, the final cause – is often called the *telikon aition* in later writings: *saphôs to telikon aition tou Platônos prosthentos* – Plato having clearly added the final cause (Simplicius, *Physics* 26.15).

telos: end, success. See *teleios*.

theologein, theologos. Not in Plato. Alexander accurately describes Aristotle's use of these terms: *theologous de legei tous peri theôn epaggellomenous legein, hôn ên Homêros kai Orpheus kai Hêsiodos* – [Aristotle] calls theologians those who claim to tell about the gods, such as Homer, Orpheus and Hesiod (Alexander, *Meteorologica* 66.13). They gave a mythological account of the creation of the world and the like, as the forerunners of the *phusikoi*, the natural scientists: *hoi men oun peri Hêsiodon, kai pantes hosoi theologoi* – the associates of Hesiod and all the theologians (Ar. *Met.* 1000a 9); *prôtous theologêsantas ... Ôkeanon te gar kai Têthun epoiêsan tês geneseôs pateras* – the first theologians ... they made Ocean and Tethys the fathers of coming-to-be (Ar. *Met.* 983b 29).

theologia occurs once in Plato, at *Rep.* 379a, where it is said by *LSJ* to mean 'the science of things divine' and by Ross 'rational theology' (*ad Met.* 1026a19). But the word occurs in a discussion of censorship of poets, and, in particular, of what they may say about the gods in their plays; it seems to mean merely 'talk about gods'. The *LSJ* sense becomes common later.

theologikê. Aristotle twice calls *theologikê* what we call metaphysics and what he called elsewhere *prôtê philosophia*, first philosophy (*Met.* 1026a 14-22 and 1064b 3). It is concerned with the *aïdion kai akinêton kai khôriston* – the everlasting and unchanging and separate [from the world of change] (Ar. *Met.* 1026a 11), since for Aristotle everything above the sublunary sphere had this character and was, as such, divine: *tria genê tôn theôrêtikôn epistêmôn esti, phusikê, mathêmatikê, theologikê* – there are three kinds of theoretical sciences, natural, mathematical and metaphysical (Ar. *Met.* 1064b 3).

theôrein: to contemplate, visually or mentally; *theôrêtikos*: contemplative, theoretical; *theôria*: (1) a spectacle or ceremony, usually with religious associations; (2) contemplation; *theôros*: a spectator or contemplator. (1) *tôn eis tous Hellênas koinêi thusiôn kai theôriôn* – the common sacrifices and ceremonies for the Greeks (Pl. *Laws* 947a). (2) *theôrous polemou tous paidas poiein* – to make the children spectators of war (Pl. *Rep.* 467c); *auton noêsei all'ouk ommasi theôrein* – to contemplate it with the mind and not the eyes (Pl. *Rep.* 529b); *theôria pantos men khronou, pasês de ousias* – contemplation of all time and all being (Pl. *Rep.* 486a); *eiê an hê eudaimonia theôria tis* – well-being must be a kind of contemplation (Ar. *E.N.* 1178b 2); *hê tou theou energeia … theôrêtikê an eiê* – the activity of God must be contemplative (Ar. *E.N.* 1178b 22); *hotan te theôrêi anagkê hama phantasma ti theôrein* – when a man contemplates he must at the same time contemplate an image (Ar. *De An.* 432a 8); *tôn theôrêtikôn epistêmôn* – of the theoretical sciences (Ar. *Met.* 1064b 3).

theos: god. Those ancient philosophers who took seriously the concept of god in their philosophy and made use of the concept of a first cause tended not to call such a first cause by the name *theos*, but quite frequently recognised a number of *theoi* not thought of in this way, but as something more like the angels and saints of Christianity. Thus Plato wrote of *auto to agathon*, the good itself, as *epekeina tês ousias*, beyond being, and the cause of being; this *autoagathon* was identified by the neoplatonists with what they called *to hen*, from which the gods proceeded (see *proienai*) like everything else. Aristotle identified his supreme being with self-contemplative *nous* (self-contemplative since contemplation of the best is superior to contemplation of anything else). Anthropomorphic gods were early rejected: *all'ei kheiras ekhon boes*

*hippoi t'êe leontes/ ê grapsai kheiressi kai erga telein haper andres/
hippoi men th'hippoisi boes de te bousin homoias/ kai ke theôn ideas
egraphon kai sômat'epoioun/ toiauth'hoion per k'autoi demas eikhon
hekastoi* – but if oxen and horses or lions had hands, or could draw
with their hands and do the works that men can do, horses would
draw the forms of the gods like horses and oxen like oxen, and they
would make their bodies like their own (Xenophanes, fr. 15).

theourgia: the art of the *theourgos*, he who is able to call up and
bring about the epiphany of gods. The art is no doubt old, but the
words are not used by Plato and Aristotle. Many neoplatonists
practised it: *pôs hai autophaneiai gignontai tôn theôn, phainomenôn tote men atupôtôn phôtôn, tote de tetupômenôn· mê gar
prosemenoi tauta tên hieratikên holên anatrepomen kai ta erga tôn
theourgôn* – how do the epiphanies of the gods come about, when
they appear sometimes as formless lights and sometimes as having
a form? For if we do not admit these we overthrow all the priestly
function and the works of the theurgists (Proclus, *On the Republic*
1.37.9). See Dodds, *The Greeks and the Irrational*, Appendix II,
'Theurgy'.

thermos: hot; *thermainein*: to heat; *thermantikos*: heating;
thermotês: heat. *psukhonta kai thermainonta* – things that heat
and cool (Pl. *Tim.* 46d); *to ... tês psukhês meta tou sômatos
thermantikon oinos* – wine, the thing that warms the soul together
with the body (Pl. *Tim.* 60d); *ou gar thermotêtos ... ergon psukhein* –
it is not the function of heat to make cold (Pl. *Rep.* 335d). In
Aristotelian physics *to thermon* is one of the four primary states,
together with *to psukhron, to xeron* and *to hugron*, that in pairs
(*suzeuxeis*) characterise the four primary elements *pur, aêr, hudôr*
and *gê*: *to men gar pur thermon kai xeron, ho d'aêr thermon kai
hugron* – for fire is hot and dry and air hot and moist (Ar. *De Gen. et
Cor.* 330b 2).

thesis has three main uses in philosophy, as well as others in
metrics etc. (1) Physical position and positioning: *eis plinthôn kai
lithôn thesin* – for the positioning of bricks and stones (Pl. *Rep.*
33b); *diapherei gar ... to de Z tou N thesei* [in this quotation the Z
and N as in codices; but see Ross's text and note *ad loc.*] – for Z and
N differ in position (Ar. *Met.* 985b 18); *to men gar aphorismon kai
metron einai theseôs ton topon kalôs oimai legetai* – I think it is well

166

said that place is the demarcation and measure of position (Simplicius, *Physics* 644.14). (2) The laying down of laws and the like: *tôn epi nomôn thesin iontôn* – those who approach law-giving (Pl. *Laws* 690d). (3a) Any thesis maintained, whether sound or not: *kai peri tou ekhthrou de hê autê thesis* – and [I maintain] the same thesis about an enemy (Pl. *Rep.* 335a). (3b) (Always in Aristotle) a paradoxical thesis: *thesis de estin hupolêpsis paradoxos* – a thesis is a paradoxical notion (Ar. *Top.* 104b 19); *ton de houtô zônta oudeis an eudaimoniseien ei mê thesin diaphulattôn* – nobody would call happy one living such a life unless in defence of a paradox (Ar. *E.N.* 1096a 1); *amesou d'arkhês sullogistikês thesin men legô hên mê esti deixai mêd'anagkê ekhein ton mathêsomenon ti, hên d'anagkê ekhein ton hotioun mathêsomenon axiôma* – of immediate syllogistic starting-points I call that a thesis which cannot be proved and which one does not need to know to learn anything, and what one needs to know I call an axiom (Ar. *An. Po.* 72a 14).

thrasutês: rashness; *thrasus*: rash: *tauta ... ha su kaleis andreia egô thrasea kalô* – those things you call brave I call rash (Pl. *Laches* 197b); *ho de tôi tharrein huperballôn peri ta phobera thrasus* – he who exceeds in confidence concerning things fearful is rash (Ar. *E.N.* 1115b 28); *thrasutetos te kai deilias* – of rashness and cowardice (Pl. *Tim.* 87a).

thumoeidês. See *thumos*.

thumos: anger; *thumousthai*: to be angry. In Homer *thumos* appears to be, among other things, any strong emotion, including anger, but also strong desire. Similarly in Heraclitus (fr. 85) *thumôi makhesthai khalepon* seems to mean 'it is hard to fight against one's heart's desire'. But in Plato, Aristotle and later authors, at least, *thumos* seems to mean 'anger': *hoi en thumôi prakhthentes phonoi* – murders committed in anger (Pl. *Laws* 867d); *aiskhiôn hê peri epithumias akrasia tês peri ton thumon* – weakness with regard to appetites is more shameful than that with regard to anger (Ar. *E.N.* 1149b 24). Proclus gives the same definition of *thumos* – *touto gar ergon thumou to antilupêseôs oregesthai* – it is the function of anger to seek for retaliatory suffering (*On the Republic* 1.208.17) – as Aristotle gives of *orgê* at *De An.* 403a 30. But there are problems: if *thumos* is mere anger, like *orgê*, (1) why is weakness about anger less shameful than weakness about appetite? (2) why is *thumos* singled out as a separate type of *orexis* alongside *boulêsis* and *epithumia* as in *orexis men gar epithumia kai thumos kai boulêsis* (Ar. *De An.* 414b 2)? (3) why is *orgê* not said to be a synonym of *thumos*? and (4) why is the *thumoeides* regarded in the *Republic* as a desirable element in the soul and the state, as in *to thumoeides epikouron tôi logistikôi phusei* – the irascible (?) element is the natural ally of the rational element (Pl. *Rep.* 441a)? It would appear that the notions of *thumos* and *to thumoeides* carry with them some notion of manliness, spiritedness and sense of honour, not present in *orgê*, which is why *to thumoeides* is often translated 'the spirited element'. Perhaps this is counted as a different form of *orexis* because both *boulêsis* and *epithumia* seek the agent's satisfaction, whereas *thumos* seeks the harm of the enemy, not the good of the agent; but, if so, this is surely not the only non-self-regarding form of motivation.

ti esti: in a question, a request for a definition. Socrates in the *Gorgias* has great difficulty in getting an answer to the question *ti esti touto tôn ontôn, peri ho houtoi hoi logoi eisin hois hê rhetorikê khrêtai* – what of all things is it that these discourses are about that rhetoric uses (Pl. *Gorg.* 451d), rather than accounts of *poia tis* – the characteristics of – rhetoric. *horismos men gar tou ti esti kai ousias* – for definition is of what a thing is and its essence (Ar. *An. Po.* 90b 30); *ta genê tôn katêgoriôn … esti de tauta ton arithmon deka, ti esti, poson, poion …* – the basic kinds of predicates … these are ten in number, telling what a thing is, how big it is, what it is like … (Ar. *Top.* 103b 20). Since the answer to *ti esti?* gives the essence of a thing or its nature, *to ti esti* was used as a substantive equivalent to *hê ousia*: *kai to ti esti kai to ei estin aporon phanêsetai* – both the nature and also the existence [of place] will appear problematic (Simplicius, *Physics* 529.10).

timan, timê, timios have a variety of uses, all connected with the notion of value. (1) Honour (a) as in 'honours list': *tôn dôreôn te kai timôn heneka* – for the sake of the rewards and honours (Pl. *Rep.* 361c); (b) as attitude: *theion gar agathon pou timê* – honour is a divine good (Pl. *Laws* 727a); *theoi timioi en têi polei* – gods honoured in the city (Pl. *Laws* 829d); *pas timatô … tous heautou gennêtoras* – let everyone honour his parents (Pl. *Laws* 932a9). (2) Value as price: *sphaira gar hê kallistê ê lêkuthos megaloprepeian ekhei paidikou dôrou, hê de toutou timê mikron kai aneleutheron* –

for a beautiful ball or a bottle is a magnificent gift to a child, but the cost is slight and trivial (Ar. *E.N.* 1123a 14). (3) Value as being worth having and to be prized: *episkepsômetha peri tês eudaimonias potera tôn epainetôn estin ê mallon tôn timiôn* – let us consider whether *eudaimonia* is something to be praised or to be prized (Ar. *E.N.* 1101b 10); *timiôteron epistêmê orthês doxês esti* – knowledge is something more valuable than correct opinion (Pl. *Meno* 98a); *homoias phêsin hapasas einai kai timêteas ex isou* – he says that all [pleasures] are alike and to be valued equally (Pl. *Rep.* 561c).

timokratia, timokratikos: timocracy, timocratic. Uncommon, but used differently by Plato and Aristotle. In Plato *timokratia* is the first and the least bad perversion of his ideal state, and results from the auxiliaries taking control: *peirômetha legein tina tropon timokratia genoit'an ex aristokratias* – let us try to say how timocracy might arise from aristocracy [the rule of the best] (Pl. *Rep.* 545c); the timocratic man is *axiôn arkhein ... apo ergôn polemikôn* – claiming a right to rule on the basis of military deeds (Pl. *Rep.* 949a). In Aristotle timocracy is where political power is based on wealth: *eisi d'hai men politeiai basileia te kai aristokratia· tritê de apo timêma-tôn, hên timokratian legein oikeion phainetai, politeian d'eiôthasin hoi pleistoi kalein* – constitutions are kingship, and aristocracy; a third is based on financial assessment, which it seems appropriate to call timocracy, though most people are used to calling it polity (Ar. *Pol.* 1160a 33); *parekbasis ... ek de timokratias eis dêmokratian* – the perversion of timocracy is rule of the mob (Ar. *Pol.* 1160b 16).

topos: place, not space, which is a possible translation of *khôra* in some contexts. *hou d'an euanthês te kai euôdês topos êi* – where there is a place with beautiful flowers and scents (Pl. *Symp.* 196b); *ekhei de pollas aporias ti pot'estin ho topos* – the nature of place raises many puzzles (Ar. *Phys.* 208a 32). Aristotle deals with these puzzles in *Physics*, Book 4, Chs 2-5. He comes to the conclusion that *to tou periekhontos peras akinêton prôton, tout'estin ho topos* – place is the immediate unmoving limit of the container (Ar. *Phys.* 212a 20). Simplicius and others found this puzzling and rejected it: *to men gar aphorismon kai metron einai theseôs ton topon kalôs oimai legetai* – I think that it is well said that place is the delimitation and measure of position (Simplicius, *Physics* 644.14). Metaphorically: *tên eis ton noêton topon tês psukhês anodon* – the upward journey of the soul to the intelligible place (Pl. *Rep.* 517b).

tragikos: tragic; *tragikôs*: in the manner of tragedy; *tragôidia*: tragedy: *tous tês tragikês poiêseôs haptomenous* – those who embark on the composition of tragedy (Pl. *Rep.* 602b); *tragikôs ... kinduneuô legein* – perhaps I am using the language of tragedy (Pl. *Rep.* 413b); *ho Euripidês ... tragikôtatos ge tôn poiêtôn phainetai* – Euripides seems the most tragic of the poets [i.e. who most arouses fear and pity] (Ar. *Poetics* 1153a 29). Tragedy is defined by Aristotle: *estin oun tragôidia mimêsis praxeôs spoudaias kai teleias, megethos ekhousês, hêdusmenôi logôi khôris hekastôi tôn eidôn en tois moriois, drôntôn kai ou di'apaggelias, di'eleou kai phobou perainousa tên tôn toioutôn pathêmatôn katharsin* – so tragedy is the representation of a noble and complete transaction, having size, with language made pleasing appropriately to each part, through action and not narrative, and through fear and pity accomplishing the purgation of [?from] such emotions (Ar. *Poetics* 1149b 24). Metaphorically: *têi tou biou sumpasêi tragôidiaï kai kômôidiaï* – the whole tragi-comedy of life (Pl. *Phil.* 50b).

tribê: literally, rubbing. In both Plato and Aristotle it is repeated practice as opposed to skill: *mê tribêi monon kai empeiriaï alla tekhnêi* – not by mere practice and experience, but by skill (Pl. *Phaedrus* 270b); *atekhnos esti tis empeiria kai tribê* – [forensic rhetoric] is an unskilled practice based on experience (Pl. *Laws* 938a). Aristotle says that before he created formal logic *peri de tou sullogizesthai pantelôs ouden eikhomen proteron allo legein, all'ê tribêi zêtountes polun khronon eponoumen* – concerning argument we had nothing previous to report, but spent much labour on unmethodical search (Ar. *S.E.* 184b 1).

tropê: literally, turning, has astronomical uses (as in 'tropics') and rhetorical uses (as in 'trope'). The term was used by Democritus as a synonym of *thesis*: *hê de tropê thesis* – *tropê* is position (Ar. *Met.* 985b 17).

tukhê: more often to be translated as luck (good or bad), or fortune, than as chance, and, when it is well translated as chance, it usually means rather 'not for any reason' than 'causeless': *esti d'heneka tou hosa te apo dianoias an prakhtheiê kai hosa apo phuseôs. ta dê toiauta hotan kata sumbebêkos genêtai apo tukhês phamen einai* – what is done by design and what happens naturally has some purpose. Things of a similar character that just happen we say

170

happen by chance (Ar. *Phys.* 196b 22). Thus if I want to meet you and might well have designed to do so, if I now meet you accidentally that is *apo tukhês*. Aristotle thinks that this is the normal and correct use of the term and that it is a confusion to think that *tukhê* implies absence of cause: *enioi gar kai ei estin* [*hê tukhê*] *ê mê aporousin. ouden gar dê gignesthai apo tukhês phasin, alla pantôn einai ti aition hôrismenon* – for some people even are in doubt whether there is such a thing [as chance]. For they say that nothing happens by chance, but there is a definite cause of everything (Ar. *Phys.* 195b 36). But, Aristotle holds, to say we met by chance is not to deny that there is any explanation of how we came to be in the same place. Luck, chance and fortune can be good or bad: *met'agathês tukhês* – with good luck (Pl. *Phaedrus* 265c; *theiaï tini tukhêi* – by some divine chance (Pl. *Ep.* 327e); *hê men gar tukhê kai to apo tukhês estin hosois kai to eutukhêsai an huparxeien kai holôs praxis* – for chance and by chance occur where there can be good fortune and in the whole field of action (Ar. *Phys.* 197b 1).

turannein: to exercise tyranny; *turannikos*: tyrannical; *turannikôs*: tyrannically; *turannis*: tyranny; *turannos*: tyrant. *hotan mête kata nomous mête kata ethê prattêi tis heis arkhôn ... môn ou tote ton toiouton turannon klêteon?* – when some sole ruler acts in accordance neither with law nor with custom ... should we not then call such a person a tyrant? (Pl. *Pol.* 301c); *hê men gar turannis esti monarkhia pros to sumpheron to tou monarkhountos* – for tyranny is sole rule aimed at the advantage of the sole ruler (Ar. *Pol.* 1279b 5); *to poiein turannounta hoti an epithumêi* – tyrannically to do whatever he wants (Pl. *Laws* 661b). Metaphorically: *tên ... tou thumou ... kai epithumiôn en psukhêi turannida* – the tyranny of anger and appetites in the soul (Pl. *Laws* 863e).

X

xêros: dry: *to men gar pur thermon kai xêron ... hê de gê psukhron kai xêron* – for fire is hot and dry ... but earth is cold and dry (Ar. *De Gen. et Cor.* 330b 3). For the general theory of the four elements and the hot, cold, dry and liquid see Ar. *De Gen. et Cor.* 2.2-3. *legetai de xêron kai hugron pleonakhôs· antikeitai gar tôi xêrôi kai to hugron kai to dieron, kai palin tôi hugrôi kai to xêron kai to pepêgos* – 'dry' and 'liquid (wet)' have more than one use; for both liquid and wet are opposed to dry, and, again, both dry and solidified are opposed to liquid (Ar. *De Gen. et Cor.* 330a 12). Aristotle explains *dieros*: *dieron men esti to ekhon allo tina hugrotêta epipolês* – wet is having some alien superficial liquid (Ar. *De Gen. et Cor.* 330a 16).

Z

zên: to live; *zôê*: life. Notwithstanding English derivatives, *zôê* is rather biological life while *bios* is more concerned with the history and way of life of persons. Thus biographers like Diogenes Laertius and Plutarch wrote *Bioi*, not *Zôai*. But, as is shown by, for example, Aristotle's statement that *eudaimonia* means the same as *eu zên kai eu prattein* – to live and fare well (*E.N.* 1095a 19) – this distinction should not be taken as very rigid. *pan zôn ekhei psukhên* – eveything that lives has a soul (Ar. *De Juv.* 470a 19); *zôên de legomen tên di'hautou trophên te kai auxêsin kai phthisin* – we call life the self-caused nutrition, growth and decay (Ar. *De An.* 412a 14); *legomen ... diôristhai to empsukhon tou apsukhou tôi zên* – we say ... that the animate is demarcated from the inanimate by life (Ar. *De An.* 413a 20); *ti d'au to zên? ou psukhês ergon einai?* – again, what is life? Is it not the work of the soul? (Pl. *Rep.* 353d). See also *zôion*.

zêtein: to search for, investigate; *zêtêsis*: search, investigation; *zêtêtês*: searcher, investigator; *zêtêtikos*: enquiring, investigative. Non-technically: *ei ... khruson ezêtoumen* – if we were searching for gold (Pl. *Rep.* 336e); *hôsper an ei zêtois tis didaskalos tou hellênizein* – as if you were to enquire for a teacher of Greek (Pl. *Prot.* 327e). Technically *zêtêsis* is, for many philosophers, the usual name for philosophical investigation: *en têi peri to dikaion zêtêsei* – in the investigation about justice (Pl. *Rep.* 336e); *pros tên tou kalou te kai agathou zêtêsin* – towards our search for the fine and the good (Pl. *Rep.* 531c); *sugkheei tên philosophon zêtêsin* – he throws philosophical enquiry into confusion (Sextus Empiricus, *Adversus Mathematicos* 8.372). Aristotle distinguished practical from theoretical *zêtêsis*: *phainetai hê men zêtêsis ou pasa einai bouleusis hoion hai mathêmatikai. hê de bouleutikê pasa zêtêsis* – not all investigation appears to be deliberation, as, for example, mathematics. But all deliberation is investigation (Ar. *E.N.* 1112b 21); *Damaskios ho ek Damaskou philosophos anêr zêtikôtatos* – Damascius, the philosopher from Damascus, a man most given to research (Simplicius, *Physics* 624.38).

zôê. See *zên*.

zôion is one of Aristotle's stock examples of homonymity, since both an animal and a picture is a *zôion*: *hoion zôion ho te anthrôpos kai to gegrammenon* – as both a man and a portrait is a *zôion* (Ar. *Cat.* 1a 2). While both plants and animals have *zôê*, only animals are *zôia*: *ta gar phuta zêi men, ouk ekhei d'aisthêsin, tôi de aisthanesthai to zôion pros to mê zôion diorizomen* – for plants are alive, but they do not have sensation, while we differentiate an animal from what is not an animal by sensation (Ar. *De Juv.* 467b 23); *tonde ton kosmon zôion empsukhon ennoun te ... genesthai* – this universe came to be as an ensouled and intelligent animal (Pl. *Tim.* 30b).

173